RABBINIC THEOLOGY

RABBINIC THEOLOGY

An Introductory Study

ROY A. STEWART

With a Foreword by
RAPHAEL LOEWE

OLIVER AND BOYD

EDINBURGH AND LONDON
1961

OLIVER AND BOYD LTD
Tweeddale Court
Edinburgh 1

39a Welbeck Street
London W 1

First published 1961

Printed in Great Britain by Oliver and Boyd Ltd., Edinburgh

FOREWORD

Rabbinics being a discipline that encourages in its cultivators a *pietas* towards their predecessors and teachers, the modern student will often be conscious of ghosts looking over his shoulder—from those of Hillel and Rabbi Judah the Prince to the seventeenth century Christian Hebraists such as Lightfoot, Pococke, and Selden and the nineteenth-century Jewish founders of modern scientific Jewish scholarship. When one thinks of the Buxtorfs, or of Zunz, one is humbled by the magnitude of what they achieved without any of the tools which we now take for granted; and as one surveys the line of earlier Talmudists one notes, with regret, the dwindling number of non-Jewish scholars, the magisterial contributions of some of whom have placed the subject permanently in their debt. As the author of this book makes clear (p. 104), both the Jewish and the Christian scholar are inevitably preconditioned to some extent in their attitude—although it is not often realised that in the present Jewish situation the Jewish scholar may be as much a negative pole of reaction against traditional Jewish institutions and values as have been certain Christian controversialists of the past, who may have been actuated by an anti-Jewish prejudice of which they have themselves nevertheless been sublimely unconscious. There are today once again some encouraging signs of a positively appreciative study of Rabbinics by Christian scholars, and as the latest example of it Mr Stewart's book deserves to be welcomed with alacrity.

Those of us who have been concerned to follow the treatment of a given topic comparatively through Rabbinic and Patristic sources have often given thanks for the numerous subject indexes to Migne's Latin *Patrology*, and have sighed for some analogous chart to the Talmuds and Midrashim. But no one could pretend that Migne's indexes, even those devoted to such engaging topics as *Virginity*, *Usury*, or *Extreme Unction*, are

bedside reading.   Mr Stewart has achieved the well-nigh
impossible, and while giving us what is essentially an index
has so leavened it with interspersed comment and explanation
as to make it eminently readable.

Of course, as he himself emphasises (pp. 18-19), the tidying
up of the source material into categories familiar to modern
western theology is of limited value.   It is, indeed, a necessary
expedient for the beginner; but the student must strive towards
the point at which he will have determined for himself the
appropriate categories that the material itself suggests.   Above
all, he must beware of forcing it into his own preconceived
categories, and he must furthermore learn how the new ones
that he will establish for himself should be so juxtaposed as to
allow for overlaps where watertight divisions are out of place.
For Rabbinic thought, though its axioms are simple enough,
is a system of remarkable fluidity.   Such a programme of
study is no simple task.   Most of us have become so conditioned
to western thought-patterns that we take it for granted that
their categories are much the most convenient yet evolved by
man, and that any others which we may encounter must be
accommodated to them; and it does not occur to us that the
advantages of using a double set of categories that are not
coincidental, can be (provided that they are more often
complementary than mutually exclusive) both intellectually
and spiritually immense.   The essential tragedy of modern
Jewry, whether it uses Hebrew or any other language as its
vernacular, is (as it seems to me) that in its haste to adopt (or
to hebraise) western thought-categories it is with equanimity
allowing the natural categories inherent in traditional Hebrew
grammatical structure, idiom, and socio-religious institutions
to become so suppressed into a secondary position that there
is a very real likelihood of their true understanding disappearing
from the popular Jewish consciousness completely.   If Mr
Stewart's book were to do no more than to draw attention (by
implication) to this state of affairs, he would be deserving well
of his Jewish public; and readers who come newly to Judaism
will owe him a debt of gratitude for guiding their steps towards
an understanding of what the word *Torah* at its most pregnant
can convey to the Jew—when logic is transcended and *Torah*,

as the field in which the dialogue of God and Man (not merely, even if preeminently, God and Jew) can take place, becomes, in a mystic way, greater than the sum of its own parts.

This book, like the *Rabbinic Anthology* of C. G. Montefiore and my late Father, H. Loewe, concerns itself exclusively with *Aggadah*, i.e. the aspect of Rabbinic literature that is neither institutional nor practical. The *Aggadah*, in addition to being (for most readers) far more engaging than the residue, is, indeed, more patient of arrangement within familiar theological categories than is the *Halakhah*. The latter, which comprises jurisprudence, ritual, and practical ethics, constitutes (it might be argued) valuable comparative material for the canonist, but not for the theologian. But it is precisely here that a word of warning is necessary. The dividing line between *Aggadah* and *Halakhah* is by no means rigid. They merge in the field of practical ethics and symbolism. Thus, the virtue of hospitality to the wayfarer is fathered on to Abraham, whose friendliness to the traveller has been read by the *Aggadah* into the biblical account; since Abraham's example is held up for emulation, the aggadist's embroidery of the text has impinged upon *Halakhah*. Again, the ram's horn prescribed for ceremonial sounding on New Year's Day ought, the *Halakhah* enjoins, to be straight rather than curly, as symbol that, at the onset of the penitential season, "the more one straightens out one's conscience, the better" (R.H. 26*b*). For elaboration of this aspect of Rabbinics the reader may be referred to the *Rabbinic Anthology*, p. xciv.

Comparison of Rabbinic Judaism with that of the Dead Sea sect fall outside the scope of this volume, but the reader interested in the Jewish background to Christianity will nowadays have to take note of the Dead Sea Scrolls as well as the Talmud. He may be referred to the Bibliography of the whole subject published in German by C. Burchard as No. 76 of the *Beihefte* to the *Zeitschrift für die A-T. Wissenschaft* (1959), and the *Revue de Qumran*.

Mr Stewart writes with such fairness and so positive an appreciation of the values of Rabbinism that, speaking as a student of Rabbinics who happens also to make Rabbinic Judaism the basis of his own personal faith and religion, I have no hesitation in commending his book to Jewish readers. If they may sometimes disagree with his conclusions they will, I think, never find just cause to object to his outline of the reasoning by which he has reached them. I would myself diffidently suggest that the author's evaluation of the Doctrine of Merits (pp. 127-8) might perhaps bear some modification in the light of internal Jewish sociology, which does not (I fancy) reveal the individual amid his own environment as inordinately self-satisfied spiritually. A folkloristic reflexion of my meaning is furnished by the tradition asserting that in every generation there are present thirty-six unidentifiable (Jewish) saints, whose nobility of character proves, unbeknown to themselves, the salvation of their age, by virtue of their example no less than of their merit (see Sanh. 97*b*; *Jewish Encyclopedia*, s.v. *Lamed-Waw*; and *Rabbinic Anthology*, p. 231).

I feel sure that I shall be expressing Mr Stewart's own mind if I venture the hope that his readers will wish to pursue the subject in greater detail than the scope of this volume makes possible. As a follow-up, they might well turn to the *Rabbinic Anthology* (now, happily, in print once again), and to the sources themselves in English translation, or better still in the original. Those who have mastered elementary biblical Hebrew need not be daunted by Rabbinic Hebrew: provided they start with a competence in grammar, they can go far in the Midrash with the aid of Jastrow's dictionary plus an explanatory index of abbreviations, such as is given by G. H. Handler's appendix to Dalman's. But no serious study of the subject can be conducted solely on the basis of the translations, and indeed one cannot hope to keep up to date with research affecting the subject without reference to such media as the Hebrew bibliographical periodical *Qiryath Sepher*, published in Jerusalem. *Ẓil Gemur—get on and study.*

LONDON   RAPHAEL LOEWE

CONTENTS

PREFACE

THE writer began the study of Rabbinics in his student days in 1943, and this has been his principal leisure time interest over the intervening years.

Work on this book began in England in August 1949, and was continued, with interruptions and difficulties, in Cairo from 1951 till 1959. In Scotland, late in 1959, some attempt was made to examine certain modern books about Rabbinics which were quite unobtainable in Cairo. At an earlier stage of the writing, these might have been used more extensively.

These pages are the work, not of a professional scholar, but of a busy working minister, living in anything but an atmosphere of academic seclusion. Mr Raphael Loewe, in his gracious Foreword, has said something about the possible usefulness of the book to Jews. It is the writer's earnest hope and prayer that it may be equally useful, and without prejudice either way, to Christian preachers and theolgical students.

The writer is himself responsible for all translations, except when these are specifically acknowledged. He has checked and re-checked the references, and hopes that the number of remaining errors, there or in the text of the book may not be unduly large.

GLASGOW   *September* 1960

LIST OF ABBREVIATIONS IN TEXT

Preliminary Remarks

The transliteration of Hebrew names and words is, in this list and throughout the book, somewhat approximate. Danby's Mishnah has been followed for the titles of all Talmudic Tractates. The exact transcription of Hebrew and Aramaic into English type is expensive to print. It saves very little labour for the student of Semitics, and it is cumbersome, unsightly and not very meaningful for the non-Hebraist. Danby's renderings, or their equivalents in other parts of the field, are accurate enough for ordinary purposes.

For details of the editions of the sources I have used, see the Bibliography. The names of the Orders of the Talmud are, in Hebrew: 1. Zeraim; 2. Moed; 3. Nashim; 4. Nezikim; 5. Kodashim; 6. Tohoroth. Some very rough indication of their scope will be found in the first chapter. For simplicity's sake, the references below are merely by ordinal number. Danby collects all the purely Mishnaic material in one convenient volume. This is easily distinguished in the footnotes, where it is cited by chapter and paragraph number. For the Gemara, the reader not conversant with the originals must turn to the Soncino translation of the entire Babylonian Talmud, 34 volumes plus Index. A glance at the list below will immediately indicate to which Order a particular Tractate belongs. It may fill two volumes or a fraction of a volume, but it will be found in its proper place—allowing for minor transpositions due to discrepant length and typographical convenience. Reference to the Gemara is always by standard pagination, as in the Venice edition of 1520, *a* representing the recto of the sheet, *b* the verso. This is clearly and completely marked in all the Soncino volumes. For the convenience of the reader, all sixty-three Tractates of the Talmud are included in the list below, though it does not necessarily follow that every single one is cited in the book.

There is a complete French translation of the Jerusalem Talmud, published from 1872 onwards by Moise Schwab, and much further material of value to which I did not have access while preparing the book. Much of the cream of these additional Rabbinic sources is to be found in the oft-cited *Rabbinic Anthology*. And the best teach-ings repeat themselves in many contexts.

The English reader will find no difficulty in using the Soncino translation of the Rabbah Midrashim. Here the Pentateuchal Books, Ruth, and Esther are divided into chapters and paragraphs which are entirely independent of their Scriptural reference.Thus the commentary on Genesis VI.9, to take a random example, will be found at Ch. xxx of the Midrash, first paragraph. Contrariwise, the Midrashim Lamentations, Ecclesiastes, and the Song of Solomon do follow the Scriptural verses or groups of verses, with a third figure to indicate paragraph number. Thus Song of Sol. R. IV.4, 9 means the ninth paragraph of the portion of Midrash on the Song of Solomon dealing with ch. IV, vs. 4.

The student scarcely needs to be told that he will gain much more from following out the rather full footnotes than from perusing the brief and synoptic treatment of the text. It is possible to go a long way in Rabbinic study with little or no knowledge of Hebrew and Aramaic.

Ab.	Pirqe Aboth, Ethics of the Fathers, Tractate in Fourth Order of the Talmud.
Arak.	Arakhin, Tractate in Fifth Order of the Talmud.
A. Zar.	Abodah Zarah, Tractate in Fourth Order of the Talmud.
B.B.	Baba Bathra, Tractate in Fourth Order of the Talmud.
Bekh.	Bekhoroth, Tractate in Fifth Order of the Talmud.
Ber.	Berakhoth, Tractate in First Order of the Talmud.
Betz.	Betzah, Tractate in Second Order of the Talmud.
Bikk.	Bikkurim, Tractate in First Order of the Talmud.
B.K.	Baba Kamma, Tractate in Fourth Order of the Talmud.
B.M.	Baba Metzia, Tractate in Fourth Order of the Talmud.
Dem.	Demai, Tractate in First Order of Talmud.
Deut. R.	The Midrash Rabbah on the Book of Deuteronomy.
Eccl. R.	The Midrash Rabbah on the Book of Ecclesiastes.
Eduy.	Eduyoth, Tractate in Fourth Order of the Talmud.
E.R.E.	*Encyclopaedia of Religion and Ethics*.
Erub.	Erubin, Tractate in Second Order of Talmud.
Esth. R.	The Midrash Rabbah on the Book of Esther.
Ex. R.	The Midrash Rabbah on the Book of Exodus.

Gitt.	Gittin, Tractate in Third Order of the Talmud.
Gen. R.	The Midrash Rabbah on the Book of Genesis.
Hag.	Hagigah, Tractate in Second Order of Talmud.
Hall.	Hallah, Tractate in First Order of Talmud.
Hor.	Horayoth, Tractate in Fourth Order of the Talmud.
Hull.	Hullin, Tractate in Fifth Order of the Talmud.
J.E.	*Jewish Encyclopaedia.* Note—As the articles are arranged alphabetically throughout the twelve volumes, the title is usually sufficient. A short relevant passage in a long article may be referred to by volume, page, and column.
Kel.	Kelim, Tractate in Sixth Order of Talmud.
Ker.	Kerithoth, Tractate in Fifth Order of Talmud.
Ket.	Ketuboth, Tractate in Third Order of Talmud.
Kidd.	Kiddushin, Tractate in Third Order of Talmud.
Kil.	Kilaim, Tractate in First Order of Talmud.
Kinn.	Kinnim, Tractate in Fifth Order of Talmud.
Lam. R.	The Midrash Rabbah on the Book of Lamentations.
Lev. R.	The Midrash Rabbah on the Book of Leviticus.
Maas.	Maaseroth, Tractate in First Order of Talmud.
Makk.	Makkoth, Tractate in Fourth Order of Talmud.
Maksh.	Makshirin, Tractate in Sixth Order of Talmud.
Meg.	Megillah, Tractate in Second Order of Talmud.
Meil.	Meilah, Tractate in Fifth Order of Talmud.
Men.	Menahoth, Tractate in Fifth Order of Talmud.
Midd.	Middoth, Tractate in Fifth Order of Talmud.
Mikw.	Mikwaoth, Tractate in Sixth Order of Talmud.
M. Kat.	Moed Katan, Tractate in Second Order of Talmud.
M. Sh.	Maaser Sheni, Tractate in First Order of Talmud.
M. T.	The Massoretic Text of the Hebrew Bible.
Naz.	Nazir, Tractate in Third Order of Talmud.
Ned.	Nedarim, Tractate in Third Order of Talmud.
Neg.	Negaim, Tractate in Sixth Order of Talmud.
Nidd.	Niddah, Tractate in Sixth Order of Talmud.
Num. R.	The Midrash Rabbah on the Book of Numbers.
Ohol.	Oholoth, Tractate in Sixth Order of Talmud.
Orl.	Orlah, Tractate in First Order of Talmud.
Par.	Parah, Tractate in Sixth Order of Talmud.
Peah	Peah, Tractate in First Order of Talmud.
Pes.	Pesahim, Tractate in Second Order of Talmud.

R.A.	*A Rabbinic Anthology*, edd. Montefiore and Loewe. Note: Quotations in the volume are numbered 1-1661. References to other matters are by page.
Ruth R.	The Midrash Rabbah on the Book of Ruth.
R.Sh.	Rosh ha-Shanah, Tractate in the Second Order of the Talmud.
R.S.V.	Revised Standard Version of the Bible.
Sanh.	Sanhedrin, Tractate in the Fourth Order of the Talmud.
Shab.	Shabbath, Tractate in the Second Order of the Talmud.
Shebi.	Shebiith, Tractate in the First Order of the Talmud.
Shebu.	Shebuoth, Tractate in the Fourth Order of the Talmud.
Shek.	Shekalim, Tractate in Second Order of Talmud.
Song of Sol. R.	The Midrash Rabbah on the Song of Songs.
Sot.	Sotah, Tractate in Third Order of Talmud.
Sukk.	Sukkah, Tractate in Second Order of Talmud.
Taan.	Taanith, Tractate in Second Order of Talmud.
Tam.	Tamid, Tractate in Fifth Order of Talmud.
Teb. Y.	Tebul Yom, Tractate in Sixth Order of Talmud.
Tem.	Temurah, Tractate in Fifth Order of Mishnah.
Ter.	Terumoth, Tractate in First Order of Talmud.
Toh.	Tohoroth, Tractate in Sixth Order of Mishnah.
Uktz.	Uktzin, Tractate in Sixth Order of Talmud.
Wis.	The Apocryphal Book of the Wisdom of Solomon.
Yad.	Yadaim, Tractate in Sixth Order of Talmud.
Yeb.	Yebamoth, Tractate in Third Order of Talmud.
Yom.	Yoma, Tractate in Second Order of Talmud.
Zab.	Zabim, Tractate in Sixth Order of Talmud.
Zeb.	Zebahim, Tractate in Fifth Order of Talmud.

CHAPTER I

INTRODUCTION

Any religion which is at the same time theistic and eschatological would undoubtedly subscribe to four important propositions: firstly, that there is a personal creator God, who must be worshipped and obeyed; secondly, that men have, at least under certain conditions, an eternal as well as a temporal destiny; thirdly, that human transgression requires expiation and divine pardon; and fourthly, that righteousness, sin, atonement, and the quality of a particular individual's immortality are closely linked in an interdependent sequence. This is the basic teaching of Christianity, Judaism, and Islam, though the emphasis on sin, and that consequent need which is felt for atonement, declines from Christianity in Judaism, and from Judaism in Islam. These are for the pious of all three creeds the foundation stones of temporal faith and eternal hope. It is when terms are more exactly defined, and the qualifications for future bliss more precisely postulated, that religious divergences become more pronounced, and that exclusive and conflicting claims are made.

Rabbinic Judaism is, like Christianity, in the line of direct descent from the Old Testament. Both of them owe something to the apocalyptic and allegorical literature of Palestinian and Diaspora Judaism, not to mention pagan sources. The thoroughgoing student of comparative religion would need to carry his studies not only backwards through the sources mentioned, but also forwards through the Christian Patristic literature, through the theology of Islam, and into many other corners of a vast field, tracing out, by parallel and contrast, a fascinating pattern of interrelationships. This book is concerned only with a tiny fraction of the whole field, the Rabbinic thought and theology in its more significant aspects. This is of interest to

Jews and Christians—to Jews as a massive and important phase of their historic faith, and to Christians as a neglected aspect of New Testament background. In selecting the material for this book, the writer has tried to focus the main attention on two kinds of Rabbinic ideas—those which are interesting in themselves, as attempts, successful or unsuccessful, to grapple with problems which are still living issues for human beings, and those—a smaller number—which have special relevance for the student of the New Testament. These will naturally be of lesser value for the Jewish reader, but their bulk is not great.

There is no articulated scheme of doctrine in any Rabbinic work of the earlier centuries, and the four propositions enumerated at the beginning did not receive the main emphasis. There was a much more burning interest in the ceremonial law, the procedure of divorce, the anachronistic Temple ritual, the Levitical discrimination of clean and unclean, the casuistry of oaths and vows, and a host of other matters little considered now. In the interminable discussions of these themes, there are scattered asides which play their part in the synthesis of the theology. The literature forms a large and chaotic museum containing many exhibits from which these pages will not attempt to wipe the dust of ages. The items selected by the writer do not form a Westminster Confession of Faith, but, allowing for certain unresolvable contradictions, they do present a reasonable coherence of pattern.

This first chapter states the main facts of literary and historical introduction, ignoring critical and specialist problems, which affect the theology very little in any case. It provides a few examples also of the legalistic side of Rabbinic thought, which becomes largely neglected in the more theological chapters which follow. The greater part of the literature is in fact composed of this very material.

The Genesis of the Rabbinic Literature

The keynote of the Protestant Reformation was the return to the Bible as the norm for faith and doctrine. In the religious history of mankind, the movement has frequently been in the opposite direction. The Roman Catholic Church has superadded to Bible and Apocrypha an extensive tradition, which it regards as equally authoritative. The earliest followers of Muhammad found the Koran sufficient for all their needs. As the Islamic empire expanded, their successors searched hungrily for, and even concocted, traditions innumerable. At a much earlier stage, the Jews, with all their reverence for the Old Testament, the written Torah, found that the Holy Book did not provide with changing circumstances that detailed guidance for all the affairs of life which their souls craved. The Talmud is the largest, though not the only monument of this search for tradition, and it attempts this task of prescription with a thoroughness unrivalled in world literature.

The meaning of the word Talmud will unfold itself in the next few pages. It may be clearer to start with the cardinal Jewish concept of Torah, which means teaching or law. This word is applied first, and always pre-eminently, to the Pentateuch, that portion of the Scriptures which the Jews regarded as the most sacred of all, and which is full of laws; then to the whole Hebrew Bible; then to the Bible and the accumulated traditional teachings of centuries. The concept was further expanded to include theological and metaphysical elements, which will be discussed in their proper place.

It may be convenient at this first occurrence of the term to say a word about the Rabbinic attitude to the written Torah, or doctrine of Holy Scripture. This varies from the most uncompromising and fanatical assertions of verbal inspiration[1] to calm admissions that the Torah is written in the language of men,[2] and not in chronological order.[3] This is exactly parallel to the division of Christian opinion between the upholder of literal inerrancy, and the upholder of free scientific textual criticism. The reader will perceive several other parallel controversies in subsequent chapters.

The origins of the Talmud, that amazing product of Jewish piety, fanaticism, and preciosity, go back to the religious teachings of the Scribes, the Oral Torah, which is probably not much younger than Ezra. This Oral Torah, which acquired with the passage of time a somewhat inflated importance,

[1] Sanh. 99ᵃ.   [2] Yeb. 71ᵃ; Ket. 67ᵇ; etc.   [3] Pes. 6ᵇ.

continued in later centuries under the Pharisaic favour and
the Sadducean frown. In the oral period as in the later documents, this teaching contained two readily differentiable
strains, the Halakhah and the Haggadah.

The contents of the Halakhah are exclusively legislative,
the series to infinity of everything that the Old Testament, and
in particular the Pentateuch, had prescribed or proscribed.
The Hebrew root verb means to walk or go, and herein lies
the extra-Scriptural traditional way of life of the Jew. The
written Law, the first Torah, is evaded or extended, relaxed
or tightened, with all the consummate skill of the most subtle
and delicate casuistry the world has ever known. The Halakhah
took within its purview jurisprudence, medicine, hygiene,
obstetrics, and many other matters which the modern mind has
divorced altogether from the aegis of religion. There is a
prevailing and tedious obsession with the minutiae of special
cases, and a resultant failure to clarify general principles.

A few random examples of Halakhoth will serve by way of
illustration. If you had been a baker in charge of an oven, and
also a good Jew of Talmudic times, your very secular vocation
would have compelled you to know a good deal about the
laws of clean and unclean. If an inquisitive cock hopped inside
your oven, it would not of itself convey defilement, even if it
died there, because it is a clean bird. But if it had just gobbled
a creepy-crawly insect, which is unclean, and then failed to
survive its explorations, the cock's last meal, not the bird itself,
would render your oven unclean and in need of purification,
because the carcass is not regarded as a tightly closed vessel
capable of circumscribing the contamination.[4] One strict
Rabbi would have counselled you to empty your mouth of
any loose saliva before walking any distance over four cubits
on the Sabbath day, lest you break the law by carrying a
burden—but his opinion was never made binding on the
community.[5] The Rabbis would legislate for your devotional
exercises, the social contacts permitted to you, the details of
your marital life, your very behaviour in the lavatory. Learned
teachers discussed solemnly such matters as the correct hand
to use in manipulating the smooth stone which served as a

[4] Kel. viii.5.   [5] Erub. x.5.

toilet roll—and still so serves in parts of the East.[6] The famous Rabbinic "fence about the Law"[7] was intended to block you at the furthest possible distance from any overt transgression. The Gentile mind feels little affinity with the Halakhic side of Rabbinic thought, and is inclined to dismiss it as learned trifling. A more sympathetic imagination can sometimes, though not always, look behind the outward rules into their inward motivation. It is undeniable that there is sometimes a double standard of obedience—adherence to the spirit and adherence to the letter.

The other strain of Rabbinic teaching, the Haggadah, signifying probably "declaration," is a much more free-and-easy affair, a medley of everything that does not fall under the definition of Halakhah. It includes history and fable, witchcraft and superstition, folklore and anecdote, parables and bad puns. A single example will suffice here, as later chapters will abound with others. The Rabbis are discussing how David could know when it was exactly midnight, in order to begin the thanksgiving postulated for that hour in the longest of the Psalms, and the following Haggadic story is introduced in explanation: "There was a lyre hanging above David's bed. As soon as it became midnight, a north wind would come and blow upon it, and it would make music of its own accord. David would immediately arise and engage himself in Torah until the dawn appeared."[8] The Haggadah is a weapon potent enough to break and resolve all difficulties of Scriptural interpretation, even the lack of alarm clocks in the days of the Israelite monarchy.

Halakhah and Haggadah doubtless existed from the earliest initiation of Scribal teaching, although the earliest surviving documents are some six centuries younger than Ezra. Rabbinism begins with a protracted and puzzling shyness of the written page outwith the realm of canonical Scripture, although the prejudice may have been disregarded on occasion. The Halakhah, in its earlier or Midrashic stage, had to depend directly on the authority of its scriptural proof-texts, which it might interpret with some freedom but could not disregard.

[6] Ber. 62[a]. Cf. Shab. 81[a].   [7] Ab. I.I.
[8] Ps. cxix.62; Ber. 3[b]. Cf. Num. R. xv.16.

Midrash, the commentary after the Rabbinic manner on the Books of the Old Testament, came in time to form a large section of the literature, though its written form is late. The Midrashim however contain, with exceptions, a higher proportion of Haggadic than of Halakhic material. At a date which cannot now be precisely determined, a new type of Halakhah, known as Mishnah, attained to independent authority, formulating its enactments without the Scriptural buttress hitherto considered essential. The word Mishnah itself means repetition, and reflects etymologically the method of its earlier transmission. The opening paragraphs of the famous Ethics of the Fathers would suggest that Mishnaic teaching began about 200 B.C., but this date may be a little earlier than the real one. Meanwhile the older Midrashic Halakhah maintained its Scripture-centricity, and continued to be operative in its own sphere. The entire Rabbinic activity was, until the destruction of the Herodian Temple in A.D. 70, merely one important aspect of the faith and learning of Judaism. But this momentous event terminated animal sacrifice, left the Sadducees unemployed, and brought the Rabbis to a position of greater authority within their own covenant.

In A.D. 200 or thereabouts, the Mishnaic Halakhic material, now somewhat voluminous, was collected and committed to writing, thus inaugurating the Rabbinic literature proper with the recognised and official Mishnah. There is a quasi-scientific arrangement in the six Orders and sixty-three Tractates, as the Tractates of each Order hinge, with exceptions, round a common theme, aspects of which they expound individually. The Mishnah codifies the discussions of six generations of Rabbinic scholars known as Tannaim, who taught from A.D. 10 till about 220—that is to say, from the time of Hillel and Shammai till the death of Rabbi Judah ha-Nasi I. The Aramaic root verb means to teach, but the noun *tanna* is used for a teacher of this particular period and milieu, whose utterances are cited either in the Mishnah or in a Baraita. A Baraita is a teaching of the Mishnaic period which failed to find its way into the canonical text, so to speak, but which is recognised as early and authoritative. The Tannaim themselves drew from earlier sources, and many of the Mishnaic traditions were of very venerable antiquity in their day. The New Testament scholar is primarily interested in the fact that the Tradition of the Elders is in fact this Tannaitic Halakhah preserved in substance in the Mishnah. The Mishnah, of course, freezes it at a stage of development later than the New Testament period, but it may still, owing to its long prior oral history, be used with discretion as valid historical background for the Gospels. The language of the Mishnah is that of the Hebrew Bible, with considerable differences of accidence and syntax, a large new vocabulary, and an intolerably bald and prosaic style. This is partly due to the somewhat prosaic nature of the contents.

After the Mishnah became written and fixed, there were further generations of Rabbinic scholars, known both in Babylonia and in Palestine, the two chief centres of Jewish culture, as the Amoraim. The word Amora, derived from the common Hebrew verb to speak, means simply speaker or interpreter. It signified first the official who translated into the vernacular Aramaic the Hebrew lectures of a distinguished scholar. Then it came to mean an expositor of the Mishnah, teaching within a fixed period, from the death of Judah I till A.D. 500. That is the sense in which the word is used here. The Amoraim expounded and expanded the work of the Tannaim, so that, both in Babylonia and in Palestine, the Mishnah became invested with a large body of commentary material, or Gemara. Mishnah plus Gemara constitutes Talmud, but geographical separation caused the Babylonian Talmud and the Jerusalem or Palestinian Talmud to become separate entities, though they incorporate the same basic document. Neither Gemara covers all the Tractates of the Mishnah, but the Babylonian enjoys the greater range and authority. The language has now become Aramaic, with differences of dialect between the two sets of Gemara. The Palestinian Amoraim are regarded as more straightforward and direct, the Babylonian as more subtle and casuistical.

The long Amoraic period was followed by the brief labours of the Saboraim, A.D. 500-540 approximately. Sabora comes from a verb meaning to reflect. They were the men of the afterthoughts—to put the root meaning another way—for they were the final editors and redactors of the Babylonian Talmud, though it was essentially complete before their time.

The functions of tanna, amora, and sabora are distinct in respects more significant than that of mere time. The words mean roughly teacher, expositor, and ponderer—originality and prestige alike diminish in passage down the time-stream.

The Babylonian Talmud took, in very round figures, some seven hundred years to reach its final shape. There was a pre-Tannaitic period, important though now a little misty, of something under two centuries—how much under, we do not precisely know; a Tannaitic period of two centuries, when the Mishnah took shape; an Amoraic period of three centuries when the Gemara was expanded in debate, and a Saboraic period of forty years, which compensates some of the unknown defect in the first period.

Rabbinic Judaism sometimes asserted that God revealed to Moses on Mount Sinai the entire Hebrew Scriptures, and everything contained in the Oral Law, placing the writing of the latter under interdict.[9] The Sinai revelation was undoubtedly the ancestor of all Jewish legislation, and the statement contains an element of poetic truth. The literal claim, however, is not taken very seriously by modern scholarship.

The story of Midrash may be told more briefly than that of Talmud. It is generally conceded that oral Midrash is earlier than Mishnah, though its written form, according to existing Hebrew documents, is later. It is probably very much earlier, for the very word is Biblical.[10] Paul's Hagar passage in Galatians is pure Midrashic allegory in Greek, and Philo of Alexandria provided voluminous earlier examples in the same tongue. The main purpose of Rabbinic Midrash was to get behind the literal meaning of the Scriptures, by exegesis, analogy, allegory, or any other convenient method, and to illuminate the deeper and richer meaning it was presumed to conceal. It has been stated already that Halakhah, though prominent in some particular Midrashim, is more often subordinate to Haggadah. That is why most of the Talmud calls for rather determined, purposeful reading—though it can be lively enough

[9] See esp. Ber. 5ᵃ, and other passages cited in C. Taylor, *Sayings of the Jewish Fathers*, Cambridge 1897, Excursus I.

[10] II Chron. XIII.22, XXIV.27.

here and there; while most of the Midrash is varied, interesting, and entertaining—though it can be dry enough here and there.

The attempt to date any particular Rabbinic teaching frequently raises problems of considerable intricacy. The pronouncements on a single page may be centuries apart in time. Fortunately, it is quite possible to perceive the general shape of the theology without detailed regard to these technicalities, and a few very broad facts may be sufficient for the reader.

If a passage contains no known name and no definite historical allusion, there may be no clue to its date beyond the niceties of Hebrew and Aramaic style—a judgment which is always, even for the expert, a little subjective. If the name of an identifiable Rabbi be given, it must be determined whether he is speaking in his own name, or on precedent; in the latter event the date needs to be pushed back before his time. Sometimes the speaker's authority may be set out in a retrogressive chain, through his teacher, his teacher's teacher, and so on. Moslem tradition requires that the *isnad* or chain should be carried right back to the Prophet or to one of his companions, but the Rabbis are satisfied with the authority of any scholar of repute. If his date be early, this is naturally regarded as enhancing the prestige of the particular teaching.

Passing more specifically to the sources cited in this volume, the reader may take it as a general rule that any quotation from the Babylonian Talmud or the Midrashim Genesis Rabbah and Lamentations Rabbah is earlier than A.D. 550, perhaps centuries earlier in specific instances, while the Midrash Leviticus Rabbah is only a little later. The remaining Rabbah Midrashim are of much later compilation, although they include early material. The writer has uniformly preferred the earlier source where there is a choice, and has always given it priority in footnote reference, but passages of particular interest from the later sources have not been excluded. It has never been considered necessary to distract the reader's attention from the main argument by discussing the dating of particular passages cited.

This volume is based on a complete and careful study of the Babylonian Talmud and the Rabbah Midrashim, with only very casual or fortuitous reference to the vast remaining bulk of Rabbinic literature. The survey of the entire field would be a somewhat gigantic task for a single book. The portions chosen are sufficiently important, typical, and voluminous to justify the claim that a study of Rabbinic theology has been made. The writer feels from his more limited acquaintance with the other sources that a complete reading of them, had this been feasible, might have furnished additional data on certain specific themes, but would not substantially have altered the general conclusions. This view is confirmed by a perusal of the *Rabbinic Anthology*, and of other books which quote extensively. Some of these books have been used, and have contributed specific points in the present study.

The Targumim or later Aramaic paraphrases of the Books of the Old Testament, which are separate from the Midrashic and Talmudic activities of Rabbinic Judaism, probably began in oral form in the days of Ezra, although the text was not written down till a much later date. They afford valuable material for the study of the contents of the Old Testament, which they often modify or expand considerably. There are a few passing references to them in subsequent pages.[11]

The Contents of the Talmud

There are six main themes in the Talmud, corresponding to the six Orders, but analogy, real or supposed, may lead any Tractate away from its official theme at any time. This is especially noticeable in the Gemara, where, more than in the Mishnah, each Order permeates and is permeated by all the others.

The first Order is mainly concerned with agricultural dues and the laws of tithe. There is no Babylonian Gemara for any Tractate in this Order except the first, which happens to be one of the five "orphan" Tractates of the Mishnah. This means merely that its topic lies outside the main theme of the Order. The subject is in fact benedictions and prayer, and this makes

---

[11] These facts may be supplemented by E. Schürer, *History of the Jewish People in the Time of Jesus Christ*, Edinburgh 1900, VOL. I, DIV. I, pp. 117-66; also articles in Hastings' *Dictionary of the Bible*, edd. J. Hastings, J. A. Selbie *et al.*, Edinburgh 1900-04, and *The Jewish Encyclopaedia*, henceforth cited as *J.E.*, New York 1901-6.

it not only one of the most interesting and readable portions of the Talmud, but also one in which the devotional side of Rabbinic piety is seen to the highest advantage. It is not necessary to detail the sacred dues here. The Roman imperial taxes were bitterly resented by a subject people, and paid only under compulsion, whereas these religious offerings were given proudly and gladly, even though they were all, with the exception of Terumah or Heave-offering, prescribed with exactitude.

The second Order deals with the set feasts of the sacred calendar. There is some measure of historical parallelism, which the present essay does not work out, between the Jewish Sabbath and the Christian Sunday; between Passover and Holy Communion; between circumcision and infant baptism. In these Tractates the Christian reader will find the historical sequel to the Old Testament teaching on the Jewish side, and, in the Mishnah at least, some valuable and contemporary Gospel background.

The third Order, on women, centres round the topics of marriage, divorce, and adultery. These Tractates and the New Testament are at variance on certain points, and a fuller understanding is valuable for those of either faith.

The fourth Order is mainly occupied with civil and criminal law, with problems of ownership and property—in short, with jurisprudence in general.

The fifth Order describes in the utmost detail the offerings and ritual of a Temple which was destroyed some 130 years before even the Mishnah was put into writing. Pious Jews treasured the splendours of every stone in the storehouse of the memory, although the vision had never been theirs in the flesh and the earthly glories had faded and vanished for ever. The pathetic and unfulfilled hope of rebuilding, with its note of expectancy and yearning, flits through Mishnah and Gemara in passage after passage, here and throughout the Talmud. The Holy One is even pictured, by a bold anthropomorphic figure, as mourning for His House.

The sixth Order deals with the Levitical laws of clean and unclean, mainly in restricted reference to Temple procedure. It is important as background for Matthew xv.1-20 and other passages, and for certain of the teachings of Paul.

The Hebrew names of the Orders and Tractates would be of little service to the general reader. The more serious student may readily familiarise himself with them. He will find some guidance on reference searching in a preliminary note to the list of abbreviations on p. xiii ff.

The Mental Climate of the Rabbinic Literature

It is not possible, without unduly enlarging this section, to offer more than a few scattered remarks on a wide subject. The reader may amplify and exemplify these for himself by a study of any portion of the literature, whether in the original or in translation.

Three features in particular intrude themselves on the consciousness of the student as he makes his way consecutively through, say, the Talmud. The first is the staccato disjointedness of it all, the lack of any obvious literary form or logical integration. The second is the unblushing juxtaposition of incompatible teachings, and the liability of every Halakhic ruling to be contradicted, in the same context or elsewhere. The uncritical moral patient must have felt, amid the disagreement of his doctors, like a cork in Charybdis. The third feature is the steady diminution of really fresh material, and the increasingly frequent consciousness of having read the same thing half-a-dozen times before. The research student must often have wished that the Saboraim had used their scissors a little more effectively. Terse obscurity of style and wearisome iteration do not make a happy combination.

In the discussion of controversial issues, many complicated examples of dialectic occur. A common type, reduced to an algebraic formula capable of infinite variation, might be represented as follows. Rabbi A said, in the name of Rabbi B, something which we will call x. Rabbi C said, in the name of Rabbi D, something contradicting x, or differing in some particular from it, which we will call y. Rabbi E reported some objection, amendment or amplification on the part of Rabbi F. The Gemara then declares that there is no contradiction: x is stated to be applicable in one set of specified circumstances, y in another. Rabbi G and Rabbi H are then cited, giving or quoting a second and a third independent resolution of the contradiction. The bewildered and uninitiated reader is left scratching his head, and wondering what the authoritative Halakhah really is. The method of reconciling the incompatibility of x and y by antithesis is important, as it occurs so frequently. A single example out of thousands will suffice. The Gemara proposes in one passage[12] that the heartless and neglectful father should be exposed to public obloquy, adding the words: "The raven searches food for its young, but that man does not search food for his children." A difficulty is raised from Psalm cxLVII.9, which is held to imply that the raven is neglectful of its young. All perplexity is removed by the statement that white ravens are neglected by their parents, whereas black ones are cared for; and then the Gemara proceeds in tranquil satisfaction. It would be interesting to secure the opinion of an ornithologist. This is the commonest method of harmonising two conflicting traditional laws, or of conforming an oral to a written law.

Owing to the long oral history of the Talmud and Midrash, and a paper-shyness which may have persisted for a long time with the conservative, mnemotechnic devices are frequent. These may employ catchwords, or the initial or medial letters of a group of words or names. Quite frequently the essential idea may be fixed in the student's mind by a paronomasia, cunning or questionable as the case may be. The lowest form of wit was sedulously used in argument as well. These aids to memory are seen in fairer perspective when it is remembered that the earlier Rabbinic student possessed neither notebook nor card index, and must needs bear a mental burden of somewhat frightening dimensions.

The Hebrew and Aramaic alphabets are identical, numerically and orthographically, and certain letter-numbers are invested with a special sanctity. By a strange arithmetical jugglery, the sum of the numerical values of the letters in a word may be used as a cryptogram for the word, or to establish some special conclusion. This device of Gematria occurs once in the New Testament, in Revelation xiii.18. The number 666 is probably the sum of the letter values of the Hebraised form of the name Nero Caesar.

[12] Ket. 49[b].

There is a complicated science of hermeneutics, whereby the written Law is casuistically interpreted and made the basis of deduced laws. The detailed study of the principles involved is a matter for the specialist. But the first of the official rules, which is also the simplest and most familiar, has a special New Testament interest. This is the argument from major to minor, or from minor to major. The first and rather less frequent form of the argument may be illustrated by a Talmudic example. The question at issue is whether the witness of two persons to the effect that a third person has unintentionally consumed forbidden fat should or should not render that third person liable to a sin offering. The affirmative argument proffered by one authority is that if the witness of two persons can render a man liable to the death penalty, which is a major matter, then it can very certainly render him liable to a sin offering, which is a very minor matter by comparison.[13] (The Jews did not actually possess the power of inflicting the death penalty in Talmudic times, but they were still deeply interested in the hypothetical basis of arguments of this nature.) The reverse form of this reasoning occurs more frequently, usually in Halakhic reference—though the Talmud sometimes queries the legitimacy of pushing it too far.[14] There are also examples in more theological contexts. If the death of the wicked grieves the heart of God, suggests one moralist, *how much more so* does the death of the righteous?[15] The essence of the persuasion always lies in the *how much more so* or *how much less so*. The Christian reader will find several arguments from minor to major in the Epistle to the Hebrews.[16]

The device of allegory is frequently used to elucidate problems or remove difficulties. The application of it may unravel the most unexpected meanings from the Peshat, or literal signification of the Old Testament text. It is found in the Talmud, despite a more stern preoccupation there with the requirements of the Law, but it is more typical of the Midrash. The verse Genesis 1.2 discloses to the allegorist in its fuller interpretation the four nations of Babylonia, Media, Greece, and Rome, with sundry of their iniquities, and also, in contrast,

[13] B.M. 3*b*.
[14] Yeb. 11*b*; Tem. 9*a*.
[15] Hag. 15*b*.
[16] Heb. 11.2-3, 1x.13-14, x.28-9.

the spirit of the Messiah.[17] For the uninitiated, this seems a good deal to deduce from so short a passage. Genesis II.10-14, on the river issuing from Eden and dividing into four heads, is the subject of an elaborate allegory, with much historical and geographical detail.[18] Scriptural and non-Scriptural examples abound throughout the sources. The chief storehouse of interpretations of this kind in all Jewish literature is found, however, in the Greek writings of Philo of Alexandria.

The argument from the silence of Scripture deserves mention here, as it is of frequent occurrence, and there is a New Testament example. If a phenomenon is mentioned for the first time at a certain point in the Scriptural narrative, it is sometimes deduced that it was unknown before that; or it is assumed that if Scripture fails to mention particular concomitant circumstances, they do not exist. The Midrash declares, in a succession of examples, that before the time of Abraham, the old and the young looked exactly alike. Abraham requested of God the appearance of old age, so that when a father and son travelled together, the father might receive the honour due to his years. Isaac asked God for bodily suffering, which was unknown before his time, that he and those who were to follow might thereby expiate some sins in the mortal state, so reducing the punishment that might await them in the after life. Jacob asked for illness before death, that a man might be warned of the approach of his last hour and meet it in a prepared state. Hezekiah asked for repeated sicknesses in the course of life, that a man might thereby find opportunity to repent.[19] The argument has considerable pictorial and homiletic value, though some might question its strict dialectic validity. It is by the selfsame reasoning that Melchizedek is declared devoid of human antecedents in Hebrews VII.3.

The fuller assessment of the value of the kinds of teaching here illustrated belongs to a later chapter. It can scarcely be denied that originality of thinking would seem to be a somewhat doubtful virtue in the Rabbinic academies, and that the pupil preferred was quite certainly the one who had developed the most tenacious and parrot-like grip on the verbal exactitudes of traditional law. As the centuries pass, the teaching

[17] Gen. R. II.4.   [18] Gen. R. XVI.4.   [19] Gen. R. LXV.9.

becomes more and more the exposition of exposition, a formal and rather stagnant exercise. In spite of all this it possesses an intrinsic value. The writer testifies of his conviction on that point in the existence of the present book.

The Importance of Rabbinic Study

Jews and Christians have a like interest in the Old Testament. Talmud, and more especially Midrash, would be of some relevance for both if only because it quotes and discusses those Books at no inconsiderable extent, thus providing another line of independent textual verification. It is not necessary to offer additional reasons to the Jewish reader—he knows already why the Rabbinic religion is significant for him. The Christian may not be equally well informed in the matter.

The New Testament scholar who desires the fullest possible understanding of his documents requires Rabbinics, at least indirectly, both for exegesis and for theology. The indirectness is due merely to the late date of the written literature, and the difficulty of disentangling its earlier strands. The exegetical side has been explored with some thoroughness by Jews and Christians, and the reader may refer to their works for details.[20] Many a problem of New Testament interpretation receives a measure of new light when its Rabbinic background is properly understood.

This essay is concerned mainly with the theological side of the Rabbinic contribution, which is equally important. If there are any doctrines which ought to lay bare the vital elements of this phase of Jewish religion, its nerve centres, the fountains of its moral and spiritual strength, they are the doctrines of God and man. The Rabbis, the Apostles, Jesus Christ Himself, sprang from a common Judaism. Was the Rabbinic faith a declension from the Old Testament? Was it the empty husk of a pusillanimous and outmoded legalism? Or was it something better and finer, even if it remained persistently blind to some aspects of the truth?

[20] Strack and Billerbeck, Abrahams, and Montefiore may be mentioned among modern writers in this field: see Bibliography.

Within about a century of the Passion[21] the two greatest religious forces of the world had finally parted, and the Cross has been the stone of stumbling for two thousand years now. Rabbinic Judaism may not explain the Jewish-Christian split, but it may give some indication of the shape of the wedge. Here undoubtedly was the prototype of the Reformation and of the separationist ethics of Anglicans, Presbyterians, Methodists, and the others. It is here perhaps that the oecumenical reformer should really begin his studies. Secession is a matter of conscience, necessary it may be, but always wasteful. The Prophet of Islam might have been a Christian, and much bloodshed and hatred saved, had the Christianity of his day and milieu been vital and sincere. The Protestant Reformation, necessary as it was, created not two Churches, but a dozen or more. The Christians of the twentieth century, deeply conscious of the scandal of manifold contemporary divisions within the Body of Christ, may do well to ponder awhile the incompatibilities of Apostolic and Rabbinic faith, and to relate them by analogy to the problems of today. A widespread and sympathetic understanding of religious divisions, with a background of historical continuity, might do a great deal for the betterment of the world of tomorrow.

[21] Various dates have been suggested for the final breach between Judaism and Christianity, including the martyrdom of James, A.D. 62; the destruction of the Temple, A.D. 70; and the Bar-Cocheba revolt, A.D. 135. See E. G. Selwyn, *I Peter*, 2nd edn. London 1947, p. 58, n. 1; C. W. Dugmore, *The Influence of the Synagogue upon the Divine Office*, London 1944, Ch. I.

CHAPTER II

THE NATURE OF GOD

IT is absolutely essential to make some study of the doctrine
of God before passing to the doctrine of man. In Judaism
and Christianity alike the two themes are closely intertwined
in every major issue, as the following fundamental questions
clearly show. God, the Creator of all, is absolutely righteous:
whence then the redness of Nature's tooth and claw, and the
stain of sin in the heart of man? Does God condemn (or pardon)
all men, or most of them, or just a few? Are the absolute justice
and the absolute love of God finally compatible? Is sinful man
a responsible and culpable agent, or do heredity and environment leave him with no fighting chance, but a very convenient
excuse? If man has the power to please God, is it by faith, or
works, or both? Why does God allow the righteous to suffer,
while the wicked frequently prosper? Are these discrepancies
adjusted in the life to come? Is salvation primarily for one sect
or creed, or is it offered freely to all men?

A book which succeeded in giving final answers to these final
questions would indeed be a best seller. The more limited task
of the pages which follow is to show how the Rabbis wrestled
with problems such as these, and to point out in passing some
appropriate New Testament comparisons. Christian theology
is not univocal on such issues, and the reader will find closely
parallel conflicts of opinion in the Rabbinic teachings—a
phenomenon already observed in the doctrine of Holy
Scripture.

Theology, like philosophy, deals with problems which
cannot be isolated. The owner of a miscellaneous library may
choose to arrange his books according to subject matter, or
authorship, or size, or colour of binding, or name of publisher—
but the strict application of one criterion may very well render

all the others inoperative. The classification of theological teachings is no more tractable. If the reader expects to find these chapters a little fluid, anticipatory, and retrospective, he will not be denied such order as the subject permits.

The present chapter deals with the nature of God—which is of course very imperfectly conceived by the human animal, Rabbinic or Christian, in the mortal state.

A Working Basis for the Doctrine of God

The shape and content of the doctrine of God depends finally on the substance of the revelation vouchsafed—it is inconceivable that man could have worked it out for himself, unaided and uninspired. There is a sharp cleavage between the historic faiths of the world as to the precise content of revelation: Christianity makes a highly significant addition to Judaism, while Islam makes a somewhat different profession. Jews do not deny that God can send His Messiah to earth—they merely deny that He has done so, rejecting decisively the Christian terminology. For the Jew or Moslem of today, the Incarnation as such is a blasphemy, and the doctrine of the Trinity something which he finds it difficult to distinguish from tritheism. The Midrash declares, in specific reference to God: "Everything which possesses issue dies, decays, suffers creation, but cannot actively create; everything which possesses no issue (i.e. by its intrinsic nature) dies not, decays not, creates actively without suffering creation."[1] This is a rebuttal of New Testament teaching which has failed to grasp fully that which it seeks to refute, but it is also the statement of a faith which is absolutely clear-headed in its own sphere, and faithful to its own premises. The Prophet of the Koran was thinking on similar lines when he declared: "Sole maker of the heavens and of the earth! How, when he hath no consort, should he have a son?"[2] For Jew and Moslem alike, the idea of the Christ is a hard one to accept.

---

[1] Gen. R. xii.7. Cf. Ex. R. xxix.5; Song of Sol. R. vii.9, 1.

[2] Sura 6,101, J. M. Rodwell's translation, London 1929. Cf. Sura 112. The Prophet's total misunderstanding of the doctrine of the Trinity is manifest in such passages as Sura 5,116: " O Jesus, Son of Mary, hast thou said unto mankind —'Take me and my mother as two Gods, beside God.' "

Jew and Christian agree on certain essential characteristics
of God. The writer prefers to avoid the word attributes, save
in a limited context below, as this will save much tedious discussion of controversial matters. A working basis for the
doctrine of God, acceptable at least in outline to either faith,
may be posited as follows. *God is One and unique, eternally existing,
endowed with limitless power and knowledge, present throughout His
creation, throned in unimaginable transcendent splendour, yet close to
every creature, supreme in His decrees, righteous, just, holy, and
merciful.* These characteristics will occupy the main portions of
this chapter.

The Unity of God [3]

The oceans and contiguous seas spread over the face of the
globe are many, yet they are also one. The limbs, bones,
arteries, and organs of the human frame are many, yet the
healthy body is also one. God is distinguished in creation,
providence, redemption, reprobation, yet He remains One in
essence. The Jew would not normally regard the Unity of
God as a matter open to debate. It was his bounden duty to
declare it twice daily in the statutory recital of the Shema, or
Hebrew text of Deuteronomy VI.4-9,[4] thus constantly reaffirm-
ing his quiet inward conviction of the fact. Heretics and
idolaters sometimes changed his tranquil acceptance into a
blazing and controversial passion.

The real sin of idolatry lay in its visible denial of the Unity
of God—men cannot worship a stock or stone and worship
an omnipresent yet undivided Deity at the same time; so
Talmud and Midrash cannot denounce the practice too sternly
or too often. The Jew must suffer martyrdom rather than
succumb under pressure or even torture.[5] Despite all the
emotion with which the subject is invested, there is also a hard-
headed facing of facts, as the cold logic of the following passage

[3] For a discussion of pagan approximations to monotheism, see W. F. Albright,
From the Stone Age to Christianity, Baltimore 1940, pp. 160-70. For the author's
claim that Jewish monotheism goes right back to Moses, see the same work,
pp. 207, 250; also his *Archaeology and the Religion of Israel*, Baltimore 1942, pp.
116, 155, 177.

[4] Lam. R. III.21-3, 8; Song of Sol. R. II.16, 1, VII.11, 1.

[5] Cf. Lam. R. I.16, 50.

demonstrates: "The elders were asked in Rome: 'If an idol does not come within God's will, why does He not destroy it?' They replied: 'If men worshipped something which was not necessary for the world, God would destroy it. But behold! they worship the sun and the moon and the stars and the planets—is God to destroy His world because of madmen?' They retorted to the elders: 'In that case, let God destroy the thing which is not necessary for the world, and let Him leave alone the thing which is necessary.' The elders replied: 'We would but strengthen the hands of those that worship the latter, for they would declare: "Know that these are gods, for they have not been destroyed." ' "[6] There are 67 words of terse Hebrew in the Mishnaic passage: it needs 122 words to represent them in English, and they then exhibit a tortuousness and a re-echoing of ideas alien to that language, though acceptable enough in the original.

For the upholder of the Divine unity, one unwelcome type of heretic was the Persian dualist, who believed in a god of light and a god of darkness. There is a clear Mishnaic prohibition, twice enunciated, against immediate repetition of thanks to God in prayer, lest this should seem to lend support to the heresy, and the whole notion is denounced in the Midrash.[7] The meticulous nature of the precaution, forbidding a phraseology not unnatural in prayer, reflects eloquently a very real fear of the notion, and of its possible effect on orthodox belief.

Another dangerous heretic threatening the unity of God, from the Jewish viewpoint, was the Christian. There are many passages containing veiled attacks on the doctrine of the Trinity, or on the divinity of Christ. They had to be veiled, in order to escape the censor. This is an interesting subject, but one which cannot be pursued here.[8]

Israel herself is not exempted from blame: the historic repudiation of the Divine unity within her own ranks is specifically recognised as one of the sins leading to the Exile.[9]

[6] A. Zar. iv.7. Cf. Gemara 54[b]-55[b]. Cf. Wis. xiii.2, 10, xiv.8 ff., etc., Ecclesiasticus xxx.19.
[7] Ber. v.3; 33[b]; Meg. iii (iv).9; 25[a]. Cf. Deut. R. ii.33.
[8] See R. Travers Herford, *Christianity in Talmud and Midrash*, London 1903.
[9] Lam. R. i.i, 1.

The Jew who asserted the unity of God was a little hampered in controversy by two features of his own Hebrew Bible. The first was the fact that the word Elohim, frequently used for God, happens to be grammatically plural, and was apt to be so interpreted by opponents. The Rabbis point out that the plural form is entirely replaced by the Tetragrammaton Yahweh in certain contexts, so as to give no handle to the heretics.[10] As the perversely-minded heretics would find plenty of plural forms elsewhere, the argument is a trifle weak. There is more cogency in pointing out that Elohim takes a singular verb,[11] which is strong evidence of a plural of majesty or excellence.[12] The second stone of stumbling is that God speaks in the first person plural in the Creation story (Gen. 1.26), in the narrative of the Confusion of Tongues (Gen. xi.7), and in Isaiah's Temple vision (Is. vi.8). The Midrash, commenting on the first passage, delineates Moses acting as God's amanuensis in recording the creation. Moses objects to the plural verb, which merely provides a pretext for heretics to cavil—that is to say, throw doubts on the Divine unity. But God specifically commands him: "Write: and whosoever desires to be mistaken will be mistaken."[13] This is a surprisingly weak line of apologetic, especially as there are several better ones available. A simple and satisfying exegesis is to regard the "we" as including either the angels with whom God discussed the act of creation, or the creative Word—*Logos* or *Memra*. These alternatives are both buttressed by adequate Jewish precedent, but the prologue to the Fourth Gospel may have rendered the latter unpopular. Some have argued the plural of majesty in these contexts also, though Gesenius rejects this.[14] Whatever line of interpretation the particular exegete may adopt, there is quite certainly nothing in any of these passages to compromise the Divine unity. In another context, probably anti-Christian in its original form, the unique creation of Adam is used as a monotheistic

[10] Men. 110ᵃ.   [11] Gen. R. viii.9; Ex. R. xxix.1; Deut. R. ii.13.

[12] F. H. W. Gesenius, E. Kautzsch, and A. E. Cowley, *Hebrew Grammar*, Oxford 1910, p. 398 f. Cf. also A. B. Davidson, *Theology of the Old Testament*, Edinburgh 1904, pp. 99 ff.; Albright, *From the Stone Age to Christianity*, p. 161.

[13] Gen. R. viii.8.

[14] Gesenius, Kautzsch, and Cowley, *Hebrew Grammar*, p. 398, n. 2, where interesting alternatives are suggested.

argument;[15] and, in one of the finest passages of the Midrash, the theme of the unique God filling the universe, just as the soul fills the body, is developed at some length.[16]

The sublimity of the concept of the unity of God does not always receive due respect in the heat and dust of controversy, and the Rabbinic teaching is on the whole vastly inferior to the noble words of Deuteronomy referred to in the first paragraph of this section.

The Eternity of God

There is little to say about the eternal existence of God, which was declared with such poetic fervour in certain of the Psalms. In the Rabbinic literature it is taken for granted, like the sunrise, and no special controversy seems to have arisen. God was before His creation came into being, and will be when it has ceased to exist. There are some scattered affirmations of the orthodox doctrine,[17] but they call for no special comment here.

The Omnipotence, Omniscience, and Omnipresence of God

The omnipotence, omniscience, and omnipresence of God were so clearly and finally taught in the pages of the Old Testament that there remained little of value for posterity to add. The impassioned sublimity and coercive fervour of the Psalm cxxxix, for example, leaves anything the Rabbis might write cold and uninspired by comparison, for they do little more than cite particular instances. The first and third of these doctrines may be discussed very briefly first: the second raises considerably wider issues.

God Omnipotent created the world without angelic assistance, that the sole glory might be His.[18] Human beings may draw pictures of their kind, but only God can impart the breath of life.[19] God's sustaining care for all creatures extends "from the horns of wild oxen even unto the eggs of lice."[20] The reader is expected to supply the tacit minor-to-major

---

[15] Sanh. 38ᵃ.
[16] Lev. R. IV.8. Cf. Ber. 10ᵃ.
[17] Cf. Ber. 28ᵇ; Ex. R. xv.10; Lev. R. vi.6.
[18] Gen. R. I.3.
[19] Ber. 10ᵃ.
[20] Shab. 107ᵇ.

argument that if God cares even for these insignificant matters, He must care vastly more for man. Certain "keys" or powers— rain, childbirth, and the resurrection of the dead—God keeps within His own hands, and entrusts to no deputy. Some would add the further "key" of sustenance, but this is included causally under rain.[21] The Rabbinic doctrine of omnipotence is thoroughgoing, but it would need to be demonstrated by the extension of a list of this kind.

God Omnipresent is frequently invested with this very title.[22] He can fill Heaven and earth, and yet become infinitely small in revealing Himself to man.[23] He fills the whole earth, even as the soul fills the body.[24] This doctrine, like the last, seems never to be subjected to any serious doubt or exception.

No Rabbi seriously doubted the omniscience of God—but he did not doubt the freedom of man's will either, and the juxtaposition of the two doctrines frequently brought him, like his Christian brother, into considerable difficulties. It is not necessary to do more than open the subject here: it will be discussed more fully at a later stage in the chapter.

It will be convenient to outline first what might be called the orthodox view of the omniscience of God, who cannot be in doubt.[25] He knows, and has ever known, the hearts of men. "From the time when the world was first formed, the Holy One, blessed be He, foresaw the actions of the righteous and of the wicked alike."[26] This is merely a statement of divine foreknowledge, without any necessary implication of pre-destination. A famous apothegm in the Ethics of the Fathers proclaims roundly and categorically that God foresees every-thing, yet leaves man with freedom of choice.[27] These passages form a consistent and logical thought pattern, with implications which will be discussed later.

There are, however, many other passages of a somewhat different tenor. It will be sufficient at this stage to refer to a single fairly lengthy one, to the effect that God first received praise from the dumb waters, then created man and endowed

---

[21] Taan. 2[a], [b].   [22] Num. R. II.19, etc.
[23] Gen. R. IV.4.   [24] Ber. 10[a]; Lev. R. IV.8.
[25] Ber. 3[a], etc.   [26] Gen. R. III.8. Cf. Ex. R. XXI.3; Num. R. XVI.16.
                    [27] Ab. III.16

him with speech for His greater praise and glory, but subsequently found him a sore trial and disappointment.[28]

The theme of omniscience has very close links with God's decree, and with the Divine attributes of Justice and Mercy. It will therefore be discussed more fully along with these related topics at a later stage in this chapter.

The Immanence and Transcendence of God

There has been much discussion as to whether the Rabbis conceived of God as immanent or transcendent, a Creator not too proud to stoop to earth and care for His creatures, or a remote and aloof Deity. The writer sees no purpose in examining the question at length, because he believes that the antithesis is artificial and false. There is ample evidence that the sources rightly depict God in both of these essential aspects of His nature, as a few typical passages will show.

God Transcendent dwells above the Seventh Heaven—the reader may examine for himself the astronomical dimensions of His abode;[29] He is exalted over everything, at the very pinnacle of His creation;[30] He is utterly different from any earthly king, as Talmud and Midrash insist with story, allegory, and precept in passages without number.

At the same time, and without contradiction, God Immanent is depicted as condescending to act as best man at Adam's wedding,[31] as taking notice of the lowly,[32] especially orphans and widows,[33] and the poor.[34] Sometimes the immanence is rather crudely anthropomorphic, as in the first example, and in another passage which not only invests the Holy One with phylacteries, after the manner of the pious Jew, but describes their very contents.[35] This is part of the dramatic and pictorial symbolism of Oriental teaching. The Western mind, trained in a different thought pattern, is inclined to dismiss it with less sympathy and understanding than it deserves.

The human perception of God Immanent is brought out

[28] Gen. R. v.i.
[30] Ex. R. xxiii.13.
[32] Sot. 5[a].
[34] Ex. R. xxxi.13, etc.

[29] Hag. 13[a].
[31] Ber. 61[a].
[33] Ex. R. xxx.8.
[35] Ber. 6[a].

very clearly also in the concept of the Shekinah, which will be discussed in the next chapter.

It may be stated without further elaboration that the Rabbis have clearly and firmly grasped two complementary truths, without either of which their theology would be incomplete. Some of the passages cited show a true religious appreciation of the love and graciousness of God.

The Righteousness and Holiness of God

It is axiomatic in the Rabbinic theology that God is not merely passively sinless, but actively righteous. As the undeniable evil in the world cannot come directly from Him, other explanations must be found—even if some highly unsatisfactory ones are rashly suggested in the heat of dialectic. Whatever happens, the character of God must never be in question.

The entire Levitical code, with all its ritual ablutions and purity laws, its distinctions of clean and unclean, and all the elaborations of Temple sacrifice and procedure, sprang from direct human consciousness of the holiness of God. Because God is so pure and so wholly Other, the human worshipper must not dare to approach His sanctuary with any lesser precautions. This was an ancient and historical form of piety, however little it may appeal to the modern spirit, and its manifestation was by no means confined to Judaism.

These two statements are inserted here for schematic tidiness, but their fuller elaboration belongs to other sections of the book.

The Decrees of God, the Attributes of Justice and Mercy, and the Divine Omniscience

The themes here linked together are all components of a troublesome yet important theological problem, anticipated already in the fourth section of this chapter, where the omniscience of God was discussed in a preliminary way. This problem is the tension between Divine predestination and human free will, the Jewish counterpart of a pertinent Christian dilemma. Stated in its crudest form, the issue is as follows. If God's decrees are fixed, man cannot be free; and if they are reversible, God cannot be omniscient. Or, beginning from the other end, God in His dealings with man cannot be just without being unmerciful, or merciful without being unjust. Many theologians, Rabbinic and Christian alike, have floundered in the mire over this issue.

The longest Talmudic discussion of God's decrees[36] ends in stalemate; but it deserves scrutiny, if only as a demonstration of the total inadequacy of logic in this context. The Aramaic is somewhat turgid, but may become clearer in a close paraphrase. The passage begins on the assumption that God's decree is absolutely unalterable. Let us suppose, says the Gemara, that Israel has been exceptionally wicked at New Year time—or that her credit balance in the Treasury of Merits[37] has become exceedingly low, and that God has therefore decreed very scanty rains in order to punish her. But Israel suddenly and unpredictably repents. What is God to do? He cannot go back on His decree, which is final and absolute, so He grants the predetermined quantities of rain without increment, but apportions them to the seasons and particular areas where they will be of maximum service—so that Israel is quite as well off as if the decree had been rescinded in her favour. Then the circumstances are considered to be precisely reversed. God's initial decree of abundant rains was framed for an Israel in good standing, but she becomes backsliding. Finally, therefore, she receives all the rain predetermined, but at the wrong seasons and in the wrong places, so that she is still punished. This ingenious argument certainly saves the decree—but what about the omniscience?

The Gemara then goes on in the same context to discuss three contrasted types of individual, successful or unsuccessful as suppliants before God. Firstly, there are those who call on God's mercy before, and those who call after, He has made the decree final. This would presuppose that the decree concerning the eternal destiny of a particular human being is finalised at some precise point of time in his earthly life, known to God but unknown to him. Secondly, there are those who make a satisfactory, and those who make an unsatisfactory, prayer. Thirdly, for those who face a final decree, God has in some cases accompanied it by an oath, in some cases He has

---

[36] R.Sh. 17b-18a.   [37] See below, Chapter X.

not—a sentiment which, considering man's rather limited knowledge of the Divine mind, sounds rather like hair-splitting.

This passage has been considered first and in detail, because it opens the problem somewhat fully but fails to come down on either side of the fence. Many teachings take a more definite stand one way or the other, and some of these may now be considered.

One viewpoint frequently advocated is that the decrees of God are both operative and absolutely immutable. This, like the sterner developments of Calvinism, produces a harsh and unlovely theology, self-consistent, but rather too like determinism when pushed to extremes. In this strain there is some very emphatic teaching, in the spirit of a classical utterance in the Book of Job, to the effect that a man must bless God for the evil as well as the good, and, coupled with it, a stern prohibition against reading mercy into the decrees of God by pointless and illegitimate prayers. The specific reference is to the lower creation, and the implication is that God brings His own will to pass, irrespective of human supplication.[38] This has been interpreted as an attack on the Pauline view of grace,[39] but the argument may not be intended to reach beyond its immediate context. Similar sentiments occur in the Mishnah,[40] with some hard-headed but incontrovertible logic. If a woman is already pregnant, for example, it is idle to pray for a male offspring—the prayer cannot make any difference to a matter which is determined before its utterance. Many human prayers are open to the precise criticism enunciated in this teaching. One further example may suffice in this context. His theological view of the decree leads a Rabbi, despite all his piety, to fear at the point of death the eternal and implacable anger of God.[41] This is a type of piety foreign to some, but typical of many earnest spirits, and as such commanding respect.

Certain passages adopt precisely the opposite view. God will Himself voluntarily rescind a decree when the man against whom it had been pronounced displays the supreme virtue of teaching Torah to the son of an unlettered man,[42] or even

[38] Ber. 33 ^{b}; Meg. 25 ^{a}.   [39] Megilla, Soncino edn., p. 149, n. 9.
[40] Ber. ix.3.   [41] Ber. 28 ^{b}.   [42] B.M. 85 ^{a}.

when he does no more than rightfully fulfil a precept.[43] God's decree may also be annulled from the human side by repentance.[44] Still more striking and suggestive is the declaration that the righteous man has the power to "rule God"—to reverse the Divine decrees by human prayer and piety.[45]

The "Calvinist" and "Arminian" teachings, as they might be dubbed, are individually logical, though of course mutually exclusive. The first and lengthy passage seems to fall between two stools, and to make God prevaricate. It may well be intended not as a solution but as a challenge to the extremists of either school. There are, however, further examples of both types of theology to follow.

The problem of this section recurs in connexion with the Divine attributes. (It has been indicated already that the precise number and differentiation of these attributes is a controversial issue bypassed in these pages. For the purposes of the present study, the technical term needs to be used in this context only.) The point to be stressed is that God possesses an attribute of Justice or Anger, and also an attribute of Mercy or Compassion. (Whether these are to be reckoned numerically as two, three, or four is of no immediate concern.) If the nature of God is to be properly understood, full allowance must be made for these seemingly opposite components.

Sometimes the attribute of Justice is supposed to be clamant and predominant. After all, what claim does sinful man possess to the mercy of God? These passages re-echo the hard "Calvinistic" realism of the unalterable decrees. The attribute of Justice is frequently represented as arguing with God, urging on Him a greater severity in dealing with men than He has actually been pleased to exercise;[46] urging also some further delay in the coming of the Messiah, because of human unworthiness.[47] There comes a point where justice has been subordinated to mercy long enough, and must now be asserted more strongly.[48] The Deluge was precisely such a time. These sinful men have been shielded too long, and must now be treated with a sterner discipline.

[43] Shab. 63ᵃ.
[44] Lev. R. x.5; Ex. R. xlv.1.
[45] M. Kat. 16ᵇ.
[46] Shab. 55ᵃ; Meg. 15ᵇ; Sanh. 103ᵃ.
[47] Sanh. 97ᵇ.
[48] Gen. R. xxvi.6.

In many other contexts, this uncompromising attitude is forsaken. God's justice may be tempered by His mercy, provided the integrity of truth is not assailed.[49] God may Himself intervene on man's behalf—His hand is sometimes spread out under the wings of the angels bearing Ezekiel's divine chariot, to protect penitents from the attribute of Justice.[50] When the world deserves by its wickedness utter annihilation, God will sometimes quit the throne of justice, and sit on the throne of mercy.[51] The Holy One is represented as praying that His own will may be such that the attribute of Mercy may prevail over the attributes of Justice or Anger, for the sake of the children whom He has created.[52] And Abraham the patriarch in his mortal state is bold enough to rebuke the Almighty, assuring Him that He cannot have it both ways: the world and absolute justice are not capable of contemporaneous existence.[53]

Another line of Rabbinic approach allows a greater importance to the human contribution: God's attitude to men, in other words, is affected radically by their attitude before Him. The doctrine of works possesses a lingering appeal for the human heart, which loves to feel itself in some measure the architect of its own destiny. An apt parable, parallel in some measure to Abraham's expostulation cited above, points out that untempered Divine mercy would encourage unrestrained human sin—a piece of psychology which cannot be called unreasonable—whereas untempered Divine justice would simply blot the world out of existence. That is why God permits some scope to both attributes, Justice and Mercy.[54] A further teaching stresses the human contribution even more. Wicked men actually turn God's mercy into judgment, whereas righteous men bring about the opposite change.[55] Most delightful of all the passages is the following, which deserves quotation in full. "Just as the pitchfork turns over the grain from one place to another, so does the prayer of the righteous

---

[49] A. Zar. 4[b]. Cf. also Num. R. XVI.22 and *A Rabbinic Anthology*, edd. C. G. Montefiore and H. Loewe, henceforth cited as *R.A.*, London 1938, No. 630.

[50] Pes. 119[a].   [51] A. Zar. 3[b].

[52] Ber. 7[a].   [53] Gen. R. XXXIX.6; Lev. R. X.1.

[54] Gen. R. XII.15.   [55] Gen. R. LXXIII.3.

reverse the decisions of the Holy One, blessed be He, from the attribute of Anger to the attribute of Mercy."[56]

The problem of Divine omniscience and human freedom has never been tidily solved, in the Rabbinic or in any other culture. That theology may seem hard and unattractive which rebukes a young man for praying that his chosen lady may become his wife—God omniscient determined the partner-to-be forty days before the embryo took shape, and any such prayer is impious and futile.[57] Yet at the same time "God so loved the world" that He ordained the breaking of the force of the winds by the mountains and hills, lest human beings should be destroyed thereby.[58] The Rabbinic God was variously conceived, like the Christian one, as anything from the hard, ruthless formulator of decrees to the loving Heavenly Father, full of compassion for even the least of His creatures. For many, the omniscience was not specifically considered, or else it remained a somewhat academic problem.

Some Curious Rabbinic Conceptions of God

The reader has seen many examples of Oriental imagery and symbolism already—an over-literal interpretation of some of these may miss the point. This section gathers together a few miscellaneous conceptions of God which seem particularly strange or amusing to Western minds. These are not of great theological importance, but they contribute to the roundness of the general picture.

Very prevalent indeed is the idea of God as a sort of super-Rabbi, more learned and industrious than any of His earthly servants. The phylacteries on the very person of the Deity have been noted already.[59] The Holy One has an exact knowledge of the clean and unclean animals.[60] Furthermore, He diligently revises His own studies in Torah, thus setting an example to men.[61] The Torah in Rabbinic eyes was a thing possessed of life and growth, never the same in any generation as in the previous one. The idea of God as its student might seem to the Gentile to compromise the Divine omniscience, but the Midrash

---

[56] Yeb. 64ᵃ. Cf. Num. R. x.5.   [57] M. Kat. 18ᵇ; Sot. 2ᵃ.
[58] Lev. R. xv.1.   [59] Ber. 6ᵃ.
[60] Hull. 59ᵃ.   [61] Ex. R. xl.1.

has forgotten that matter for the moment, and is asserting the paramount importance of the Torah.

The apparent lapses of God from Rabbinic rectitude are justified from the Halakhah in answer to the taunts of sectarians. When the heretics accuse God of breaking the Sabbath law by carrying burdens, inasmuch as the winds and storms He causes may lift entire objects, even on the holy day, the Rabbis are quick to retort that even the most pious Jew is permitted by the law to carry burdens on the Sabbath, provided he does so only within his own courtyard. The entire earth is the courtyard of God—therefore He does not break the law.[62] The response of the heretic is not recorded, but the ingenuity and wit of the answer were beyond his power to deny. For two specific "transgressions" God is supposed to require atonement. He diminished the size of the moon after its original creation—a fact deduced by very Rabbinical methods from Genesis 1.14 and 16, and He also permitted the moon to trespass on the sun's domain[63]—which is what happens presumably every time a shadowy moon is seen in a daylight sky.

Rather more open to criticism is the statement that when God created Adam, He deceived the ministering angels, revealing to them only the righteous posterity that would spring from him, and concealing the evil one. Otherwise the attribute of Justice would have thwarted the creation of man.[64] This is one of those ill-considered remarks that may slip out in dialectic, not really meant in the heart, but actually derogatory to the Deity they are meant to honour.

The Rabbis and the Deity both come off well in the last example to illustrate this topic, which has a laugh in it. A Roman matron happened to enquire as to how God had spent His time since the six days of creation, and was informed by the Rabbinic authorities that He had spent it in making human marriages. The lady did not believe that this task required special abilities, so, anxious to display her semi-divine potential, she promptly coerced a thousand male and a thousand female

---

[62] Gen. R. x.5; Ex. R. xxx.9.
[63] Hull. 60b; Sheb. 9a; Gen. R. vi.3. See *J.E.*, VOL. x, p. 621, col. 2.
[64] Gen. R. viii.4. See below, Chapter IV.

slaves into matrimony in a single day. Unhappily the sun rose next morning on a sorry crop of broken heads and scratched eyes, accompanied by eager beseechings for an equally rapid divorce. Thus was the once confident lady reduced to admit that God's reputed task was not quite so easy as she had imagined.[65]

[65] Lev. R. viii.1; Num. R. iii.6.

CHAPTER III

THE MANIFESTATIONS OF GOD

THE Rabbinic view of the nature of God has been established in general outline, and the particular vehicles or channels of God's self-revelation to man, or the direct agents of His purposes must be considered next. The chapter title calls these the manifestations of God. There are several other possible words, appropriate in varying degrees, but the one chosen is as convenient as any. In this part of the doctrine of God, later Judaism diverges much more radically from Christianity than in the part discussed in the last chapter. Some of the concepts about to be discussed have little or no foundation in the Old Testament. In other words, while Christianity developed doctrinally towards the Trinity, Judaism also expanded its canonical theology, but in a different direction. The present chapter is concerned principally with that development.

The first and most important manifestation of God, from the Jewish point of view, is the Torah. The first section of this chapter attempts, not to exhaust the vast diversity of Rabbinic ideas about this, but to place the more important of them in a wider religious context. This is a topic significant for Jew and Christian alike, and formative in the history of faith.

Torah, Wisdom, and Logos

The Torah as a code of laws and teachings, Scriptural and extra-Scriptural, was discussed in the first chapter. But it meant for the Rabbis, at least occasionally, something more than this, and something very much older than the Sinai revelation. Moses is declared to have gone to heaven to receive a Torah which had been in existence for 974 generations before the creation of the world, and which the angels did not at first consider flesh and blood fitted to receive.[1] Another figure given is 2000 years.[2] The applicability of mundane time mensuration to the eternal sphere is a bold assumption—but this is the pictorial thinking of the Orient once again. The essential part of the claim is that the Torah has temporal priority over the realm of mankind. This is of course nonsensical except in a special or extended meaning of the term—a mere corpus of law could not logically precede in time those expected to obey it. At the time of the Sinai promulgation of the Torah —a late stage in its history, according to this view—the sound was heard over the entire earth.[3] This is a touch of the spectacular, to emphasise the relevance of this lawgiving, as the Jews conceived it, to all the earth.

Wisdom was regarded by many of the Rabbis as a synonym for Torah, and many statements about the Torah are referred to texts in the Book of Proverbs, of which Wisdom is the subject.[4] Sometimes the identification is even more explicit in the text of the Midrash,[5] sometimes they seem to be closely connected, but endowed with a separate existence.[6] It is perfectly clear that the two words held the same meaning in certain contexts. Before attempting further examination of the Rabbinic material, it is necessary to pause for a moment to consider briefly the growth and definition of the Wisdom concept in Judaism.

The monuments of Jewish Wisdom literature are the Books of Proverbs, Job, and Ecclesiastes in the Old Testament, and the Wisdom of Solomon and the Wisdom of Jesus ben Sirach, frequently known as Ecclesiasticus, in the Apocrypha. These books were the product of a special school in Judaism, which held itself aloof from the burning current issues of nationalism and the prophetic teaching, trying rather to view mankind with detachment, as man rather than as Jew, and thus rising above the usual rather exclusive interest in compatriots. King Solomon may well have been the ancestor of this kind of

---

[1] Shab. 88 *b*-89*a*. Cf. Zeb. 116*a*.
[2] Gen. R. viii.2; Lev. R. xix.1; Song of Sol. R. v.11, 1. See *R.A.*, p. 169 f.
[3] Zeb. 116*a*.   [4] Cf. Lev. R. xxv.1; Song of Sol. R. i.1, 3; etc.
[5] Lev. R. xi.3; Deut. R. xi.6.   [6] Cf. Esth. R. 1.17.

teaching, although the precise determination of his personal contribution to the contents of the Old Testament is a matter for the critic to decide. Suffice it here to say that these writers form the nearest Hebrew equivalent to Plato and the Greek philosophers, although their interest in metaphysics was much less elaborate and sustained. Human psychology and ethics were nearer to their hearts—in other words, the practical rather than the merely speculative aspects of philosophy. The Book of Job is a detailed and careful exploration, couched in the terms of Hebrew poetry, of a significant ethical and theological problem: why does God permit the righteous to suffer? It is a monumental contribution to world literature, but its style and method are radically different from those of the Timaeus.

In the Jewish Wisdom literature the personified concept of Wisdom not only goes back before the Creation, being "a breath of the power of God, and a pure emanation of the glory of the Almighty,"[7] but is sometimes regarded as God's co-worker in the very act of forming this world and its inhabitants.[8] This is merely a variant of the familiar creative *Logos* or Word, which is also found in the Apocrypha.[9] Philo of Alexandria greatly elaborated the idea, mingling Hebraic and Hellenistic elements in a synthesis potentially acceptable to the wider Graeco-Roman world, but thereby rendering himself suspect among his more conservative Palestinian co-religionists. The *Logos* terminology was very widespread in the first Christian century, as familiar in Greek philosophy as in Jewish theology. Implicitly or explicitly, it pervades Paul and the Epistle to the Hebrews. The Prologue to the Fourth Gospel is of purely Hebraic origin, and the creative *Logos* is nothing new. Even the connexion with light and life has Jewish parallels. But the personality, eternity, and divinity of the *Logos* incarnate in Jesus Christ are shatteringly new. The third verse of the prologue traces its direct ancestry from the Hebrew Bible—not only from the Wisdom literature but from the Psalm xxxiii, the Creation story, and many other passages. The link passes

[7] Wis. vii.25, R.S.V.

[8] Cf. Prov. iii.19-20, viii.22-31; Wis. viii.4, ix.9; Ecclesiasticus xxiv.9.

[9] Wis. ix.1. For the probable origins and later usage of the *Logos* concept, see Albright, *From the Stone Age to Christianity*, pp. 145 f., 285 f.

through the apocryphal Wisdom, and on into the Targumim, which are even more explicit. It is doubtful if there is much direct dependence on Philo, although his writings and ideas may possibly have been familiar to the Evangelist. The Wisdom element in the Christology of Paul is a commonplace to every reader.

With such ample Jewish precedent, particularly in the Old Testament, it is not surprising that the Rabbis make use of the concept of the creative *Logos*, though sometimes under other names. Anti-Christian or even anti-Alexandrian prejudice may have caused them to dislike the word, and even the Aramaic Targumic equivalent, the Memra. But they themselves mean much the same thing by Wisdom, which they freely equate with Torah, as indicated above. The Mishnah does refer to the world being created by the ten verbal commandments of God recorded in the Genesis story, which is a very close approximation,[10] and also to the Torah specifically as the instrument of creation.[11] There is a still more explicit acceptance of the doctrine in the opening paragraph of Midrash Rabbah on Genesis. Wisdom, equated with Torah, is describing her association with God in the work of creation, and a possible though very conjectural pointing in a key word in Proverbs viii.30 enables the Rabbis to declare her the master-workman or architect, the precision tool of the Holy One in His task. This is a more elaborate instance of the creative *Logos* in the Rabbinic literature.[12]

There are two passages of opposite tendency, which might or might not be counter-propaganda to the Christian *Logos* of the Fourth Gospel. The first declares the Torah less complete than heavenly Wisdom[13]—a sentiment scarcely open to serious dispute, which may denote merely zeal for monotheistic religion. The second speaks in disparagement, it may be of wisdom rather than Wisdom, and is only possibly controversial.[14] Its etymological arguments are quite unsound.

Much as the Torah is exalted in certain passages, Israel is exalted over her in others. The seeming contradictions may

---

[10] Ab. v.i.   [11] Ab. iii.15.
[12] Also *R.A.*, No. 454.   [13] Gen. R. xvii.5, xliv.7.
[14] Ex. R. xli.3.

frequently be removed by a consideration of the various meanings of the concept already indicated: sometimes the Rabbis are thinking solely of the written and oral law, sometimes also of the metaphysical, theological, or emotional elements superadded. When they declare, as they frequently do, that the world was created for the sake of the Torah, it may be presumed that they are giving the word its fullest and richest content.[15] In one passage it is declared that Israel would not be accepted or even considered by God save only for the sake of the Torah, without which she would be classed with the idolaters.[16] This places her on a clearly lower level. On the other hand, it is stated with equal confidence that the Torah was conceived by God not only after, but for the sake of, His people Israel, who must therefore take precedence.[17] If the meaning be restricted here to the code of law, this need not necessarily contradict the last passage—the code would be meaningless without the existence of those under its obligation, and Torah in the wider sense is not under consideration. This precise limitation of meaning is very clear in the reputed desire of the angels to observe the Torah in place of sinful and unworthy man. God points out to them that they do not die, beget, eat, or conduct business, and that they therefore cannot observe it.[18] It is only fair, in each significant context, to consider the particular meaning of Torah the teacher has in mind. This will greatly reduce the number of seeming contradictions.

Montefiore declares that "God, Israel and the Law form a sort of triad, linked together by the closest ties of affection."[19] Israel cannot receive the Torah, God's "daughter," without receiving God as well—hence, by implication, the need, in their respective ages, for the Tabernacle, the successive Temples, and latterly the synagogue.[20] This beautiful concept comes out in some of the best passages.

Of still greater interest is the idea of the Torah as intercessor on behalf of Israel,[21] and on behalf of the heathen for the

[15] Cf. Gen. R. 1.4, 10, etc.   [16] Ex. R. XLVII.3.
[17] Num. R. XIV.11; Eccl. R. 1.44.
[18] Shab. 88b-89a; Song of Sol. R. VIII.11, 2. Cf. also R.A., No. 99.
[19] R.A., p. 171.   [20] Ex R. XXXIII.1, 6.
[21] Song of Sol. R. v.16, 3.

ultimate sake of Israel, that she be not destroyed through their sins.[22] Coupled with the implicit creative *Logos* concept, this would suggest some measure of correspondence in scope and function between the Rabbinic Torah and the Second Person of the Christian Trinity. There is no link whatever with the Incarnation, or with the divinity of Jesus Christ.

The Torah links closely with the theme of revelation. The Christian Word of God in its written form is now fixed, closed, and sufficient for each succeeding age, at least in Protestant theology. The teaching and atonement of Jesus Christ was full and final—there is no need for further revelation, only for fuller understanding. The Rabbinic Torah is by contrast a growing, evolutionary thing, ever expanding, and never fixed.[23] The Christian greatly prefers the "once and for all" theology of Paul and of the Epistle to the Hebrews.[24] The Jew finds something of this comfort in the classical interpretation of the Sinai lawgiving mentioned earlier (p. 8).

Summing up, the Torah meant for the Rabbis more than a law code—rather the sum-total of human knowledge, wisdom, and philosophy. To this may be added pre-existence, a share in the task of creation, and intercessory powers between God and man. Though not in itself divine, the Torah was one of the holiest things God had created, a projection of His Own mind into the spatio-temporal realm, not to be worshipped by men, but requiring from them a high degree of reverence.

The Shekinah

The idea of the Shekinah is found in the Old Testament in passages such as Exodus xxxiii.22-3, and the root verb *shakhan*, to dwell, is Biblical. The noun Shekinah is not found in the Hebrew Bible, but is freely used in the Targumim, in translating or paraphrasing passages such as the one cited above.[25] The word may signify the Presence of God abiding in the Temple, particularly in the Holy of Holies; or some earthly manifestation

[22] Song of Sol. R. viii.14, i.
[23] Cf. J. Jocz, *The Jewish People and Jesus Christ*, London 1949, pp. 290-6.
[24] Cf. Rom. vi.10; Heb. vii.27, ix.12, x.10; etc.
[25] Cf. Targum Onkelos, Ex. xxxiii.14; Targum Yerushalami, xxxiii.23; etc.

of the hidden and heavenly glory of God; or simply the radiance of the Divine Presence dwelling on earth.

The historical revelation of the Shekinah in Israel is sometimes associated with the Sinai lawgiving,[26] but it is carefully stipulated in another context that this manifestation did not fully descend to earth, for it stopped short ten hand-breadths above the summit of the holy mountain.[27] This is an attempt to bring Mount Sinai into the picture without abandoning the more usual view, namely that the historical revelation of the Shekinah begins with the erection of the Tabernacle.[28] One passage adds that the Shekinah had been vouchsafed to Adam, had departed from the world when he sinned, and had never returned till the time of the Tabernacle.[29] This is typically at variance with the frequent accrediting of experience of the Shekinah to the various Patriarchs. Adam is forgotten when Abraham, about to offer Isaac on Mount Moriah, is said to have been the first recipient.[30] Jacob enjoyed the privilege at Bethel,[31] and so did Moses before the completion of the Tabernacle, both as an infant[32] and as an adult.[33] This tangle of contradictions is only partially unravelled by the distinction of personal and corporate manifestations, which would allow certain of the statements about the Patriarchs to stand. The very itch to harmonise such discrepancies is a Western one: the Oriental mind has a larger capacity for floodlighting the significant point of the moment, without undue regard to what may have been said on another occasion. One inconsistency, however, is very easily explained. Those of Sadducean descent or sympathy would naturally prefer to bring the Shekinah to earth in connexion with the Tabernacle, thus stressing the priestly side of their religion, whereas the Pharisees would naturally prefer Mount Sinai, thus exalting the Law. The stipulation of ten hand-breadths of "no man's air" above the summit of Mount Sinai suggests an undoubted gift for compromise.

The Rabbis had a prevailing and cardinal teaching about

---

[26] Sot. 5ᵃ; Eccl. R. viii.1, 3.   [27] Sukk. 5ᵃ.
[28] Shab. 87ᵇ; Ex. R. xxxv.1, lii.2; Num. R. xii.6.
[29] Num. R. xii.6. Cf. xiii.2.   [30] Gen. R. lxv. 10.
[31] Gen. R. lxix.7.   [32] Sot. 12ᵇ.
[33] Shab. 87ᵃ, etc.

the Shekinah, which is of much greater religious significance: namely that human sin drives the Shekinah farther away, whereas human virtue brings it closer. In other words, God is more Immanent to the righteous than to the unrighteous. This applies equally in the corporate and in the individual realm. A mixed example may serve for the first illustration. The Shekinah is said to have ascended from earth through the seven heavens, one at a time, because of the successive sins of Adam, Cain, the generation of Enosh, the generation of the Flood, the generation of the confusion of tongues, the Sodomites, and the Egyptians. It was brought down to earth again in reverse stages by the successive lives of righteousness of Abraham, Isaac, Jacob, Levi, Kohath, Amram, and Moses.[34] It is easy to laugh at the acrobatic feats of the Shekinah, but the theology behind the quaint imagery is reasonable and cogent. A similar teaching of more priestly emphasis is that the Shekinah departed from the Temple by ten stages, because of the sins of Israel. This occurs both in Talmud and in Midrash.[35] The Midrash, however, retains the Shekinah at convenient recalling distance on the Mount of Olives, while the Talmud sends it right back to heaven, after it has tarried six months in the wilderness vainly hoping for the repentance of Israel. There is some controversy as to whether the final destruction of the Temple in A.D. 70 did or did not drive the Shekinah irrevocably away from Jerusalem. Some hold that it still hovers round the Wailing Wall.[36]

The glory of the Rabbinic teaching is that, whatever national disasters may have befallen the Jews, the Shekinah is still available for the individual, who can attract or repel its presence by his own conduct. There are scores of passages of this tenor which are ethically and spiritually irreproachable. Scoffers, liars, hypocrites, and slanderers are said to be excluded, but this is hardly unreasonable.[37] Exception might be taken in a few instances, as when the stipulated requirements are too formal or Halakhic,[38] or when they depend on purely

---

[34] Gen. R. xix.7; Num. R. xiii.2; Song of Sol. R. v.1, 1. The sin of the Egyptians refers to Gen. xii, and should have come before the Sodom reference.

[35] R.Sh. 31ᵃ; Lam. R. Proem xxv. [36] Ex. R. ii.2. Cf. Num. R. xi.2.

[37] Sanh. 103ᵃ. [38] Cf. Ber. 5ᵇ, 27ᵇ; Shab. 63ᵃ, etc.

physical endowments[39] or on genealogical claims.[40] In the overwhelming majority of relevant cases, the Rabbinic teaching is sound, gracious, and wise.

The Shekinah is fundamentally an outward manifestation of God Himself, endowed with something of His power. It is frequently declared that its own radiance feeds and sustains the angels.[41] The earth does not yet enjoy the full lustre as it might, because of sin, but the Shekinah will itself one day fill the world.[42] In this life the beholding of the radiance is for the elect only, but in the life to come the privilege will be extended to all.[43] It is good to find these tolerant and universalistic teachings in sources which contain so many of rather opposite tendency.

It is scarcely necessary to labour the point that the Shekinah holds in Judaism a place parallel to that of the Third Person of the Christian Trinity. There are also some slighter resemblances of office between the Torah and the Second Person of the Trinity, but these cannot be pressed too far, as the divinity of the Torah has never been claimed by Jews. There is the germ of a metaphor here for those who care to consider it further.

The Holy Spirit

Another manifestation of God in human life is the Holy Spirit—which has nothing to do with its Christian namesake, and proves a somewhat barren concept by comparison. The Rabbinic Holy Spirit is simply the gift of prophecy or divination, regarded as deriving from God.[44] According to one authority, this disappeared in large measure with the last of the canonical prophets, but was replaced by the Bath-Qol, or voice from Heaven[45]—which is also a manifestation of God. In scores of passages in Talmud and Midrash, it is recorded that a Bath-Qol was vouchsafed in such-and-such a circumstance, but no significant theological teaching is worked out.

---

[39] Cf. Shab. 92*a*; Num. R. x.5.   [40] Num. R. xii.4.
[41] Gen. R. ii.2, etc.   [42] Esth. R. i.4.
[43] Lev. R. i.14.   [44] Erub. 64*b*; Meg. 14*a*; etc.
[45] Song of Sol. R. viii.9, 3. For the connexion of Bath-Qol with the dove, and its relationship to the Baptism of Jesus, see I. Abrahams, *Studies in Pharisaism and the Gospels*, VOL. i, Cambridge 1917, pp. 47-50.

The familiar New Testament counterpart is the voice from Heaven at the baptism of Jesus Christ and also on the Mount of Transfiguration. The Holy Spirit was taken away from idolaters.[46] It was endowed with the grace of pity, for it might weep over human suffering.[47] Its chief attribute of prophecy is associated with the Shekinah in one context[48]—which demonstrates the fluidity of much of the Rabbinic terminology. Beyond these facts, there is little to say.

The Name of God

Even in English, name may mean more than mere appellation, as when a man is said to make a name for himself. The Hebrew word *shem* is very much richer in significance, including the elements of reputation, fame or glory, memorial or monument, and, more important, character or essence. The Name of God above all means much more than something which can be written on paper, as the next paragraph will indicate. It is associated in the history of Judaism with many heroic martyrdoms, with unflinching honesty in the face of unscrupulous extortion—and also, in sad contrast, with a curious jumble of deceitful casuistry, esoteric nonsense, and crass superstition. The juxtaposition of the noble and the calculating is by no means untypical.

Underlying the Rabbinic treatment of this theme, there is a long history of Oriental name-significance and name-theology, in primitive and in later times. The name, human as well as divine, was very generally regarded as the foundation and prerequisite of personality,[49] of the possession of a soul,[50] and even of life itself.[51] Knowledge of a proper name was supposed to give a certain measure of power over its bearer,[52] so that mere mortals suitably endowed might enjoy some control over the spirit world and over the souls of the departed.[53] In the case of God, the association between His Name and His Being

---

[46] Num. R. xx.1.   [47] Lam. R. 1.16, 46, 50.   [48] Pes. 87ᵇ.

[49] Cf. *Encyclopaedia of Religion and Ethics*, henceforth cited as *E.R.E.*, Edinburgh 1908-26, VOL. IX, p. 130, col. 1; p. 180, col. 2.

[50] J. P. E. Pedersen, *Israel*, London 1926, VOL. I, pp. 245, 248; C. G. Montefiore, *The Synoptic Gospels*, London 1927, VOL. I, p. 111.

[51] *Op. cit.*, p. 256.   [52] *E.R.E.*, VOL. IX, p. 180, col. 2.

[53] *Op. cit.*, p. 132, col. 2.

was generally thought to be very close indeed,[54] so that God and His Name are often virtually equivalent. It would be interesting to know whether any members of the priestly caste believed that their knowledge of the secret Name made God's decrees reversible, at least for them.

To return to the Rabbinic sources, it may be noted that the reputed Ineffable Name, consisting of seventy-two letters, enjoyed the highest sanctity, and was a closely guarded secret.[55] Next in holiness came the Tetragrammaton, approximately Yahweh in English letters, then Adonai, El Shaddai, and the other substitute names. The familiar Jehovah is, of course, a hybrid containing the consonants of Yahweh and the vowels of Adonai.

Although God's dominion extends over the entire earth, His Name is regarded as the peculiar possession of Israel.[56] On the one hand, this Name was deeply reverenced, and blasphemy was regarded as a grievous sin.[57] Death must be preferred to profanation if need be. Yet despite a stringent casuistical fencing of the law,[58] the Name of God might in practice be coupled with wilful deceit, of which one Rabbi gives an unedifying example. He desires to extract a therapeutic secret from a Gentile woman, who requires him to swear *by the God of Israel* that he will not divulge her prescription. He takes advantage of the fact that the preposition she uses also means *to*. Thus he merely swears mentally that he will not divulge it *to the God of Israel*, and fully intends to use it in his next lecture. The Talmud rightly condemns this as a profanation of the Name, and modern parlance might aptly describe the Rabbi as "no gentleman."[59] Parallels of an equally objectionable nature may be found elsewhere, and it is against this background that the New Testament exegete must read the Dominical command: "Swear not at all."

There is another side to the picture, which comes out in a long discussion about evading customs.[60] It is agreed that it is morally wrong to evade by deceit the payment of lawful state dues—implying, even if they are payable to the hated Roman

[54] *E.R.E.*, p. 177.   [55] Deut. R. 1.11; Num. R. xi.8; Kidd. 71ᵃ.
[56] Ruth R. Proem 1.   [57] Yom. 86ᵃ; Sanh. 60ᵃ; Ab. iv.4; etc.
[58] Shebu. iv.13; Num. R. xxi; etc.
[59] Yom. 84ᵃ.   [60] B.K. 113ᵃ.

overlords. The rapacious personal cupidity of tax-farmers was notorious, and some Rabbis felt that it was permissible to try to escape some of their extortions when these were for private gain. Yet Akiba would prohibit even this if it involves profanation of the Name. Very great nobility of character is reflected in this advice. In further contrast to the deceiver of the Gentile woman mentioned above, it is only fair to remember his colleague who declared that even delay in the payment of the butcher's bill dishonours God's name.[61]

On the whole, it is true and fair to say that the Rabbis did hold God's name in reverence.

[61] Yom. 86^a.

CHAPTER IV

THE MESSIAH

JUDAISM still expects that God will one day send his Messiah or Anointed One to earth, and still denies that He has already done so in Jesus Christ, as Christians claim. This is an anticipated manifestation of God on the Jewish side, and might for that reason have appeared in the last chapter. But the manifestations there were conceptual, whereas the Messiah is essentially personal. Furthermore this is a topic of special importance both to Jews and to Christians, and the particular matter on which they differ most radically. It claims therefore a brief separate chapter, which rounds off the doctrine of God in its wider aspects.

The word Messiah is adjectival in the Old Testament. The noun usage is later. It may describe the anointed priest or king; a patriarch or even the non-Jewish Cyrus, considered as God's special agent; a representative of the royal line of David; or finally, in the familiar words of prophecy, the king-to-be of David's line, who would deliver the people and set up God's kingdom on earth. Apocryphal, apocalyptic, and other usages may be ignored here, as the Rabbinic development only is under consideration.

The Time of Messiah's Appearing

There are two types of Rabbinic opinion regarding the time of Messiah's advent, mutually exclusive from a logical point of view, but typical of that elasticity of thinking found in other connexions. One places God in absolute control, denying to man any share or influence in the matter whatsoever; the other regards man as the principal agent, affecting the entire issue for good or ill by his own conduct. This is a fresh reflexion of the

46

old tension between the absolute and the reversible decrees, between divine omniscience and human free will—a problem which neither Jewish nor Christian thinkers have as yet finally solved.

In accordance with what might be dubbed the "predestinarian" view, there is a teaching to the effect that Messiah will not come till all the unborn souls have attained their sojourn on earth:[1] in other words he will not come until life in this world has told its full story, until the final curtain is lowered on the human drama. This is the most extreme of the views which deny to man any share in the shaping of the event. Yet this very argument is by implication amusingly turned round in the opposite direction. If a man's children die, he must, declares one authority, beget more, because it is part of his duty as a human being to keep the world inhabited. A demurring voice, however, asserts that this man has reduced the number of unborn souls, has thereby hastened Messiah's coming, and has therefore fulfilled his duty in life, whether his children be living or dead. Men may therefore further eschatological ends merely by sedulous propagation.[2] This is in logical disharmony with that other Eastern doctrine of metempsychosis or transmigration of souls—the number of the unborn cannot be reduced if each life goes through many successive manifestations; but it is not the task of this book to unravel such discrepancies.

There are a few more passages implying that man is powerless to hasten or affect Messiah's coming. A Bath-Qol is said to restrain that presumptuous Rabbi who would dare to reveal the secret date by means of a Targum on the Book of Daniel.[3] According to yet another authority, Messiah will not come till certain predicted cycles of human suffering and distress have run their course: these have not yet been fulfilled in their proper order, though men have mistakenly believed otherwise, thereby revealing their lack of exact knowledge.[4] These "pangs of the Messiah" will call for a further reference below, in

[1] Yeb. 63[b]; Gen. R. xxiv.4; Lev. R. xv.1; Eccl. R. 1.6, 1.
[2] Yeb. 62[a].   [3] Meg. 3[a].
[4] Sanh. 97[a] et seq.; Song of Sol. R. ii.13, 4. Cf. also Shab. 118[a]; Pes. 118[a].
Cf. Mk. xiii, etc.

another context. Other attested signs are not such as to make the date more predictable. The sharp prior decline in human morals has been fulfilled countless times in human history, but without its end result.[5] It is said also that the appearing will be to a generation which is either wholly righteous or wholly wicked.[6] In order to fulfil the first alternative, the Messiah would need to believe only the propaganda of each nation about itself—for the second, only its propaganda about others. There is another teaching to the effect that Messiah will come when men least expect him—which is the more prosaic equivalent of Paul's "thief in the night."[7] The prevailing moral of these passages is that men should wait with patience for the promised coming, and not attempt to prognosticate independently, for this is beyond their powers.

In sharp contrast to this is the opposite view—namely that the time of Messiah's coming is directly influenced by human faith and conduct. This kind of belief is always dearer to the heart of man, whatever theologians may teach in a contrary direction. Those who are pessimistic about man's character declare that the attribute of Justice causes the desired advent to be delayed merely on account of human sin, that the date formerly appointed is already past, and that it may be brought into the proximate future only by repentance and good deeds, or by the sufferings of Israel.[8] Those who are more optimistic regarding man's moral potential teach in a more comforting manner. Every precept properly fulfilled hastens Messiah's coming,[9] and one Sabbath strictly observed—presumably by the whole community of Israel—would bring him forthwith,[10] as would one day's true repentance.[11] This consummation would equally be effected by the united prayers of Abraham, Isaac, and Jacob, were Elijah so incautious as to wake the three of them from sleep simultaneously in the life which they now enjoy.[12]

Once again the whole problem remains indeterminate in the Rabbinic sources, chiefly because there is no agreed solution to the relationship between the divine and the human will.

[5] Sot. IX.15.
[7] Sanh. 97ᵃ. Cf. I Thess. v.2.
[9] Deut. R. VI.7.
[11] Song of Sol. R. v.2, 2.

[6] Sanh. 98ᵃ.
[8] Sanh. 97ᵇ; A. Zar. 9ᵃ.
[10] Ex. R. xxv.12.
[12] B.M. 85ᵇ.

This particular theme is the nearest Jewish equivalent to the Christian doctrine of the Second Coming of Christ, and the interested reader may be left to work out the fuller comparison for himself.

There is a third choice of opinion which may be mentioned for completeness, though it is not important—namely that Messiah has come to earth already. This links up with the topic of the next section, and some representative passages will be cited there.

The Nature of the Expected Messiah

The question as to the kind of Messiah the Rabbis expected resolves itself into two more specific queries: firstly, did they associate him with the future or with the past; and secondly, did they look for an ordinary mortal, selected by God for special mission and office, or for some divine or semi-divine being? Both questions are capable of double answers, according to the evidence chosen.

It was suggested hypothetically in one place that the Messiah might be enjoying mortal life even then,[13] or actually dwelling incognito in Rome, which is frequently disguised under the name of Edom.[14] Some say that he must be hidden for a period, like the infant Moses.[15] Or his advent may be pushed back more definitely into the past. One teacher dates it in the days of Hezekiah[16]—an unorthodox view which might well have been motivated by anti-Christian propaganda. There was also a tradition that he was already born when the Temple was destroyed in A.D. 70.[17] It is probable that all these passages visualise a Messiah with at least the appearance of an ordinary man.

Two last pieces of evidence may be cited, pointing in opposite directions. Like Abraham, Job, and Hezekiah, the Messiah made successful but autonomous efforts to know God—which would scarcely be necessary if he possessed any measure of divinity at all.[18] On the other hand it is stated several times over that the Name of Messiah was created before the world.[19]

---

[13] Sanh. 98^b.   [14] Ex. R. 1.26.
[15] Ruth R. v.6.   [16] Sanh. 98^b, 99^a.
[17] See H. J. Schoeps, *Aus frühchristlicher Zeit*, Tübingen 1950, p. 183.
[18] Num. R. xiv.2.   [19] Pes. 54^a; Ned. 39^b; Gen. R. 1.4.

Despite the strenuous denials of Moore,[20] this may be taken as tantamount to a claim for pre-existence, in accordance with the principles mentioned in the fourth section of the previous chapter. Such a claim would imply a status which was very much more than human.

It is clear then that the orthodox and adoptionist Christologies may both be paralleled amongst the Rabbinic utterances concerning the Messiah. The total weight of emphasis would seem, however, to favour the concept of an ordinary human being, ordained by God to special office.

The Character of the Messianic Age

The keynote of the Messianic Age for Israel is usually regarded as political triumph with social supremacy, a time of reversal and revenge. Christians are apt to regard some of the sentiments expressed as abominable—but their own hands have not always been clean, and neither side can throw stones without provoking answering ammunition.

In general, the Messianic Age is regarded as an era in this world, quite distinct from the world to come[21]—though there are a few apparently exceptional teachings.[22] This is further underlined by the repeated statement that Old Testament prophecy related only to the mundane era, and not to that which is to follow.[23] The Messiah is depicted in one context as bringing only a limited improvement to the existing order of things: Israel will be released from bondage to foreign powers, but some measure of poverty and suffering will continue to afflict her sons.[24] Other schools of thought are more optimistic. The resurrection of the dead,[25] the cessation of physical death,[26] the termination of the troubles and afflictions of the normal mortal state,[27] are conditions which suggest a vastly greater difference than the first passage would allow. It will be an age of peace,[28] of Messianic sway over seas and lands,[29] of night

[20] G. F. Moore, *Judaism*, Cambridge, Mass. 1927, VOL. II, pp. 344, 349.
[21] Ruth R. v.6. Cf. Montefiore, *Synoptic Gospels*, p. CXLV f.
[22] Cf. Ruth R. II.10, which will be discussed in a later chapter.
[23] Ber. 34^b; Shab. 63^a; Sanh. 99^a.   [24] Ber. 34^b.
[25] Sot. 48^b.   [26] Ex. R. XXX.3; Eccl. R. I.4, 3.
[27] Ex. R. XXIII.11.   [28] Lev. R. IX.9.
[29] Num. R. XIII.14.

turned into day,[30] and of wondrous manifestations of light.[31] The power of temptation over the human heart will be finally broken,[32] the very Torah improved,[33] and the existing natural order reversed by such phenomena as winds blowing in opposite directions at the same time.[34] The main weight of evidence therefore inclines to an era radically different from the existing one, though still mundane. The Old Testament miracles—the dividing of the waters for the Israelites before the hosts of the Egyptians, the resurrection of the dead, and so forth—constituted a partial and anticipatory experience of the better things to come.[35] It may be noted further that there will be special divine protection for Israel,[36] that those buried in the Holy Land will be the first to enjoy resurrection,[37] and that the divine blessings lost through Adam's sin will be restored.[38]

Nothing in the last paragraph is open to any particular exception. In other passages, however, the Rabbis are more particularistic and aggressive, just as Christians are apt to be in similar contexts. It is stated, for example, that the door will be completely barred to proselytes in the days of Messiah, because Israel will then be prosperous and powerful, as she was in the time of David and Solomon, and she will have no further need for recruits to her ranks[39]—a sentiment which is rather the antithesis of the missionary spirit. It will then be the turn of the heathen to become the servants and underlings of the triumphant chosen race,[40] and Israel will enjoy a delicious reversal of circumstances, and a rich revenge on all those who have insulted or persecuted her.[41] Life will be far from happy for the Gentiles, however delightful it may be for the faithful.[42] These sentiments do not make pleasant reading, whatever their provocation may have been. They are, however, a part of the Rabbinic vision of the nature of the Messianic Age.

[30] Ex. R. xviii.11.
[31] Gen. R. 1.6; iii.6.
[32] Gen. R. xlviii.11. Cf. lxx.8.
[33] Eccl. R. xi.8, 1.
[34] Esth. R. ii.14.
[35] Eccl. R. iii.15, 1.
[36] Ex. R. xxiv.4.
[37] Gen. R. lxxiv.1, xcvi.5. Cf. 1 Thess. iv.16.
[38] Num. R. xiii.12.
[39] Yeb. 24ᵇ. Cf. Eccl. R. 1.7, 6.
[40] Eccl. R. ii.8, 1.
[41] Num. R. ii.13.
[42] Song of Sol. R. vii.5, 3.

The Messiah, Jewish and Christian—Some Parallels

No reader who is familiar both with the Rabbinic traditions concerning the Messiah and with the Gospels can fail to see the parallels, both in verbal echo and in concomitant circumstance. The likenesses are interesting, even if they be a little superficial.

The term "the Comforter" is used in both faiths, though not quite so frequently in Judaism. It derives ultimately from certain familiar passages in the Old Testament, which explains the fact of parallelism.[43] The ass of the Triumphal Entry likewise features in prophecy, and it is hardly surprising that the Rabbis should make use of it from their point of view.[44] There is even a passage which, like the First Gospel, seems to interpret Zechariah ix.9 as signifying the use of two animals.[45] The prophet, however, is merely using the accepted parallelism of Hebrew poetry, and does not mean to suggest any impossible feat with a pair of mounts. Of somewhat greater interest is the fact that the Messiah ben David, the personal symbol of Israel's final hopes, is sometimes represented as destined to follow a forerunner, the Messiah ben Joseph, sometimes called the War Messiah, who occupies a place exactly corresponding to John the Baptist in Christian theology.[46] The careful exegete may find it of some profit also to compare the Rabbinic statements regarding Messiah's ancestry[47] with the Dominical genealogies of the First and Third Gospels. In fact, all the passages footnoted above are worthy of his fuller investigation.

The pangs of the Messiah—the human sufferings that are to attend his advent according to the expectation of some—have been noted already, and references are given in the fourth footnote to this chapter. The idea that the Messiah should suffer in his own person is usually regarded as a Christian rather than a Rabbinic one, yet there are traces of it in the sources—traces also of a doctrine of vicarious suffering.[48] In

---

[43] Num. R. xiii.5; Lam. R. i.16, 51. [44] Cf. Sanh. 98b; Gen. R. lxxv.6.
[45] Gen. R. xcviii.9.
[46] Sukk. 52a; Num. R. xiv.1; Song of Sol. R. ii.13, 4.
[47] Cf. Gen. R. xcvii, alternative version (Soncino translation, pp. 901, 906); Num. R. xiv.1; Ruth R. vii.2.
[48] Sanh. 98a, b.

another source, possibly rather more medieval in date, there is an interesting Messiah, complete with subambient ass, who by terrible voluntary suffering makes vicarious atonement for every son of Israel.[49] Anti-Christian sentiment may have rendered the Messianic interpretation of Isaiah LIII unpopular in some quarters, but it cannot be denied that there are clear traces of it here and there in the sources. Were it but possible to demonstrate a somewhat earlier date for the last passage, its teachings would be both impressive and important.

There are two sharply contrasted viewpoints regarding the relationship between the Jewish Messiah and Jesus of Nazareth. Evangelical Christians have always maintained that Jesus Christ fulfils in His own person the highest Messianic expectations of Judaism, that the bare Gospel record, read in the light of the Old Testament, proves this over and over again. Jews on the other hand, together with certain Christians of more liberal theological opinion, have frequently argued that the canonical Gospels have been manipulated to some extent, to make the career of Jesus of Nazareth look more like the fulfilment of Old Testament prophecy than it really is. It has been glibly stated that the Bethlehem Nativity, the Flight into Egypt, and other narratives are merely apologetic fabrications; that the "legend" of the Virgin Birth springs solely from the Septuagint "mistranslation" of Isaiah VII.14; and so forth. The reader quite certainly has his own firm convictions in one direction or the other, and must always allow for the element of bias when he considers the evidence.

[49] *R.A.*, No. 1618, pp. 584 ff.

CHAPTER V

ANGELS AND DEMONS

THE subjects of angelology and demonology, which are closely related, despite their seeming antipathy, are less interesting to the modern reader than most of the other topics considered in this volume, simply because contemporary theological emphasis has changed. Their importance in the past, their unquestioned place between the doctrine of God and the doctrine of man in any scientific exposition, and their continued if more limited interest in the present, justify historically some reference to them. An interest in angels has never harmed mankind, but an interest in demons has frequently been linked with various pseudo-sciences of the occult, with terrible and unreasoning fears of the supernatural, and with the foolish if harmless superstitions of simple minds. The survey of the present chapter is both synoptic and Rabbinic: those who desire to know precisely why people throw salt over the left shoulder after spilling it, or perform similar strange rites, will need to delve more deeply into sundry cultures. The most interesting demonic personality of all, Satan himself, will be considered more fully in a later chapter in connexion with the origin of sin.

An angel is by definition a messenger of God. Demons are variously regarded as fallen angels, as departed human spirits, or as separate and independent existences. They may also be conceived as human or animal in form. Langton and other authorities may be consulted for fuller detail—the Rabbinic interest does not range over the whole field.

Modern man, to his loss and gain, is much less interested in angels, or in the Devil and the demonic host, than was his grandfather. If this means a lessening of certain unhealthy preoccupations, it also means a lessening of interest in religion as a whole.

Angelology

Angels are normally conceived of as an order of rational beings higher than the human, but lower than the divine, probably immaterial, certainly immortal, potentially sinless in perfect obedience to God, with capacities of action, intellect, and locomotion superior to those of man, but still inferior to those of the All Highest. It is frequently admitted in other cultures, including other Jewish cultures, that angels, possessing free will, may sin and rebel against God—a notion which, significant and full of consequence as it may be for some, seems to have made surprisingly little impression on the Rabbinic mind. There is an obvious half-heartedness about the temporary Midrashic banishing of certain angels from their proper circles and surroundings for revealing divine secrets,[1] as also about the imputation in another source of adultery in this lower world of humanity.[2] There is no proper doctrine of the Fall in the angelic realm in the Rabbinic literature. The numerous passages which specifically play down the holiness or potential of the angels have a different motive, which is usually the exaltation at their expense of either God or man. It would almost seem as though certain teachers were a little jealous of these higher creatures.

Three sets of contrasting viewpoints may be noted: one in each case is disparaging.

1. The statement that the angels are immortal[3] rouses no particular disagreement in the mind of the reader—it falls within the category of the expected. When it is declared several times over that certain angels possess a life more ephemeral than that of the flies in this mundane state, a life which is terminated after a single song, a conclusion based on the Rabbinic interpretation of Lamentations III.23,[4] a measure of counter-propaganda may perhaps be suspected. (In one context, the higher angelic ranks are specifically exempted from so transitory an existence,[5] and in another the notion is re-written as a new doctrine of daily rebirth, founded on the self-same Scriptural passage.[6]) It is difficult not to interpret as

---

[1] Gen. R. L.9, LXVIII.12. [2] *R.A.*, No. 772.
[3] Ex. R. XXIII.7; Num. R. XVI.24. [4] Hag. 14^a; Lam. R. III.21-3, 8.
[5] Gen. R. LXXVIII.1. [6] Ex. R. XV.6.

"anthropolatry" the notion that God consumed in anger those angels who dared—not without some reason from their point of view—to counsel Him against the creation of man.[7] Notwithstanding these exceptions most people, including most Rabbis, have regarded angels as immortal beings.

2. Similarly, while angelic obedience to the divine commandments is declared in one context to be perfect,[8] a disobedient Gabriel or Metatron is made elsewhere the recipient of forty or sixty fiery lashes—a notion very displeasing to popular sentiment.[9]

3. Again, while angels are normally represented as beneficent,[10] even as the guardians of individual human beings,[11] or at least as acting towards men in accordance with their ethical deserts,[12] there are also contrary teachings to the effect that they are guilty of actual jealousy towards humankind[13]— another sentiment which seems to strike the wrong note. This is not to be confused with the orthodox and regular teaching that every human life, irrespective of fault or merit, is terminated by the Angel of Death, who is no respecter of persons,[14] and who is superior even to the stubborn resistance of a Moses.[15] This is a fundamental aspect of the mortal ordering of events, and resentment is futile under any circumstances.

These three contrasts may be supplemented by a few further passages which seem, for the greater glory of God or man, to adopt a slightly disparaging attitude towards the angels. The discussion as to whether they were created on the second or on the fifth day[16] has the clear theological purpose of establishing God's unique and unaided initiative in the task of creation. Yet their pre-mundane existence is normally inferred from the "we" of Genesis 1.26, from Job xxxviii.7, and from other passages of the Old Testament. This might justly be taken as the more orthodox doctrine, and the Rabbinic notion as a piece of special pleading with a particular purpose. Still more

---

[7] Sanh. 38[b].   [8] Lev. R. i.i.
[9] Yoma 77[a]; Hag. 15[a].   [10] Meg. 15[b], etc.
[11] Sanh. 94[a]; Ex. R. xxxiii.6, etc.   [12] Shab. 88[a], 119[b].
[13] Ber. 20[b]; Hull. 91[b]. Cf. also below and n. 17.
[14] M. Kat. 28[a]. Cf. Ned. 41[a]; A. Zar. 5[a], 20[b], etc. In the last passage and elsewhere, there are harrowing details.
[15] Deut. R. xi.5.   [16] Gen. R. i.3.

derogatory is the statement that the angels were jealous and resentful when the Torah was given to man, though their intrinsic superiority and their freedom from physical limitations makes them circumstantially and by nature incapable of obeying a law intended for humanity. There is a strong implication that this is something of a dog-in-the-manger attitude.[17] Rabbi Safra's prayer for peace among the angels would suggest perhaps that he considered its utterance necessary.[18] It is declared that righteous human beings are greater than angels —which sounds a little presumptuous.[19] Adam before his sin was closer to God than any of the celestial host,[20] and this honour is humanly recoverable.[21] These sentiments are virtually contradicted elsewhere by the statement that angels are exempt from the power of temptation—which would certainly imply a status superior to that of humanity.[22] It might be inferred that this particular teacher chose to reject the apocalyptic belief in fallen angels in a rather definite manner, and that many of his colleagues were merely agnostic. Surely any Rabbi with a real desire to disparage the angels could scarcely find better weapons than those available in the wider context of his own faith.

Two other ideas may be mentioned which play down the angelic capacity rather less directly, but quite subtly for all that. The celestial messengers are often regarded as the mediators who bear human prayers to God—though the Jerusalem Talmud emphatically denies the necessity for this, in a sentiment reminiscent of some of the best teachings of the Epistle to the Hebrews.[23] Yet the Babylonian Talmud declares that angels are wholly unacquainted with Aramaic, the common speech of the day, which limits the use of effective prayer to those versed in the sacred tongue.[24] This particular polemic may be pro-Hebraic rather than anti-angelic, and the attribution of linguistic incapacity may be altogether secondary. The other notion is that if evil men are minded to depend too much on invoking angels in prayer, God may actually re-allocate the

---

[17] Song of Sol. R. VIII.11, 2.
[18] Ber. 17^a.
[19] Sanh. 93^a.
[20] Gen. R. XXI.1.
[21] Ned. 32^a.
[22] Gen. R. XLVIII.11.
[23] *R.A.*, No. 48.
[24] Shab. 12^b; Sot. 33^a.

angelic names and functions, so as to render these unworthy human petitions null and void.[25] However effective the divine subterfuge, it would unquestionably undermine the personality and individuality of the celestial beings, and import instability and impermanence into their ranks.

Most of these derogatory passages are vagaries of individual opinion, and must not be taken as orthodox or general.

Certain angels are mentioned by name and characterised so often as to become almost familiar figures. Of the immense detail available, only a few typical references are given here. There is Metatron mentioned above,[26] and Sandalphon who weaves the prayers of the righteous into crowns for God—an idea beautifully worked out by Longfellow in his poem about this angel.[27] Michael is the defender of Israel,[28] Gabriel above-mentioned the sternest of all the host.[29] Michael is declared metaphorically to be made of snow—he cools God's anger against Israel, whereas Gabriel is made of fire—he inflames it.[30] There is an unpleasant vindictiveness about Sammael, the wicked angel, who is a prototype of Satan, and seems a little out of place in the unfallen hierarchy.[31] There are many further names and functions.

The speculations as to the physical or non-physical form of angels are interesting, and more in accordance with the nature of beings supra-human but infra-divine. The Biblical association with fire is often enough echoed (Ps. CIV.4). They do not possess a back, as they are capable of looking in all directions at the same time. They are unacquainted with physical weariness, and exempt from the human weakness of requiring to sit.[32] They have no need to eat or drink, as they are fed by the radiance of the Shekinah.[33] When they appeared to accept the hospitality of Abraham, this was merely a piece of tactful deception.[34] When Moses had to be temporarily raised to the status of the ministering angels, the remains of food and drink

[25] Lam. R. II.2, 5.

[26] Hag. 15*a*; A. Zar. 3*b*; Lam. R. Proem XXIV; etc.

[27] Hag. 13*b*.   [28] Ruth R. Proem I.

[29] Lam. R. II.1, 3.

[30] Deut. R. V.12; Song of Sol. R. III.11, 1. For Gabriel's hot temper, see also Sot. 12*b*.

[31] Deut. R. XI.10; Sot. 10*b*.   [32] Hag. 15*a*. Cf. Gen. R. XLIX.7.

[33] Gen. R. II.2; Ex. R. XXXIV.4; etc.   [34] B.M. 86*b*; Ex. R. XLVII.5.

in his human body had to be miraculously consumed.[35] Angels possess the further power of becoming visible or invisible at will.[36] According to the Midrash they share four special attributes with man—which does not of course exclude them from the possession of other and greater ones. These are the capacity for upright stance, speech, understanding, and sight.[37] According to the Talmud they share three capacities with demons, which may be remembered below in their proper context, and three with man, which are partly repetitive of those above. Like the demons, they are winged, they can fly from end to end of a world still frequently presumed to be flat, and they have a measure of foreknowledge; like man, they possess understanding, the power to walk erect, and knowledge of Hebrew.[38]

Very widespread is the idea that each individual is equipped with two guardian angels.[39] When a man attends to a call of nature, he must, according to some schools of opinion, take courteous and temporary leave of his celestial attendants; according to others, he must invoke their special help.[40] Under certain circumstances, a man may be accompanied by a good and an evil angel at one and the same time, both jealously watchful of his actions.[41] The notion is extensible into that of guardian angels for nations.[42] Similar ideas are very familiar in Christian cultures, as Mt. xviii.10 clearly shows.[43]

It is difficult to build up an orthodox doctrine from these divergent strains, but the consensus of opinion would doubtless accord to angels their proper status between God and man. Everything not in harmony with this may be regarded as individualist and unorthodox.

Demonology

Demonology is singularly unattractive as a special study. Apart from the figure of Satan, which is rather carefully considered at a later stage in this volume, it possesses only a

[35] Yoma 4[b].
[36] Num. R. xvi.1.
[37] Gen. R. viii.11.
[38] Hag. 16[a].
[39] Sanh. 94[a]; Hag. 16[a].
[40] Ber. 60[b].
[41] Shab. 119[b].
[42] Cf. Deut. R. 1.22.
[43] Cf. Montefiore, *Synoptic Gospels*, vol. ii, p. 248.

minor theological interest. It is important for the student of superstition and magic, not to mention other things more abominable. Fortunately for the modern reader of the Bible, ethical monotheism was not the soil most favourable for the growth of the grosser demonic conceptions; but these formed a large element of contemporary pagan preoccupation, and the sacred writers are not unaware of the facts.[44] The Rabbis were plagued by a somewhat more luxuriant growth of superstition in this direction, and this accounts for some of the very dreariest folios in the Talmud and elsewhere.[45]

The Rabbinic theories of the origin of demons are scattered, incidental, and inconsistent. Three of them call for special mention. (1) God fashioned the souls of the demons on the sixth day of creation, but was caught unawares by the intervention of the Sabbath and the consequent cessation of work: He was therefore unable to supply them with bodies, and they remained for ever creatures incomplete and uncorporeal, which accounts perhaps for their evil and malevolence. The reader may be left to supply his own criticism of this aetiology.[46] (2) A second version is that Adam and Eve severed physical relationships with one another for one hundred and thirty years after their expulsion from Eden. During this period, however, Eve repeatedly became pregnant by male demons, while Adam impregnated numerous female ones—thus each had a large and independent demonic progeny.[47] The notion scarcely commends itself as attractive. (3) A third independent idea is that certain of the human beings who rebelled against God in building the Tower of Babel were transformed into demons.[48] It is difficult to take any of these notions very seriously. The doctrine of fallen angels is considerably more acceptable than any of these—it is not easy to determine why it so failed to commend itself to the Rabbis. As they use the demonic names of beings who are fallen angels in other branches of Jewish literature, there may have been some tacit acceptance

[44] Cf. Ps. xci.5-7; Is. xiii.21, xxxiv.14; Lk. viii.30, xi.24-6; etc.

[45] The following notes are independent. For a fuller treatment, see E. Langton, *Essentials of Demonology*, London 1949.

[46] Gen. R. vii.5. Cf. Pes. 54[a].

[47] Gen. R. xx.11, xxiv.6. Cf. the statement and contradiction in Erub. 18[b].

[48] Sanh. 109[a].

among some of them.[49] They certainly have no satisfactory alternative to offer.

The claim that Psalm XCI—especially verses 5-7—makes specific reference to demons is probably correct; the claim that Moses composed the psalm whilst ascending Mount Sinai, to protect himself from his demonic tormentors, certainly is incorrect.[50]

The demons may be numbered in infinite legions, and those who wish to see their footprints, or, at considerably greater personal risk, the demons themselves, are fully instructed in the precise procedures required by black magic.[51] The creatures may be found by the unfortunate in ruins,[52] in drainpipes,[53] and in other strange places. (The inhabitant of the drainpipe turns out an amusing, voluble, and legally astute character.) Demons are harmful to men,[54] and become more harmful to those who sin.[55] Man's best safeguard against their malevolence is the recital of the Shema,[56] or a torch, or moonlight, or company,[57] or the avoidance of night travel.[58] The numerous precautions of imagination, superstition, and black magic would be of little interest to the modern reader.[59]

The trained scholar will find a larger number of lacunae in this chapter than in most of the others. These are quite deliberate—a larger and more exhaustive treatment would not be in place in this particular volume.

---

[49] Cf. Asmodaeus or Ashmedai, prince of demons, Gitt. 68[a, b]; Pes. 110[a]. Cf. Langton, *Essentials of Demonology*, pp. 120 ff.

[50] Num. R. XII.3.

[51] Ber. 6[a]. Cf. Ps. XCI.7.

[52] Ber. 3[a, b].

[53] Hull. 105[b].

[54] Gen. R. XXIII.6, XXIV.6.

[55] Deut. R. IV.4.

[56] Ber. 5[a].

[57] Ber. 43[b].

[58] Pes. 112[b].

[59] Cf. Ber. 51[a]; Shab. 151[b]; Pes. 110[a]; etc.

CHAPTER VI

CREATION

THE doctrine of man proper begins in the second section of this chapter: one further preparatory topic remains. Man is corporeal, and cannot therefore come into being without a physical home. The theme of this chapter falls in consequence into two familiar aspects, the cosmological and the anthropological—the creation of the world or universe, and the creation of man. A scientific materialist, who believed only in a process of evolution generated by a "chance collocation of atoms," would accept the resultant distinction, even if he rejected the term "creation." The Rabbis were quite certainly innocent of modern science, of modern scepticism, and of modern Pentateuchal source analysis. The contemporary findings of Apologetics and Old Testament criticism, higher or lower, are therefore irrelevant in the present context: it may be taken for granted that the Rabbis accepted the main outlines of the Genesis story of creation, and regarded Adam as a discrete individual, endowed with that name. This is not the place to argue whether the legitimacy of the proper name usage be intrinsic or acquired. If "Adam" be translated as "a man," or even as "mankind," no violence is done to Hebrew etymology, and the essential meaning of the doctrine of the Fall is not in any way invalidated. The third chapter of Genesis teaches that man's original innocence and potential righteousness were lost through sin, and whether Adam and Eve were two individuals, or the human race in parable, makes no real difference to the doctrine. In dealing with the Rabbinic theology, it would be pedantic and unnecessary to alter the Adam terminology, or to discuss the historicity of an Old Testament figure whom they undoubtedly took, and whom many still take, for granted.

When Paul designated Christ as the Second Adam, he is making use of a figure of speech known as typology. This may be defined as the particular kind of allegory which pinpoints the essential likeness between two personages quite different perhaps in other respects, and widely separated in time. The earlier example is known as the type, the later as the antitype. The type is often the more striking figure—when some modern general is compared to Alexander the Great, he is scarcely accorded an equal greatness and genius. Yet where Christ is made the antitype in the New Testament, He is always inconceivably greater than the type who foreshadows Him. It is because Paul's typology is the most famous of all, and because it has become so integral to Christian theology, that the Rabbinic treatment of Adam is examined in considerable detail—it would scarcely possess an equal Jewish interest. A further example of typology will be found in a later chapter. The figure need not be rigidly restricted to persons, but may be validly applied to institutions and even things.

The two aspects of creation outlined in this chapter belong in their own right to any synopsis of theology. The first is rather less important, and only its more interesting features are mentioned. The second forms necessary prolegomena for the theme of the next two chapters, the doctrine of Sin. The details of the original state of Adam clearly possess greater interest for the Christian than for the Jew, though the latter cannot hold them altogether without significance. They would, however, receive considerably less emphasis in his outline of theology.

A much fuller presentation of the literary evidences for the subjoined themes, in a wider context, will be found in the first two chapters of Ginzberg's *Legends of the Jews*, which are both interesting and readable.

The Rabbinic Cosmology

The Old Testament, reasonably interpreted, is remarkably free from what the modern scientist might describe as blunders. The ages of the patriarchs and the recorded miracles have occasioned some controversy, but the Bible as a whole is amazingly up-to-date for an age which believed in a flat earth at the very centre of the universe, and in other notions now discarded. The Rabbinic imagination was a trifle less restrained, though it formulated a partially consistent pattern, and frequently attempted to explain things in its own way. A typical kind of reason, here adduced to account for the vast ages of the early patriarchs, is cogent and ingenious. They lived so long, it is claimed, by divine dispensation, so that certain astronomical observations and calculations impossible in the normal human life-span might be made once and for all, for the benefit of posterity.[1]

The numbered propositions which follow will indicate certain of the leading ideas of the cosmology. In the interests of brevity, several closely related ideas may be grouped under one heading.

1. Knowledge of the facts concerning creation is the sole prerogative of Israel—a fact which makes her the envy of the nations.[2] Her teachers have therefore divided these facts into two categories, those suitable for public teaching, and those which are esoteric, and therefore to be kept secret.[3]

2. The earth on which mankind dwells was not the first one to be created by God, but it was the first which happened to satisfy Him. Time is therefore prior to this world, which was preceded by one or more experimental ones.[4] Apart from being somewhat antagonistic to the Platonic tradition, this would seem to cast doubt on God's omnipotence by representing Him as a bungling workman. It would take too long to defend the thesis, but theologians are generally on safer ground when they ascribe the defects of the created order to man rather than to God. Another view is that God is Lord of other worlds which are in contemporaneous existence even now—whereas Plato and Philo Judaeus teach that this is a unique world, and that all the available matter was used up at its creation.[5] If the passage really means that other orbs in stellar space are inhabited by intelligent beings, then available resources are not sufficient to verify or disprove the opinion.

[1] Gen. R. xxvi.5.   [2] Ex. R. xxx.12.
[3] Hag. ii.1. See Soncino edn., p. 59, note 3, and refs.
[4] Gen. R. iii.7, ix.2, etc.
[5] Song of Sol. R. 1.9, 4. Contrast Plato, *Timaeus*, 31*a, b*, 32*c*-33*b*. Also Philo, *De opificio mundi*, 171.

3. God created the world alone and unaided,[6] *ex nihilo*,[7] without effort or striving,[8] by His uttered fiat alone[9] which was expressed in the Hebrew language,[10] and by His own eager desire.[11] These statements contradict a number of other teachings. The first proposition would rule out the collaboration of the Torah, mentioned in the third chapter, or of angels, mentioned in the second. (The participation of angels in creation is sometimes asserted, sometimes denied. Ginzberg may be right in suggesting that the positive line, when it is used, is aimed against the Christian claim that the "we" of Gen. 1.26, etc. foreshadows the Trinity.) Creation from nothing is inconsistent with several other statements—with the unresolved dispute as to whether the source of matter is earth, or heaven, or both;[12] with the assertion that the earth was created from the dust below the Throne of Glory;[13] with the statement that it was compounded of the four elements.[14]

4. Certain things preceded this world in the order of creation. The Talmud specifies seven: the Torah, discussed in the second chapter; repentance—though the occasion for its existence prior to that of sinful beings is not explained; the Garden of Eden—which must have been extra-mundane in that case; Gehenna; the Throne of Glory; the Temple—presumably either a heavenly counterpart, or the conception; and the Name of Messiah.[15] The Midrash gives a similar list, resolving some of the difficulties by distinguishing between, yet boldly equating, immediate creation and volitional contemplation.[16] The real Rabbinic purpose is to invest these seven things with a special holiness. It is the Western rather than the Eastern mind which is over-preoccupied with merely logical difficulties.

5. The light of creation was such that it was possible to see from one end of the world to the other. (The Rabbis obviously visualised a flat earth.) Owing to the immediate sin

[6] Gen. R. 1.3.   [7] Gen. R. 1.5, 9.
[8] Gen. R. XII.10, XXVII.1.
[9] Erub. 13[b]; Meg. 21[b]. Sometimes the ten specific fiats are distinguished, as in Ab. v.1, etc.
[10] Gen. R. XXXI.8.   [11] Num. R. X.1, XIII.6.
[12] Gen. R. XII.11.   [13] Ex. R. XIII.1.
[14] Num. R. XIV.12. Cf. *Timaeus*, 32[c].   [15] Pes. 54[a].
[16] Gen. R. 1.4.

E

of Adam and the sins of his posterity, foreseen by divine omni-science, this light was stored away for the Messianic future and a serviceable but less glorious light provided for the sons of men.[17] There is an unresolved dispute in two passages as to whether the world or light was first created.[18] The second passage adds that light is the refulgence of the garment of God. There is a similar dispute as to whether earth or heaven was created first. This is always resolved by the statement that they were created simultaneously, like a pot and its lid.[19]

6. God created all things for His glory,[20] and His handiwork, unlike that of mortals, does not suffer from the ravages of time—witness the unfading glory of the heavens.[21] (This is not entirely consistent with the next paragraph.) Everything God has created has a purpose, even fleas and gnats. Several legends are cited to support this claim.[22] Yet such are the mercy and goodness of God towards His beloved Israel that He will even on necessity reverse the created order for her sake.[23]

7. The world is not destined for eternal duration. One passage boldly predicts a total span of 6,000 years, followed by 1,000 years of desolation[24]—a span already long surpassed, according to modern science, in the days of the Talmud. The ultimate passing of this temporal realm is familiar Biblical teaching,[25] amply borne out by the expectations of modern science. Men have been trying to predict the date all through the ages. The Psalmist showed a wise reticence. However limited the duration of the physical state may be, it is never doubted that God Himself exists from eternity to eternity. The expectation of human immortality is affected only if it be interpreted in terms of a purely corporeal resurrection—which was the precise belief of many of the Rabbis.

8. Palestine was the first land to be created, and God continues to supply its prior claims for water by His direct action, whereas He leaves His messengers to divide the water the Holy Land does not require amongst the lesser nations of

[17] Hag. 12ª; Gen. R. III.6, XLII.3; etc.   [18] Gen. R. III.1; Ex. R. L.I.
[19] Hag. 12ª; Gen. R. I.15; etc.   [20] Ex. R. XVII.I.
[21] Gen. R. XII.13.   [22] Gen. R. X.7; Lev. R. XXII.2 *et seq*.
[23] Ex. R. XXXVIII.4; Eccl. R. III.4, 1.
[24] R. Sh. 31ª. Cf. Sanh. 97ª, ᵇ, which differs in detail.
[25] Ps. CII.25-7, quoted in Heb. I.10-12.

the earth.[26] There would be numerous physiographical difficulties in connexion with such a procedure, even under the assumption of a flat earth. But the underlying idea is considered important, not the physical means. Several alternative schemes are discussed in another passage: (a) that the formation of the earth began from a stone cast into the primeval ocean by the hand of God; (b) that God began from the circumference of the earth, and worked inwards; (c) that He began from the centre and worked outwards; (d) that the act of creation began with Jerusalem—which is an amalgam of (c) and the preceding passage.[27]

There are numerous subsidiary notions, none of them without at least antiquarian interest, and several Rabbinic elaborations, in greater or less detail, of the six days of creation, which the interested reader may peruse for himself.[28] One further idea deserves a passing mention—the world is shaped like a ball, and the sea like a dish.[29] Though still far from accurate, this is a nearer guess than the old Greek notion of a flat earth with the River Oceanus flowing round it.

Few modern readers would take the foregoing cosmology very seriously: the noble opening chapters of Genesis are vastly superior, and the greater reticence of the Scriptures in general shows a ripe wisdom.

The Original Physical State of Adam

The special Pauline importance of Adam was mentioned in the introduction to this chapter. In Judaism, the father of mankind is accorded a significance somewhat inferior to that of Abraham, and vastly inferior to that of Moses. Yet the Rabbinic views about him are of fascinating interest to the Christian, whereas in a volume of this type the much more voluminous material on the Patriarchs must pass unrecorded. Adam's sin will be considered carefully in the next chapter: of immediate interest are the endowments, both physical and mental or spiritual, ascribed to him before his sin. The latter

[26] Taan. 10ᵃ.   [27] Yom. 54ᵃ.
[28] Gen. R. xi.8, xii.5; Ex. R. xv.22. Cf. also Sukk. 49ᵃ; Hag. 12ᵃ, ᵇ; Ruth R. ii. 3.
[29] Num. R. xiii.14.

are of considerably greater interest, but the former must not be neglected. Here the Westerner finds himself in difficulties not unfamiliar. Because Oriental metaphor is more exuberant and exaggerated than anything within his own thought categories—the East is more colourful anyway—he is apt to dismiss as nonsensical that which he has failed to understand. He should remember two things: firstly, that the teacher who is trying to get his essential idea across in a striking way is supremely uninterested in the validity of the Aristotelian syllogism; and secondly, that the first Adam is sometimes Rabbinically glorified in apologetic counterblast to the Christian exaltation of the Second Adam—though he may on another occasion be vilified with an equal energy. The reader may now be left to form his own judgment on the material sub-joined.

All living things of the original creation, the Talmud teaches, were brought into being in full maturity.[30] The old riddle "whether first the egg or hen . . ." has never been answered with finality, and this claim, though not directly demonstrable, is not necessarily absurd, unless certain Darwinian hypotheses be regarded as absolutely infallible. Thoroughly consistent is the statement that Adam and Eve were created already endowed with the maturity which human beings normally attain at the age of twenty. The adult status still comes a little earlier in the Orient.[31] The first couple then did not undergo the normal period of mental and ethical immaturity, but stepped into the world as fully responsible beings. On a literal interpretation of the Genesis story, this point of view is rather essential in maintaining both the reality of the first sin, and the justice of God. It would be surprising to find any contrary opinion.

Adam's physical beauty surpassed anything ever known to his descendants. This is expressed pictorially by the repeated statement that the ball of his heel outshone the sun in splendour.[32] Sarah, Eve, Adam, and the Shekinah are arranged in an ascending order of beauty: so great was the gap that each made the successor in time, the predecessor in enumeration, look a mere monkey by comparison; while Sarah, the least

[30] R.Sh. 11ᵃ.   [31] Num. R. xii.8; Song of Sol. R. iii.11, 1.
[32] B.B. 58ᵃ; Lev. R. xx.2; Eccl. R. viii.1, 2.

distinguished of the four, makes us all look like monkeys. This was because Adam had originally received the direct likeness or image of God, which became diluted, so to speak, in successive transmissions.[33] According to this curious theory of Darwinism-in-reverse, men do not evolve from simian ancestors, but progressively approximate towards simian brethren. If this idea were expressed in more ethical and less physical terms, and in cold logic, it could well provide a topic for serious debate.

Various passages attempt to describe the original size of Adam's body. According to the Talmud, he reached to the firmament in stature, and his extended form stretched from one end of the world to the other—the earth, of course, is here regarded as flat.[34] This merely postulates infinite height—he might or might not have been exceedingly thin in comparison. The former is extremely unlikely, as Oriental taste prefers the skeleton to be well covered. The Midrash goes further, and asserts that his frame filled the entire earth, adding various refinements and discussing the inert mass from which he was created.[35] Adam's punishment after his sin consisted partly in having his stature reduced to one hundred cubits.[36] The Western mind jumps at once to logical difficulties—how could a man, whatever his size, be confined in a space scarce bigger than himself? And where was his partner Eve to find rest for the sole of her foot? And what about their progeny? And the animal kingdom? The Eastern mind, supremely untroubled by such discrepancies, merely enjoys the magnificence of the hyperbole, receiving and appreciating the essential and intended concept of tremendous size, and ignoring all else.

The Talmud assigns the various parts of Adam's body to different regions of the known world, which need not be fully detailed here. Israel, it may be noted, has the credit of producing his head, while his sexual organs are attributed to a town with a special reputation for immorality.[37] The last statement may be of greater interest when the next section has been read.

[33] B.B. 58^a.   [34] Hag. 12^a.
[35] Gen. R. xxiv.2; Lev. R. xiv.i; etc.   [36] Hag. 12^a; B.B. 75^a; Sanh. 100^a.
[37] Sanh. 38$^{a, b}$.

The character of Adam at the time of his creation will be considered in a later section of this chapter.

The Creation of Eve

The Rabbis are agreed that the first pair of mortals were not fashioned apart, for Eve was taken from the body of Adam, even as Scripture teaches. It is added, however, that God "intended" to create them separately.[38] This is a little compromising in respect to the doctrine of divine omniscience, and it is difficult to see any real necessity for the statement.

There are two main Rabbinic theories as to the manner of the creation of Eve. The first is really borrowed from Plato, but the Rabbinic sources cast it into a Hebraic mould, and base it ostensibly on the exegesis of Psalm cxxxix.5a. The words are usually translated: "Thou hast beset me (or hemmed me in, or besieged me) behind and before"—a meaning which is not particularly appropriate to the immediate context, though harmonious enough with vss. 7-12. The verb part might equally well come from another weak verb with the same strong radicals, and mean: "Thou hast formed (fashioned) me behind and before." Neither rendering enjoys the unanimous approval of modern scholarship, but the Rabbis used the second when it suited them, and deduced therefrom that Adam was originally created with two faces, or two body fronts, looking opposite ways, and that in due course Eve was formed from him simply by the process of fission. The Talmud discussion is tangled up with a controversy as to whether Eve was fashioned from Adam's spare face, or from a tail which has disappeared in the course of his corporeal evolution. The essential and emergent idea, plain in the Midrash and doubtless implicit in at least part of the Talmud passage, is that they were originally like Siamese twins, only joined back to back, and that they became two individuals when they were sundered. If the proposition were accepted, this would furnish an interesting argument for the equality of the sexes. It should be remembered that all this and more has been argued in more general terms in the *Symposium*.[39]

[38] Ber. 61*a*; Erub. 18*a*; Ket. 8*a*.
[39] Ber. 61*a*; Erub. 18*a*; Lev. R. xiv.i. Cf. Plato, *Symposium*, 189*d*-193*e*.

The second and perhaps more acceptable Rabbinic theory regarding the creation of Eve is the familiar Scriptural one, namely that she was fashioned from a rib of Adam while he was in deep sleep. The Almighty is accredited with the best intentions in securing a partner for the lonely man, and with careful prior reflexion on the matter, but the prevailing Rabbinic opinion seems to be that Eve was a sad mistake on His part. The preliminary thoughts of the Holy One are summarised in the following manner: "I will not create her from the eye, lest she be coquettish; nor from the ear, lest she be an eavesdropper; nor from the mouth, lest she be talkative; nor from the heart, lest she be of a jealous nature; nor from the hand, lest she be thievish; nor from the foot, lest she be a gadabout; but from the hidden part in man, for even in the moment when a man stands stripped, that part of him is covered."[40] (The mere concealment of any part of the body is a mark of modesty, and a virtue in itself.) The passage immediately goes on to demonstrate from Scripture how Eve and her descendants turned out to possess all the evil qualities the Almighty had endeavoured so scrupulously to avoid. This is somewhat forced exegesis—and most ungallant.

Despite all the imperfections alleged in women, men are charged with the categorical imperatives of marriage and procreation,[41] and some very hard things are said about bachelors and their sins of omission.[42] There is also the widespread idea that a celibate adult life is a life of sin, at least in thought and perhaps in act also.[43] The same opinion prevails more strongly in the Moslem lands of today, and many hard judgments on quite innocent people result therefrom. Yet the important sect of the Essenes required celibacy, though this was contrary to the majority tradition of Judaism. Against this near-compulsion to marriage must be set the deep-seated religious conviction that everything associated with sex and the sex life is fundamentally unclean, that husbands and wives alike need elaborate ritual purification to keep themselves free from Levitical sin. This is perhaps a little less bewildering when it is remembered that a dead body, a

---

[40] Gen. R. XVIII.2.
[41] Yeb. VI.6.
[42] Yeb. 63ª.
[43] Kidd. 29ᵇ.

leper, the flesh of the pig, and a number of other things were unclean in precisely the same sort of way as sexual matters —that is to say, ritually rather than morally. The Moslem who washes at the lustral fountain before praying in the mosque is performing an analogous religious action.

While it is freely admitted that the female mind is quicker and more perceptive than that of the male,[44] women are yet frequently stigmatised as possessing qualities of a most unpleasant nature.[45] They are said to require perfume, which a man does not require, because they were created from a putrefying bone, whereas man was formed from pure and wholesome earth.[46] Yet it can scarcely be denied that the bone was drawn from the man's body, and must go back ultimately to the same constituents. Men should, and many still do, give daily thanks in their prayers because they were not born as females.[47] Of the two Jewish compilers of the *Rabbinic Anthology*, one feels that this phrase, long incorporated in the Prayer Book, can be justified, the other that it cannot be justified.[48] The only conceivable line of apologetic is to urge that thanks are expressed to God, not for any intrinsic superiority of the male sex, but simply for the man's privilege of observing a greater portion of the Law than is possible for the woman. The words are of course liable, justly or unjustly, to much less fortunate interpretations.

The Westerner is inclined to criticise the very high divorce rate in Rabbinic circles. It must be remembered that if the husband was zealous for the Law, it was his bounden if unfortunate duty to divorce a hopelessly barren wife, no matter how tenderly he loved her, for the sake of perpetuating the race. The story of one devoted couple, ten years married, but childless, and about to part for ever, is worth recording. The counselling Rabbi insisted on a farewell feast, where the lady encouraged her spouse into a condition of drunkenness, under the influence of which he gave her authority to remove from his house to her father's home, where she must needs repair, any single article she might care to choose. While the man lay

---

[44] Gen. R. xviii.i.   [45] Cf. Gen. R. xlv.5; Deut. R. vi.ii.
[46] Gen. R. xvii.8.   [47] Men. 43 b.
                    [48] *R.A.*, pp. xcviii, 507, 656 ff.

in unconscious sleep, the woman superintended his bodily removal to the home of her youth, assuring him when he returned to sobriety that there was nothing else in the house she desired so much. So they remained married, were blessed with a child after all, and lived happily ever afterwards.[49] There must have been many similar stories with a less happy ending.

It is difficult for the Westerner who is pre-conditioned by a romantic approach to the whole relationship of the sexes to judge fairly how far the average Rabbinic marriage was an external legal contract unemotionally undertaken, and how far it was the joyous union of two people who deeply loved each other. No doubt it could partake of either character, as it has in fact done in the West also, depending on the individuals concerned. In the twenty-third chapter of the *Rabbinic Anthology*, the reader will find some charmingly tender passages, contrasting strangely with certain of those deprecated above.

For Jew and Christian alike, the relationship between man and woman forms a large area of potential sin, but the Jewish fusion of the ethical and the ceremonial, together with certain fundamental differences in viewpoint, makes the criteria of judgment radically different in the two cultures. The average Rabbi certainly maintained a fanatical personal purity, perhaps at a high emotional cost, which is reflected in the many long discussions of every conceivable sexual theme in the literature. In theory and law, the penalty for adultery was death, though this could not be inflicted under Roman rule. Family limitation was regarded not merely as contrary to the law, but as equivalent to child murder. Yet with all this, there remains a certain inner uneasiness, reflected in a passage cited in the last section, where the sexual organs of the still innocent Adam are said to come from a town with a particularly unsavoury reputation. Much of the Rabbinic attitude to sex is thoroughly healthy, though it often rests on completely un-Western presuppositions, yet it contains also an element of potential neurosis.

The creation of Eve raised the whole question of sex—that is why it has been briefly discussed here. It belongs also to the

49 Song of Sol. R. 1.4, third section, par. 2.

doctrine of sin—but theological themes never fit neatly into watertight compartments.

The Original Nature of Adam

The original nature of Adam interested the Rabbis less perhaps than the nature he acquired through his sin. There are, however, some comments worthy of note. No specific fault was imputed to him, unless indirectly in the possession of sex organs—a matter which was scarcely of his choosing. So superb was the intelligence with which he was endowed that he was appointed to name the animals—a feat which the angels were unable to perform. He also named himself, and addressed God as Lord.[50] God taught him the use of fire, the manner of cross-breeding animals, and many other things.[51] The various parts of the world have remained populated or barren according to his original and personal decree.[52] The Rabbis visualise the time between his creation and his sin as of a few hours' duration only. His intelligence must therefore have been the direct gift of God, not something gained by empirical methods. This would deprive him of any really personal credit.

Without certain divine precautions Adam, the crown and consummation of creation,[53] might have been mistaken for God.[54] Before his sin, he could listen to God's voice gladly and unafraid, because he had not offended against his Maker.[55] God had personally appealed to him not to sin,[56] for he was created upright,[57] and the faithful observance of one commandment would have earned his immortality[58] even as Elijah was later to earn his.[59] For Adam was intended for immortality,[60] created to serve God,[61] and yet, with Eve, to rule over the rest of creation.[62] Sustained obedience to the will of God would have meant unspoiled felicity for him and for his descendants, with continued enjoyment of all the delights of the Garden of

[50] Gen. R. xvii.4; Num. R. xix.3; etc.
[51] Pes. 54ᵃ.
[52] Ber. 31ᵃ; Sot. 46ᵇ.
[53] Gen. R. xiv.1.
[54] Eccl. R. vi.10, 1.
[55] Num. R. xi.3; Song of Sol. R. iii.7, 5.
[56] Eccl. R. vii.13, 1.
[57] Eccl. R. vii.29, 1.
[58] Num. R. xvi.24.
[59] Eccl. R. iii.15, 1.
[60] Ex. R. xxxviii.2.
[61] Lev. R. xx.2.
[62] Num. R. xii.4.

Eden.[63] The wistful note of the might-have-been rests over the entire Rabbinic contemplation of the still innocent Adam. Whatever view the modern reader may hold regarding the opening chapters of Genesis, he will recognise their abiding moral, namely that the sufferings of mankind originate for the most part within the domain of human nature.

An interesting speculation with a slightly metaphysical flavour may be cited in epilogue to this chapter. A reflective Rabbi once watched the manufacture of tongs, noting that the blacksmith required existing tongs to hold the glowing metal from which the fresh implement must be fashioned. Who then, he asked himself, made the first tongs that ever were? His colleagues found it possible according to temperament to answer that the first manufacture was by means of a mould —though this merely raises further questions—or to argue alternatively that tongs were a special creation of God, which, with a number of other things, came into being on the eve of Sabbath.[64]   A fuller report of the debate would be of considerable interest.   Some minds at least were alert to imponderables.

[63] Gen. R. xv.5.   [64] Pes. 54^a. Cf. Ab. v.6.

CHAPTER VII

THE ORIGIN OF SIN

I F a Rabbi were to partake of the flesh of the pig, or to wear a garment of mingled linen and wool, the sin might seem nearly as great to him as that involved in a deliberate act of theft or adultery, for these are equally an infringement of the Law. The modern Gentile world does not share these particular scruples, and in this brief account of Rabbinic hamartiology stress is laid on those aspects for which some common ground of ethical judgment exists. The other side of the story has been illustrated already, in the Halakhic enactments cited in the first chapter and elsewhere. The present chapter, which is largely aetiological, will deal with the historical origin of sin in the human race, with its psychological initiation in the individual, with its supernatural background as this was conceived by the Rabbinic mind, and lastly with the thorny question of the relationship of God to human sin. The eighth chapter will deal with the more concrete and workaday aspects of sin in its common Eastern and Western understanding, and will contain some comparisons between Rabbinic and New Testament ideals.

The Historical Origin of Sin

Sin began, the Rabbi would declare, with the disobedience of Adam to the divine commandment, and it has continued historically ever since—though he might choose to mention a few individuals who were in his opinion exempt from the almost universal taint. The sources are unanimous, and Scriptural also, in holding that the first transgression took the form of eating the fruit of some plant divinely proscribed, though there are varying opinions as to its identity. The vine, the fig, and wheat are all suggested,[1] but some would argue more strongly for the vine, inasmuch as it has caused considerably more harm in the world than either of the others.[2] None of these plants possesses in contemporary experience the peculiar quality claimed by Scripture, that of imparting the capacity to distinguish between good and evil. But this is not the place to pursue the matter further.

There is a curious fluctuation of opinion in assessing the culpability of Adam and the heinousness of his sin. One passage declares that he was not nearly wicked enough to merit death, and that God killed him only through foreknowledge of his evil posterity.[3] On being charged with his fault by righteous descendants, and upbraided because of bringing mortality upon the human race, he is said to have retorted that he had committed only one sin, whereas the best of his posterity, including even Moses, have been guilty of several sins.[4] By the argument from the silence of Scripture, this is Rabbinically correct. Yet the excuses that are found for the father of mankind in one context may give place to the most violent vituperations in another. For Adam is also declared to be ungrateful to God,[5] a complainer,[6] stubborn and blasphemous in his unrepentance,[7] a bringer of death who himself deserved immediate extermination,[8] and—most serious charge of all in Rabbinic eyes—one utterly unfitted to receive the 613 precepts of the Torah, seeing that he could not observe the few simple injunctions laid upon him.[9]

The results of the first sin are also emphasised. The innocent Adam could listen to God's voice standing upright and unafraid, but his transgressions rendered him a slinking, frightened creature, even as Scripture points out.[10] Moreover the glory with which he was created did not abide with him overnight.[11] Nevertheless the splendour which was taken from him will be restored in the Messianic future.[12]

---

[1] Ber. 40^a; Sanh. 70^a, ^{b}; Gen. R. xv.7.
[2] Lev. R. xii.1; Num. R. x.2; etc.   [3] Gen. R. ix.5.
[4] Num. R. xix.18.   [5] A. Zar. 5^b.
[6] Lam. R. iii.34-9, 9.   [7] Num. R. xiii.3.
[8] Num. R. xxiii.13.   [9] Gen. R. xxiv.5; Eccl. R. iii.11, 2.
[10] Num. R. xi.3; Song of Sol. R. iii.5.   [11] Sanh. 38^b; Gen. R. xi.2; etc.
[12] Num. R. xiii.12.

It will be readily perceived that Adam is to some extent a controversial figure, and that various interpretations might be built up from separable strains of tradition. The question which particularly interests the Christian is whether Judaism does or does not regard the sin of Adam as involving abiding consequences for his posterity in the moral, as distinct from the merely practical, sphere. In other words, is there any counterpart to the Christian doctrine of original sin?

Most men have committed a sufficient number of personal transgressions to bring upon themselves the responsibility for their own physical death, the Rabbis would teach—and here they are on safe ground. Yet many would go on to make a few individual exceptions. Elijah is said to have abstained from sin, and to enjoy in consequence uninterrupted life.[13] Yet the acute nervous breakdown in I Kings XIX and other incidents of his recorded life reveal a man dedicated to God, but certainly not without mental and physical weakness. Other men, guiltless in themselves, are said to have died solely through the evil machinations of the serpent: "There exists a kind of death unaccompanied by sin, and a kind of chastisement unaccompanied by wrongdoing."[14] Moses pleads for his life before God, affirming that he has committed no sin worthy of death, and God replies that he is to die because of the sin of Adam, the instigator of human death.[15] The passages so far cited acknowledge merely the physical consequences of the first transgression, tacitly or specifically denying any universal or ineluctable taint in the moral sphere. They constitute, therefore, not an endorsement but a rebuttal of the Christian doctrine of original sin. This links up with an idea which is prevalent in Judaism, namely that a man may render himself guiltless by keeping the whole Law. There is thus a diametric opposition of honest conviction between the two faiths.

There are two contrasting but much less widespread ideas which approximate more closely in certain directions to New Testament teachings. The first is that the serpent copulated with Eve in the Garden of Eden, though Scripture does not record the fact, thereby infecting her and her descendants with

---

[13] Lev. R. XXVII.4.   [14] Shab. 55ᵇ. Cf. B.B. 17ᵃ.
[15] Deut. R. IX.8. Cf. *R.A.*, No. 620.

an abominable lust, usually interpreted as a tendency to bestiality. Those who received the Law on Mount Sinai were purged from this unclean thing, but the heathen are still under its chains.[16] The idea is itself ugly and repulsive, but the theology behind it is significant. The second notion is that the real fall of mankind occurred, not through our first parents, but through the worship of the golden calf under the slopes of Sinai. The taint of this most heinous of all acts of idolatry has been passed on from generation to generation, and no human being ever receives any punishment which does not contain an element of retribution for that particular sin.[17] It is interesting to note elsewhere the attempt to clear the good name of the pure stock of Israel in this connexion by blaming the proselytes for the entire incident,[18] and to find yet another passage treating the same event as a shining example of the power of penitence.[19] A third and somewhat fainter parallel may be found in certain Rabbinic attitudes to sex, briefly discussed in the last chapter. There is a fourth and slightly stronger analogy in the statement that parents pass on merit or guilt as the case may be to their children and children's children.[20] This could well be interpreted as a character legacy, in harmony with the modern psychological stress on heredity. There is much general truth in this, provided a number of individual exceptions be recognised.

The Pauline concept of original sin is clearly foreshadowed in the Genesis record itself, and elsewhere in the Old Testament. It was also a commonplace in certain strains of Judaism long before the Apostle's time, and clear statements are found in certain books of the Apocrypha.[21] The previous paragraph demonstrates the existence of certain ideas which, if widely accepted and applied, would lead to somewhat similar results. When Rabbinic Judaism elected to soft-pedal the idea, or to shift its centre of gravity away from the person of Adam, this was not due to ignorance or lack of precedent but to deliberate choice, which may have been dictated by opposition to the

---

[16] Shab. 145^b-146^a; Yeb. 103^b; A. Zar. 22^b.
[17] Sanh. 102^a. Cf. Ex. R. xxxii.1, xli.7, xliii.2; Lev. R. x.3; etc. Note the casuistic praise of Aaron in the last passage cited.
[18] Lev. R. xxvii.8.   [19] A. Zar. 4^b.
[20] Yom. 87^a.   [21] Cf. notably Ecclesiasticus xxv.24.

teaching of Paul. Through these or other circumstances, it is approximately true to say that the doctrine of original sin does not belong to this particular strain of Judaism.

On the Scriptural evidence, it is not possible to place the historical origin of sin and of human immortality anywhere but on the shoulders of Adam. The Midrash carefully stresses the potential of atonement by declaring that God took his dust from the future site of the Jerusalem Temple.[22] Despite these impressive facts, Adam has never become a foundation stone of Jewish, as he has of Christian, theology. A few individual teachers regard sin as hereditary, but they are not in the main stream of strictly Hebraic thought. The more usual view is that men are given a clean sheet at birth, and that if they allow it to become dirty, they are themselves responsible. It is unfortunate that, through the sin of Adam, all are condemned to die. In a few cases, this is by misfortune rather than by fault, but the vast majority of men render themselves culpable by their own actions. There is an underlying implication here and there that certain of the more saintly of mortals have not quite had a square deal, though other contexts recognise the universality of sin.[23]

There is in another source a fascinating and detailed account of the destiny of the soul about to be born into a human body, which is partially relevant to the immediate theme, and certainly worthy of mention. It is fully summarised by Ginzberg,[24] and certain of its ideas are reflected elsewhere. It states in brief that every time a woman conceives, Lailah, the Angel of Night, carries the sperm before God, who precisely fore-ordains all the physical characteristics of the body that is to be—the environment is largely predetermined already by the selection of the mother. Freedom of choice is granted to the destined human being in the moral and spiritual sphere, and there only. (This is also familiar Talmudic teaching.)[25] Lailah then brings a soul which is destined without option to enter the human sperm, despite its unwillingness to quit the joys of Paradise. A comprehensive preview is granted, of heaven, hell,

[22] Gen. R. xiv.8.   [23] Cf. Lev. R. xxxvii.1.

[24] Ginzberg, *Legends of the Jews*, Philadelphia 1913-28, VOL. I, pp. 56-9, citing Tanhuma Pekude 3, or Midrash Yetzirat ha-Walad.

[25] Nidd. 16ᵇ.

and the mortal life awaiting with all its dangers; only amnesia is thereupon induced by a blow on the head. This is a variant, more elaborate in certain particulars, of Plato's proof of immortality by recollection—the incarnate soul recalls with difficulty the things it knew directly in its former state.[26] The import of the Rabbinic passage is, of course, that sin means the abuse of the freedom of the will granted to the personality in the moral sphere.

On the whole issue of the historical origin of sin, it is roughly true to say that whereas Paul teaches that Adam sinned, *therefore* all men sinned by consequence, Talmud and Midrash teach rather that Adam sinned, *and then after that* all men, or most of them, sinned in their turn, but without any direct causal relationship.

The Psychological Origin of Sin

As the Rabbis seem little inclined to lay the full burden of the world's sin on the shoulders of Adam, they are constrained to find some other explanation for the proneness of human beings to transgression, individually and corporately. The principal theory offered is that every person is born with an impulse or inclination towards evil, the *yetzer ha-ra* which enters into his nature the moment he emerges from the womb—some say even before that, in the embryo state.[27] This is more or less equivalent to what the Christian would call the power of temptation, though that is usually regarded as operating a little later in life. It is, or should be, counterbalanced in the Jew by the good inclination, the *yetzer ha-tobh*. But this is only granted to him at the age of thirteen, when he undertakes the responsibility of observing the Law.[28] Victory in the struggle is by no means assured, for the enemy is insidiously strong.[29] Exact minds even located the good inclination in the right kidney, and the evil one in the left.[30] According to one view, there were originally two evil inclinations, one leading men to idolatry, the other inducing unchastity; but, so far as Israel is concerned, the first has been uprooted, and battle with the second remains the

[26] Plato, *Phaedrus*, 249ᵉ-250ᵉ; *Phaedo*, 73ᵃ-76ᵉ; and sundry other passages.
[27] Gen. R. xxxiv.10. Cf. Eccl. R. iv.13, 1, ix.15, 8.
[28] Eccl. R. iv.13, 1, ix.15, 8.   [29] Ned. 32ᵇ.   [30] Ber. 61ᵃ.

F

order of the day.[31] The Rabbinic literature is not univocal regarding the cessation of the sin of idolatry, and it would be extremely naïve to class all remaining sins under the single label of unchastity. For all practical purposes, the evil inclination may be regarded as a single force urging the soul into transgression, whatever be the precise nature of its fault. This is the fundamental working theory of sin in the Rabbinic writings. The Scriptural foundation of the entire concept is clearly revealed in the Hebrew text of Genesis VIII.21.

According to the Talmud, each individual is endowed with two guardian angels.[32] In a more detailed and circumstantial passage, one of them is declared to be good, the other evil.[33] Maimonides [34] later propounded the hypothesis that the Rabbis equated these respectively with the good and evil inclinations, basing his deduction principally on the last passage cited. The notion is a most interesting one, and it gains colour from that particular reference, but it can scarcely be demonstrated that it was the official theological position.

In dealing with the evil inclination, the Rabbis make several psychological points which are of very great interest. The first of these is that a human being is only tempted, not compelled, to yield to the solicitations of this internal disturber of his peace, although most men are too weak by nature to offer any very effective resistance. The inclination is not in itself a sin, original or otherwise, only a tendency towards sin, and no guilt or punishment inheres until it is translated into specific action. There are wise and sound elements in this principle, but the Rabbis sometimes push it too far. Thus God is declared not to reckon against a man even a fixed intention to do evil, provided it happens, through no virtue in himself, to remain unfulfilled.[35] The thwarted murderer may remain guiltless in the eyes of the law, but he is scarcely cleared at the judgment-seat of God. The Rabbis declare further that moral conquest over the evil inclination honours God,[36] that men can achieve it and have achieved it,[37] and that they may enlist the good inclination, the Torah, and other spiritual allies on the side of

---

[31] Song of Sol. R. VII.8, 1.   [32] Taan. 11^a. Cf. Ber. 60^a, *init.* Cf. Mt. XVIII.10.
[33] Shab. 119^b.   [34] Ginzberg, *Legends of the Jews*, VOL. V, p. 20.
[35] Kidd. 40^a.   [36] Sanh. 43^b.
[37] B.B. 17^a, 78^b; Song of Sol. R. IV.4, 1; etc.

victory.[38] There is something very attractive in the theory mentioned in the last section, namely that men start life with a clean sheet, and are able to keep it clean by obedience to the Torah. The Christian, in denying this particular postulate, does not deny that the heart and will of man are well able to overcome many specific temptations to evil. This pearl of wisdom and truth is well worthy of segregation and emphasis.

A second interesting psychological view regarding the evil inclination is that a man is tempted by what he sees with his own eyes, whereas he is not tempted by what he does not see directly.[39] If there is no visible enticement, a man does not sin. The immediate reference is to lust, but if the principle is true, it is obviously capable of extension. Tangible opportunity leads to many more crimes than abstract planning, but the premeditated deed may be of an infinitely more dangerous character. With this qualification, the psychology is sound. It follows logically that those who, by deliberation or careless-ness, place temptation in the path of others share some measure of the guilt—a careless master readily makes a thieving servant. The really strong-minded Rabbi may safely expose himself to temptation, by deliberately walking past a brothel, for example, knowing that his future resistance will be strengthened by this new moral victory.[40] Others may prefer to go round by a different street.

A third and absolutely undisputable psychological point is the growing power of sin once the evil inclination has taken hold of a man. When he has fallen once, he will fall again. The specific reference is to idolatry, but the general principle is of much wider validity—conscience does become blunted by the mere fact of transgression.[41] Lamentably true also is the statement that the inclination seems to grow stronger in the course of a man's life, and that pre-eminence of character makes it the more subtle and dangerous.[42] It is a cobweb which becomes a cable.[43] Yet just before that, in paradox, it is a vast obstacle which the righteous have overcome, and a slight impediment which the wicked did not honestly try to resist.

---

[38] Ber. 5[a]. Cf. Kidd. 30[a]; B.B. 16[a]; A. Zar. 5[b].   [39] Sot. 8[a]; Sanh. 45[a].
[40] A. Zar. 17[a, b].   [41] Nidd. 13[b].   [42] Sukk. 52[a, b].
[43] Sukk. 52[a]. Cf. Sanh. 99[b]; Gen. R. xxii.6.

The first promptings to sin are easily overcome, but an impeccable standard throughout life is hard to maintain. The proselyte is declared to stand in especial danger, because his faith is not ancestral, and his evil background cannot be eliminated.[44] Even for the righteous Jew, the struggle against the evil inclination lasts throughout this mortal life, and peace and victory come only at the moment of death.[45] Yet the Ethics of the Fathers, in a passage of eloquent but rather sombre fatalism, declares that it is mere wishful thinking to imagine that the grave terminates the sorrows of this fight, for judgment follows after that.[46] It is clear that certain of the Rabbis did not take the external and rather light-hearted view of sin suggested in some contexts, and strongly condemned by Christians. They could be sober and even pessimistic, declaring, for example, that the evil inclination has continued, generation after generation, to destroy the sons of men,[47] that it brings the innocent to death, and has caused such national disasters as the Exile and the destruction of the Temple.[48] Yet the more optimistic cherished the hope that one day this evil thing would be uprooted from Israel, and the glory of the Shekinah restored.[49] Some continued to believe, or, as the Christian would maintain, delude themselves that sinlessness is possible even in this mortal life under its present conditions.[50]

The Rabbis frequently asked why God had ordained this troublesome and unnecessary disruptive force within the human personality. It is roundly declared in one context that God repents of having created it at all,[51] and, more boldly still, by forced exegesis, that He has wronged sinners by so doing.[52] Petitionary prayers for the complete removal of the evil inclination from the hearts of men follow by natural sequence, but God's answer is that this may be achieved only in the life to come—meanwhile, the sons of Israel must continue to fight the good fight.[53]

Two freak views may be mentioned in passing. It is solemnly

[44] B.M. 59 *b*.
[45] Gen. R. IX.5.
[46] Ab. IV.22.
[47] Eccl. R. IV.16, 1.
[48] Yom. 69 *b*.
[49] Deut. R. VI.14.
[50] Cf. Deut. R. VII.5; Pes. 87 *a*.
[51] Sukk. 52 *b*.
[52] Ber. 31 *b*-32 *a*.
[53] Ex. R. XLVI.4. Cf. Ex. R. XLI.7; Eccl. R. II.1, 1.

declared that the evil inclination is a good thing—even a very good thing—because without it there would be no marriage or procreation, and the human race would cease.[54] Surely the answer is to maintain the legitimacy of sex without sin in its proper place. How could a righteous God ordain a good end by sinful means?

The second and equally objectionable view is fortunately an individual one, that of Rabbi Ilai the Elder, but it is perpetuated in at least three Tractates.[55] If a man is utterly unable to resist the evil inclination—that is to say, overwhelmingly tempted to commit some particular sin—he is urged to put on black clothes, go to a strange place and sin in secret, rather than cause his profession of religion to dishonour God by his actions. Did this Rabbi profess the religion of external convenience, that sin or abstinence is unimportant provided there is no human witness? As secret sin is roundly condemned in other contexts,[56] it may be taken for granted that this view, like its Christian counterpart, is only a freak one.

The Supernatural Origin of Sin

It will be clear from the two preceding sections that a selective interpretation of the Rabbinic literature provides a broad explanation for the phenomenon of sin on the terrestrial plane. With a little change of emphasis and nomenclature, much of the teaching would be acceptable to thinking minds today, whether Jewish or Christian. But the religious temperament has never been contented with the purely mundane sphere. There are still many references, serious or jocular, to the world, the flesh, and the devil, and it is not so very long since the latter element of the triad was securely established in Christian theology. The writer has no desire to argue in this context for or against the validity of the concept of a personal devil, but it may be remarked in passing that even if certain schools of thought have confidently argued him out of existence, the

[54] Gen. R. ix.7; Eccl. iii.11, 3.
[55] M. Kat. 17ᵃ; Kidd. 40ᵃ; Hag. 16ᵃ. In the last passage, secret sin has just been condemned, and the view criticised in the text of the chapter is offered as an alternative.
[56] Cf. Kidd. 31ᵃ.

effects formerly attributed to his machinations still flourish abundantly. In other words he stands for a reality, whatever its metaphysical nature. The Rabbinic view of Satan is of special relevance to the topic of this chapter, and the salient facts must be stated, though it is not necessary to go beyond the immediate sources. The doctrine of the celestial Fall—sin, pride, and rebellion in the heavenly places, resulting in the expulsion of certain angels from Paradise—was quite certainly not unfamiliar to the Rabbis. But it belongs primarily to the apocalyptic strain of Judaism, leaves only minor traces in the Rabbinic literature, and therefore falls outside the scope of this book. Milton has given this concept an enduring monument in the epic literature of the English language. Langton's volume on demonology, cited earlier, will give the curious reader all the wider background he may require, for all the strains of Judaism and beyond.

There is little to say about the Old Testament material. Satan was first of all the adversary, the potent factor in human stumbling, but he is scarcely endowed with a distinctive personality in the earlier canonical books. In Job and Zechariah he does become a personal agent, but is still subject to the will of God. In the First Book of Chronicles, he appears to have attained a greater independence.[57] In the Rabbinic, as in other branches of post-Biblical Jewish literature, his sway and power advance considerably.

The first comprehensive doctrine of the supernatural origin of evil is the simple or popular one, not unknown in Christian cultures, which represents Satan as the malevolent enemy of the human race, inspired in his vindictive deeds by nothing beyond sheer ill will, and quite unable to remain passive in the contemplation of any human happiness or contentment.[58] If this cannot be backed by any adequate reason or revelation, it is a rather lazy way of accounting for human transgression and misfortune.

It is sometimes declared by way of encouragement that the fulfilment of a divine precept is like an arrow in the eye of Satan. This word of good cheer needs an accompanying warning: boasting or jubilation over the supposed arrow

[57] Job I. II; Zech. III.1-2; I Chron. XXI.I. [58] Cf. notably Gen. R. XXXVIII.7.

finding its supposed mark may only lead the enemy of mankind to a more determined onslaught on the rash individual who seeks to defy him.[59] Early marriage is another means of discomfiting Satan, it is confidently claimed, because this protects a man from the impure thoughts which are so bad for his soul.[60] This may be linked with other teachings which have been cited on the same theme. In general criticism of this particular approach, it may be said that the conception of human righteousness as a constant battle against a vindictive and unsought enemy of vastly superior power, who serves no useful purpose whatever, is intrinsically unsatisfying. The presupposition of the apocalyptic doctrine of the fallen angels would provide at least a logical foundation for such a view, though this would still have to be related to the justice, providence, and permissive will of God. The vivid personality and motivation of the Miltonic Satan, admired despite the strongest resistance of the will, is unknown in the Rabbinic literature. This is in any case the least satisfactory of the three theories offered.

The second version of the Rabbinic doctrine of Satan, as it may conveniently be dubbed, gives him a function, or rather a threefold function, and makes him theologically significant. He is conceived in one key passage in the treble role of the seducer, accuser, and destroyer of men: in other words he entices human beings to sin, then arraigns them before God, and finally, by divine permission, destroys them.[61] On the Day of Atonement, however, he has no power to accuse.[62] The three cardinal activities are separately ascribed in numerous passages, but it is sufficient to mention the one in which they are made so much more impressive by their co-ordination. On this view, the Book of Job might be significantly regarded as an epic of ultimate Satanic failure in a particular case. The Rabbinic psychology reaches a profound level of truth in this interpretation. The seemingly sombre pessimism need not be pushed to extremes, for it is nowhere suggested that man is merely helpless in the face of Satan's enticings. Given free will and personal pugnacity, he will resist the

[59] Sukk. 38ᵃ; Men. 62ᵃ.
[60] Kidd. 29ᵇ-30ᵃ.
[61] B.B. 16ᵃ.
[62] Yom. 20ᵃ.

assaults of the adversary, and this ethical gymnastic will build up his moral and spiritual stamina. The solemn note is due to the fact that so many are overcome in the struggle. These are noble teachings, and it is probably more wholesome and less misguided to stress the challenge to man's personality rather than the supposed "unfairness" of the Deity in permitting human beings to be tempted in the first place. The vehicle of language is never adequate to the deeper mysteries of man's nature—still less can it properly describe the things that concern God.

The third version of the Rabbinic doctrine of Satan is the most interesting of all, for it shows a wide imaginative sweep, and a grasp of the significant and essential. It also aligns itself with some of the most modern theories. Satan, the angel of death, and the evil inclination are boldly and confidently equated—they are all one and the same thing.[63] This statement, thrown out so tersely and incidentally, could form the foundation for a whole philosophy of sin—and it must certainly have seemed in its day a major revolution in the Rabbinic theology. It is only a step to the thoroughly modern concept that Satan is not a fallen angel, not a personal devil, not an external force of evil, but an inward spiritual and psychological disharmony in the very nature of man, making him his own adversary, his own seducer, the final moral agent of his own death. This notion is further endorsed by the interesting Talmudic statement that the Tempter dwells within the personality of man.[64] The amazing theological comprehensiveness and ethical adequacy of this theory cannot be denied. Many would still prefer the more colourful apocalyptic view: it is not for this book to argue one way or the other. It would be quite wrong to imagine that Rabbinic Judaism as a whole had attained to this very modern opinion propounded by one or two advanced thinkers.

The interest of the present chapter in Satan is limited to the pinpointing of the three significant views of his person and function: the vindictive personal devil, who spoils so much of human life and effort, and leaves man more sinned against than sinning; the seducer, accuser and destroyer, against whose

---

[63] B.B. 16ª. Cf. Ex. R. xxx.17; etc.   [64] Shab. 105ᵇ.

onslaughts the man of moral calibre may yet triumph; and the wholly subjective force, equivalent to the evil inclination, inherent in the nature of man. The main theme of this chapter is the origin of sin, and this section provides another theory— or rather three alternative theories.

God and Human Sin

The second chapter raised briefly a familiar paradox: God is absolutely righteous, yet the world He has made is full of evil. Now that the principal Rabbinic theories regarding the origin of sin have been outlined, it is appropriate that the paradox should be considered again. It is very unlikely that the Rabbis ever faced it squarely as a separate issue, or thrashed it out to the utmost of their logical powers. It may be that they would have advanced no further, that the solution is beyond the grasp of the finite brain. Yet men will keep trying to find an answer as long as they have any interest in final issues. It is only possible here to consider hypothetically the kind of approach the sources might have made.

The Rabbis would certainly agree that the first sin took the form of disobedience to God under the pressure, perhaps the severe pressure, of external and unsought temptation. God permitted Adam to transgress, but he possessed within himself the potential of obedience and righteousness, and could have strengthened and ennobled his own character by victory over sin. His free will was God-given, and was abused solely by his own fault and weakness: God is therefore utterly dissociated from his guilt. The same thing has continued to happen all through history, whenever a human being has knowingly succumbed to temptation. Yet how could it be otherwise when the essence of human personality is ethical freedom? If men were not capable of sinning, their righteousness would be automatic, and not truly virtuous. The ferocity of the tiger and the gentleness of the dove do not receive moral censure or approval, because they are not characteristics of rational and free creatures, whereas the actions of man spring from intelligent volition. Yet over and above this fact, God is ever active in influencing men to right the wrongs they have committed.[65]

[65] Lam. R. 1.16, 49.

The matter is complicated by the concept of the evil in-clination, though the same line of apologetic would be valid. It might be added that, owing to the repeated abuse of the freedom of the will throughout successive generations, each child starts with a heredity which is at least partially bad. If Satan be regarded as a cryptogram for the evil inclination, or as a spiritual adversary who can be successfully resisted, no difficulty, or at least no greater difficulty, arises. The first or popular view of Satan, pushed to extremes or expressed in careless ways, could be interpreted as detrimental to the justice and holiness of God. Many would reject that view in any case, for there is something inherently unsatisfactory about it.

The statements of the paragraphs above are a little too sharp and definite for chapter-and-verse substantiation in the sources, but the general direction of the Rabbinic answer might well be similar. The less happy sort of approach may be typified in a parable which the wiser and more perceptive of the teachers would reject. A father, according to this parable,[66] strikes and injures his son, then binds up the wound with plaster, assuring him that he will suffer no harm so long as he leaves the plaster intact. In like manner God created the evil inclination, to the bitter sorrow of His people, and without any recorded reason, providing also the Torah as an unfailing antidote. This ascribes an unfatherly action to God, makes Him the Author of sin—the pons asinorum of the careless theologian—and fails utterly to get down to the real problem.

The relationship between a man's conduct and the treatment he receives at the hand of God is a cognate and hotly debated problem. It may be worth while to look closely at a serious though not wholly successful attempt to "justify the ways of God to man."[67] Moses has asked God why prosperity and adversity are both found without apparent discrimination among the righteous and among the wicked alike—the implica-tion being that each man should be rewarded according to his deeds. God is represented as giving two slightly different answers, which are really successive Rabbinic attacks on a problem still unsolved. The first answer is: "Moses, the righteous

---

[66] Kidd. 30[b]. Cf. R.A., No. 332, p. 125, with notes thereon and cross-references.
[67] Ber. 7[a].

man with whom things go well is himself righteous, and is the son of a righteous man. The righteous man with whom things do not go well is in himself righteous, but he is the son of a wicked man. The wicked man with whom things go well is, though wicked himself, the son of a righteous man; the wicked man with whom things do not go well is not only wicked himself, but is also the son of a wicked man." After further discussion, the difficult verse Exodus xxxiv.7 is declared to refer to children who persist in the evil ways of their fathers, while the apparently contradictory but morally satisfying verse Deuteronomy xxiv.16 is declared applicable to those children who abandon the evil parental ways. This is merely an application to Scripture of the familiar Halakhic method of reconciling two apparently contradictory statements x and y, a matter discussed in the first chapter. This leads to an emended version of God's supposed words to Moses: "The righteous man with whom things go well is an absolutely righteous man; the righteous man with whom things do not go well is not an absolutely righteous man. The wicked man with whom things go well is not completely wicked; the wicked man with whom things do not go well is completely wicked." The first dictum ascribed to God is unjust and unsatisfying; the second is inadequate and untrue. It is only the human comment in between which offers any moral conviction. But God is not to be judged by the words placed in His mouth by men.

This passage raises wide issues. There can be no valid personal ethic if a man is to be treated according to the deserts of his father, because, so far as human information goes, he never possessed the power to choose his father. Logic does not seem to ordain that the partially wicked should be regarded as preferable to the partially righteous—if indeed the two can be distinguished. But there is some reason for supposing that the child bears his own moral responsibility in so far as he may rise above or sink below the environment he did not initially select, thereby placing himself under judgment. There is excellent Scriptural authority for this. The passage Exodus xxxiv.7 has a partial doublet in the Decalogue, Exodus xx.5, where the iniquity of the fathers is visited upon the children unto the third or fourth generation *of them that hate me*. There is no vindictiveness or injustice here—the children are punished only if they bring guilt upon themselves. If this may be regarded as the implication of Exodus xxxiv.7 also, a serious stone of stumbling disappears from the exegesis of the Old Testament. This would harmonise well with the eighteenth chapter of Ezekiel and other passages, where the individual nature of responsibility is declared in no uncertain terms. Other passages cited elsewhere set forth the effectiveness of righteous prayer, and the readiness of a merciful God to answer it. This, with the important concept mentioned above, furnishes a doctrine acceptable to Jews and Christians alike.

It would be outside the scope of this essay to discuss the relationship of God to natural catastrophe or sudden death, or to the predatory nature of the human, animal, and vegetable kingdoms. Certain it is that a large proportion of the evil under the sun, though not all of it, arises directly through man's fault. The innocent are frequently involved along with the guilty, but it is idle and impertinent to blame God because the freedom of man's will brings results which are only to be expected while he remains sinful. Rabbinic Judaism, like Christianity, does not confine man's existence to this transient mortal state, and that is perhaps formative of the ultimate answer.

CHAPTER VIII

THE FACT AND MEANING OF SIN

ON a large number of specific transgressions of the
moral law, the ethical judgments of the Rabbi and of
the Christian would coincide, or else differ only in
degree. This is natural and proper, because their respective
definitions of sin overlap throughout an area larger than that
in which they diverge. The Rabbi recognises a wider area of
potential sin in certain directions because of a ceremonial and
consuetudinary code which the Christian does not accept as
binding on him. On the other hand, the Rabbi may sometimes
justify by dubious casuistry actions which the Christian would
condemn. The most fundamental differences of ethical outlook
are to be found in the realms of marriage, divorce, and
adultery.[1] In these matters it is far from easy for the Westerner
to arrive at a fair judgment—he is all too ready to condemn
that which he does not properly understand. He has lived and
matured in an utterly different society, with a moral code based
on altogether different social customs and circumstances. He
is apt to forget also that the Talmud preserves archaic legisla-
tions for institutions, such as Levirate marriage, which had
ceased to be operative by the time it was committed to writing.
It would be a grave anachronism to make this a basis for
adverse criticism. Allowing, however, for such broad and
important exceptions, the Rabbinic and Christian moralists
would still find a great deal of common ground in other
directions, with differing specific emphases. This chapter is
concerned with the common ground, with the more practical
aspects of the subject, and with some direct comparison between
Rabbinic and New Testament teachings.

[1] On the whole subject, see L. M. Epstein, *Marriage Laws in the Bible and Talmud*,
Cambridge, Mass. 1942.

The Definition of Sin

It would be easy to draw up from the Rabbinic literature a very long list of particular sins which the Jew and the Christian would condemn univocally. No right-thinking person on either side would hesitate to arraign procrastination, carelessness or partiality in the seats of public justice, perjury, bloodshed, incest, and obscenity;[2] likewise rape, sodomy, murder, forgery, and other misdemeanours.[3] There would be general agreement too that it is a sin to tempt Providence by exposing one's life to unnecessary danger—the example given is specific, but the general principle holds—or to allow one's self-righteousness and censoriousness to reach the pitch of praying God to bring destruction on an offending neighbour.[4] These are random examples. It may be taken for granted that every conceivable variety of theft, dishonesty, violence, adultery, drunkenness,[5] and vice would be equally condemned by either side, and that the sensitive human conscience, Jewish or Christian, would give precisely the same answer in facing many of the serious and slight temptations which beset mankind.

In their definition of sin, the Rabbis make two clear but quite independent classifications, both of them useful. First they make the sharp distinction that each particular sin of any individual must be committed either against God (frequently expressed as against heaven), or against a fellow man.[6] This is cogent and self-explanatory. A few specific offences, such as the mishandling of Temple funds or the equivalent, might fall under both headings at one and the same time, but the majority of human misdemeanours could be readily and un-ambiguously assigned to one category or the other. The Jewish and Christian conceptions sometimes diverge in detail in the first class, the sins against God, because of the radical difference in the content of revelation accepted as valid. Nevertheless, allowing fully for this, the agreements in particular instances would still form a large numerical majority.

The other distinction is between those sins which are

---

[2] Shab. 33[a].   [3] Sukk. 29[a, b].
[4] Ber. 55[a].   [5] Cf. Lev. R. xii, *passim*; Num. R. x, *passim*.
[6] Yom. 86[b]; Eccl. R. ix.12, 1.

deliberate and wilful, and those which are unintentional.[7] The wilful sin is always regarded as blameworthy in a higher degree, irrespective of end results. In special cases, the unwitting offender may conceivably do much more harm, but this is not a valid ethical criterion. A modern cyclist of otherwise excellent character may find that his rear light has failed in the dark, miles from home, and may ride on without either ill effect or police intervention, whereas a scrupulously careful motorist may kill a pedestrian by sheer accident. Technically, the first is more guilty than the second, though he has much less on his conscience. Open-eyed wrongdoing normally carries unsparing censure, whereas there is some sympathy or leniency for the unfortunate victim of circumstances. The Talmud makes this very clear in its allocation of penalties for particular offences. The Rabbis note also what may be regarded as a special class of unintentional sins—those of which the transgressor himself has no awareness at all, either at the time or later, and which are therefore known to God alone. Before the final destruction of the Temple, the ritual of the Day of Atonement took special care of the expiation of such offences in its statutory sacrifices.[8] As the average man stumbles in this way many times, the scrupulosity of the precaution is not to be dismissed as mere pedantry.

The prevalence of the terrible scourge of leprosy led some to ask whether this might not normally be God's punitive visitation on sinners.[9] Certain Old Testament narratives, such as those of Miriam and Gehazi, lent at least a superficial colouring to such an interpretation. There has been much discussion regarding the precise nature of the Biblical leprosy, whether it be the incurable *Elephantiasis Graecorum*, the malady known as leprosy today, or the curable *Psoriasis vulgaris*. Possibly it included both of these, and certain other skin diseases as well. The curious reader will find fuller details in the standard Bible Dictionaries, and in commentaries on Leviticus XIII. The Biblical disease, whatever its precise medical definition, was something frightening and revolting. Nevertheless, cold scientific observation does not bear out that the

---

[7] Shebu. 67[b]-69[b]; Shebu. 7[b]-8[a].   [8] Shebu. 9[a]; Ker. 25[b]-26[a].
[9] Shebu. 8[a]; Lev. R. XVII.2 ff., XVIII.4; Num. R. VII.5. Cf. Montefiore, *Synoptic Gospels*, VOL. I, p. 43.

blackest sinners necessarily become afflicted with leprosy, or that the greatest saints are necessarily exempted. Furthermore, the aetiological implication may be grossly unfair to many innocent sufferers. The seriously religious mind has always regarded leprosy as a parable of sin—the contamination is just as horrible, though the results remain outwardly invisible; but it is nothing more than a parable, except perhaps in one or two specific instances of the Scriptural record.

One commonplace assumption of Christian apologetics is that the Jewish conception of sin is completely external and ceremonial, limited to specific acts, and totally unconcerned with the mind and heart. It would not be difficult to fill this volume with quotations selected to point in that direction. The Dominical denunciations of the Scribes and Pharisees, or rather of certain of their number, justified in their proper context and reference, have been universalised in a manner which was never intended by their Author. A considerable portion of this volume could also be filled with quotations reflecting a deep, inward, spiritual, contrite conception of sin—the Rabbis were not all legalists. Neither selection by itself would give a fair and rounded picture. An attempt is made throughout this book to show something of the best, and something of the worst. In the next paragraphs, and later in the chapter, some of the flowers will be found.

It is roundly declared that it is a sin to fail to take the opportunity of praying for one's fellow[10]—a sentiment which beautifully expresses the Godward and manward duty of the persevering saint. This law is operative in the practical sphere also: leprosy is considered a fitting punishment for the sin of refusing to lend and share one's goods.[11] Rabbinic Judaism probably knew little of the vast and growing class of deliberate and professional beggars in the East of today, of simulated lameness, of faked and bloody bandages, of straining the ingenuity to avoid work above all other evils. All these co-exist with desperate poverty. There was once an unclouded beauty in the giving, unmarred by exploitation in the receiving. The Jew did not usually fail to help a co-religionist in his distress, and honesty and integrity are inculcated in all dealings with

[10] Ber. 12 *b*.   [11] Lev. R. xvii.2.

Gentiles—though active charity towards the latter might perhaps have been considered a little unnecessary.

It is interesting to note arrogance[12] amongst the sins specially castigated. Some Rabbi had the right idea, for this sin is rather discernible among certain of his colleagues. Even stronger language is used about loss of temper, which is said to deserve in punishment nothing less than the torments of Gehenna.[13] Significant also is the recognition of the need for atonement for impure thoughts, even though these have not been carried into outward act.[14] Adultery of the eye is likewise strongly condemned, in a passage which will be cited below.[15]

There is enough evidence here to show that the Jew and the Christian may discuss together the doctrine of sin, resting assured that they mean broadly the same thing.

The Philosophy of Sin

The Rabbinic reflexions about sin are too numerous for any exhaustive examination—only a few distinctive ones are selected here.

Much attention is given throughout the literature to the major issue of temptation, and to the respective results of mere yielding and of successful resistance. It is declared that either of these courses may become an ingrained habit and eventually second nature, so that the righteous man becomes absolutely immune and the sinner unable to stop himself from committing the accustomed sin.[16] Both halves of the proposition are reiterated categorically in more than one context. Even purely ritual measures are claimed to be potent enough to bring complete freedom from the chains of transgression.[17] On the other hand, when a man persists in a certain indulgence or wrongdoing, his conscience becomes blunted, and he fails eventually to retain even the awareness of his guilt. He is described in Scriptural terms as a dog returning to its vomit.[18] Nobody is likely to question the growing power of sin, the cobweb aforementioned which becomes a cable,[19] but the

[12] Sukk. 29^b.   [13] Ned. 22^a.   [14] Shab. 64$^{a, b}$.
[15] Lev. R. xxiii.12.   [16] Yom. 38^b-39^a. Cf. the notable Mishnah Ab. iv.2.
[17] Men. 43^b.   [18] Sot. 22^a; Yom. 86^b, 87^a; Kidd. 40^a.
[19] Cf. Sanh. 99^b and other passages cited below.

Rabbis are inclined to overestimate the beneficent power of good habits. The least blameworthy of human beings can maintain his integrity only by constant struggle and watchfulness. More modest, and at the same time much more sound psychologically, is the idea that the sensible man will at least put up a fight when he is faced with temptation, and not just weakly and immediately yield.[20] Equally to be commended is the recognition of the worthwhileness of the minor victory,[21] and of its spiritual value.[22] These discussions are all made more relevant and important by the clear claim that a man's deeds, good and evil alike, follow him into the world to come, and are present with him at the time of judgment.[23] Eschatological consciousness gives a much deeper meaning to the religious teachings of any faith.

Among the worldly-wise sayings of the Rabbis, in a passage on betrothal and divorce, is a terse aside to the effect that no man enters into sin without the expectation of some profit therefrom.[24] The point under discussion is the ready credence granted to the man who declares himself to have been betrothed to a certain woman, but is now willing to give her the divorce necessary under Jewish law, where betrothal was as binding as marriage. Why should he create gratuitous trouble for himself on the basis of a lie? What conceivable gain could there be, to himself, to the woman, or to anybody else? It follows that he must be speaking the truth. This is another piece of acute psychological observation, lacking only the necessary qualification to make it applicable in other spheres—few statements about human beings ever attain to universal validity. There are a number of sins due to lust, weakness of character, even devilry, but the motive of financial gain or personal advancement is unquestionably one of the most frequent. Equally penetrating is the dictum that the beginning of sin is sweet, whereas the end is bitter.[25] The deceiving and alluring glitter of the first temptation is a very different thing from the final sordid outcome. Very clear and emphatic also is the recognition that there is something worse than any sin a man can commit

---

[20] Ex. R. xlii.8.
[22] Song of Sol. R. iv.4, 3.
[24] Kidd. 63 *b*.

[21] Num. R. x.8.
[23] A. Zar. 5 *a*.
[25] Eccl. R. iii.2, 3.

by himself—namely, the act or persuasion of leading another person from innocence into transgression.[26] This passage will be discussed later, as it has close links with the teaching of the New Testament.

The Rabbis are not usually capable of sustained metaphysical thinking on abstruse questions, but they sometimes take a more direct way to the heart of the matter. When faced with the problem of the relationship of soul and body in the specific act of sin, they do not argue like a Plato or a Kant, but offer instead a crystal-clear parable of rare and pungent insight. They tell the story of a king who possesses an orchard with fine early figs worthy of special protection. He selects, with what would appear to be great cunning, two watchmen presumably incapable of abusing their trust, one being blind and the other lame. The lame man, however, sits on the blind man's shoulders, and they commit a joint felony, pleading their separate disabilities as a proof of innocence. But their trick is unmasked. So it is with human sin. In the final judgment the body will try to blame the soul, and the soul the body, for all their united transgressions. But God will not be deceived, and will judge them as one.[27] The combined learning of all the philosophers could not have found a more telling and memorable way of putting a fundamental truth.

The next section may be regarded as a subdivision or special topic of this one.

Intention—an Important Ethical Criterion

The Rabbis realised very clearly that the major intelligent actions of rational human beings are accompanied by an intention, a purposive will to bring about some desired result, good or evil as the case may be. The righteous man who is supposed to become immune against temptation is one whose intentions are habitually good, while the confirmed transgressor is his opposite in all respects. Closer ethical thinking would

[26] Num. R. xxi.4.
[27] Lev. R. iv.5. The 13th-century Christian use of this parable by Alexander Neckam is interesting. See R. Loewe, " Alexander Neckam's knowledge of Hebrew," in *Mediaeval and Renaissance Studies*, Warburg Institute, vol. iv, London 1958.

distinguish motive from intention, recognising its possibly greater importance. Brutus and Cassius, as Shakespeare portrays them, have the same intention to murder Caesar—but Brutus has the motive of a noble and self-effacing patriotism, Cassius that of base jealousy. It is a little difficult to legislate about motives: they are seldom tangible, and not always clearly discernible even to the person concerned, who may be torn this way and that. The Rabbis formulate their precepts on the slightly firmer ground of intention. Examples of their concrete discussions are most frequent in the technical Halakhoth, which would appeal little to the general reader, and would require much detailed explanation. This section confines itself to the broader and more interesting examples and principles.

It may be instructive to open the subject with a seeming contradiction. It is laid down that a man is liable to make full civil restitution for any damage whatsoever caused by him, directly or indirectly, wittingly or unwittingly. (Witting and unwitting transgressions, discussed a few pages earlier, may now be conveniently re-defined as sins accompanied or unaccompanied by a purposive intention.) If a farmer's ox breaks loose while he is asleep, he is liable to pay for all the damage caused, however carefully he may have tried to secure the beast.[28] And yet, strange as it may sound to those unfamiliar with the historical background, the same Talmud decrees that if Jones intends to kill Smith, but kills Brown by mistake, and if it can be proved that he had no specific intention of evil against Brown, he escapes all punishment.[29] This goes much further than the passage referred to in the last chapter,[30] which exculpates the man whose evil intention remains unfulfilled. On the purely penal side, the discrepancy is simply explained. The ideal conviction of the Rabbis was that full condemnation should be effective only when evil intention and evil act are quite indisputably combined. This is a magnanimous principle which could be fully applied only in a better world than this, and one which would be particularly unworkable in the realm of civil law, where any kind of culpable negligence would have to be excused on the plea that there was no specific intention of harm. The Rabbis perceived clearly that it is better

B.K. II.6, 3[b], 26[a, b].   [29] Sanh. IX.2, 79[a].   [30] Kidd. 40[a].

to allow the above-mentioned farmer and others like him to suffer occasionally through sheer misfortune, than to allow him and others to become so grossly careless that the recognition of personal responsibility and the exercise of individual foresight might become weakened throughout the community. This is forensic common sense, severe as it may be in some cases. This makes it seem all the more incredible to split hairs over the definition of Jones's intention, and to release a deliberate murderer on a point of casuistry. For it was the same Rabbis who stressed intention sufficiently at other times to regard the man who thought he had the right to kill as next-door to a murderer.[31] This theme is sufficiently important to justify a short digression on capital punishment, which will explain this discrepancy, and a number of other things in the Talmud.

In theory the Talmud recognises, in descending order of harshness and pain, four legitimate ways in which the death penalty may be inflicted—stoning, burning, decapitation with the sword, and strangulation. There is some controversy as to whether the last pair should be transposed. As the first three methods are Pentateuchal and the fourth superadded by the Rabbis in mercy, the matter would scarcely seem to call for discussion.[32] Burning would seem rather more barbarous than stoning, though it may have taken place in many instances after death.[33] The seeming harshness and severity of the Biblical legislation—which will be discussed further below—was always a little foreign to the Jewish temperament,[34] and many casuistical brakes were applied to prevent its enforcement long before the Romans took away from the Sanhedrin the power of pronouncing the death sentence at all. This last deprivation may have taken place soon after Judea became a Roman province in A.D. 6, though some Rabbinical traditions would place the date somewhat later.[35] That is why the Crucifixion could not take place without the co-operation, willing or unwilling, of Pilate. The stoning of Stephen was unquestionably an act of mob violence, not the legal outcome of a judicial sentence. The reputedly harsh Pentateuch itself requires two

[31] Makk. 7^b, 9^a. [32] Sanh. VII.1, 41^a, 51^b, etc.
[33] Cf. Josh. VII.25. [34] Cf. Makk. I.10.
[35] Schürer, *History of the Jewish People in the Time of Jesus Christ*, VOL. I, DIV. II, p. 188 and n. 515.

witnesses to secure conviction in any capital charge.[36] As sins are normally furtive and secret, this is a stiff requirement in murder, adultery, or any other crime. A certain Rabbi once pursued an assassin into a ruin, found his sword dripping with the expiring victim's blood, yet lacked the evidence necessary to bring the miscreant to justice.[37] He was not even a witness —he arrived some fifteen seconds too late to see the fatal thrust—and he was one person, not the necessary two. To this Biblical requirement of double human beholding and attestation was added the Rabbinic one of official warning immediately beforehand—though this was supposed to be superfluous for a Rabbi.[38] The ordinary malefactor, before he could be condemned, would thus need to fulfil three conditions —secure a prior warning, then act immediately, and make sure there were two witnesses. It may be presumed that he would either give up the unequal struggle, or else postpone his crime to a more convenient occasion.

No Jewish judges cared to condemn a man to death: they had grave religious fears of bringing some guilt upon their own heads, and also, in most cases, innate humanitarian promptings. Capital punishment might well have become a farce even without the Roman embargo. There may well have been a conflict of emotions in the minds of the legislators— delight at rationalising out of existence something they hated with all their hearts, together with a deep resentment at the galling fact that this power had been wrested from them by a hated Gentile conqueror.[39]

The purpose of all punishment is frequently declared to be not reformatory, but retributive. Of greater significance is the fact that it is exemplary and deterrent. The death penalty for murder is not inflicted to secure a life for a life—that would do little good, but to try to protect society from criminal violence, which is apt to grow if it is not checked. This the Mishnah recognises.[40] When the Rabbis exact the full penalty for negligence, yet allow a very guilty Jones to go scot free,

[36] Num. xxxv.30; Deut. xvii.6, xix.15.   [37] Sanh. 37[b].
[38] Sanh. 8[b]; Shebu. 3[b].
[39] In addition to Schürer, see Moore, *Judaism*, vol. ii, pp. 184-8; *J.E.*, art. "Capital Punishment."
[40] Makk. i.10 *fin.*

they would seem to be neglecting an important duty to their fellows, however distasteful its fulfilment might be to themselves. But the pronouncement is an abstract ratiocination about a hypothetical law, uttered by the waters of Babylon by men who merely dreamed of a restored Israel, and who lacked the power to bring Jones to justice in any case.

After this necessary digression, it is fitting to return to the official topic of this section. If the Rabbis are a little reluctant to attach a sufficiently black mark to the man whose evil intention remains unfulfilled, they certainly hasten to bestow full credit on his well-meaning brother who does not quite succeed in carrying his excellent intentions into specific action. The man who meant to fulfil a precept, but was circumvented by force or accident—or might it be forgetfulness or laziness? —still receives his full meed of praise.[41] There is great hope too for those purposes and motives which are not yet perfected. A man should always be encouraged to study Torah, even if his initial spiritual approach is altogether wrong: from this unpromising beginning, purer intentions and deeper piety may ultimately be born.[42] The psychology of this is sound and wise. Indifference and ignorance are the foes of all true religion, but a beginning of interest, even a casual one, may grow to more—though the Torah should normally be studied with intent to practise its precepts.[43]

There is another interesting saying, embodying much paradoxical truth, but needing many qualifications as a guide to action. It is declared to be better to commit a definite sin from a good and pure intention than to fulfil a precept with an evil intention.[44] It may be just in certain circumstances to restore to their rightful owners the ill-gotten gains of grafters and exploiters—it is certainly just to hang the wilful and cold-blooded murderer. But these things must never under any circumstances be left to private judgment or action: they are community duties. For mere private individuals, the teaching cited above could be full of very terrible dangers.

This section, like the preceding one, may be fittingly closed with an attractive story.[45] Rabbi Johanan b. Zakkai foresaw

---

[41] Ber. 6ᵃ; Shab. 63ᵃ; Kidd. 40ᵃ. [42] Pes. 50ᵇ; Naz. 23ᵇ; Hor. 10ᵇ; Arak. 16ᵇ.
[43] Lev. R. xxxv.1. [44] Naz. 23ᵇ; Hor. 10ᵇ. [45] B.B. 10ᵃ.

in a dream that his nephews were going to lose seven hundred dinars within the year—probably all their worldly wealth. He therefore constrained them, without revealing his dream, to give most of the money to charity, which they did either obediently or generously. Very soon afterwards the government ruthlessly confiscated their seventeen remaining dinars, and the delighted Rabbi explained to his nephews how much more virtuous he had made them by preserving the disinterested nature of their initial act of charity. It is to be hoped that these reflexions brought them some comfort in their loss.

The general tenor of this body of teachings is sound and wise, though occasional exception might be taken to particular passages. It is fundamentally just that a man is to be judged not only by his discernible actions, but also by his inner compelling purposes and intentions, which are the real key to his character.

Some Rabbinic and Christian Teachings on Sin

The earnest Jew or Christian is sometimes too thoroughly preconditioned by his own religious training to assess the other faith quite objectively. Montefiore's suggested expedient of bringing in a Mohammedan or a Buddhist would scarcely be satisfactory either, as the formative Judaeo-Christian elements would be lacking in his mental heritage and approach. It cannot be denied that uninformed Christians have all too frequently dismissed the Rabbinic religion as worthless, devoid of the breath of the spirit, while Jews have declared with equal readiness that the entire teaching of Jesus and the Apostles is borrowed directly from Judaism, save for those doctrines concerning the Person of Christ, and contains no intrinsic virtue, apart from being "nicely put." The two views are erroneous in equal measure. But every writer on either side must feel the tremendous difficulty of being scrupulously fair in a discussion of this kind.

Much discussion on the respective merits of the Dominical and Rabbinic teaching has started from the Golden Rule. Jewish teachers had enunciated the negative version over and over again before Jesus: in his famous advice to the facetious proselyte who desired to learn the entire Torah while standing on one leg, Hillel was merely quoting.[46] The Christian tends to assume that the positive form of the Rule marks an incalculable advance on the negative one—a claim which the Jewish commentators deny, not without arguments on their side. In an appraisal which is scholarly, balanced, and admirably fair, Abrahams concludes that the negative form is "more fundamental," whereas the positive form is "the fuller expression of practical morality."[47] Montefiore quotes German scholarly opinion in support of the thesis that any specific difference between the two expressions belongs to modern rationalisation rather than to ancient consciousness.[48] There may be an element of truth in this interpretation, though it seems a rather arbitrary severing of the Gordian knot. The idea of positive welldoing always possesses a stronger emotional appeal, however it may be circumscribed by circumstances, but there is grandeur also, and a wider reference, in the will to abstain from evil towards any living creature. It is needless to deny to Jesus the credit and originality of making the Rule positive, and thereby infusing something new and challenging into it. It is needless also to regard the two forms as antithetic when it would be much more profitable to regard them as complementary.

In the sixth chapter of the Epistle to the Romans, Paul discusses the general and unparticularised aspect of sin. He certainly never intended to imply that human beings in their mortal state possess the omniscience necessary to keep them from all of what the Rabbis would call the involuntary or unwitting transgressions: in this respect they are bound to remain sinners, though a careful scrupulosity may reduce the number and seriousness of their lapses. What he does assert very strongly—again borrowing Rabbinic terminology—is that any dabbling in wilful transgression must be utterly unthinkable for the Christian. It is the text Ecclesiastes VII.17: "Be not wicked overmuch" which brings the Rabbis face to face with Paul's problem. The modern expositor might declare

[46] Shab. 31ᵃ. See C. G. Montefiore, *Rabbinic Literature and Gospel Teachings*, London 1930, p. 150, for full translation and other references.

[47] Abrahams, *Studies in Pharisaism and the Gospel*, VOL. I, p. 22.

[48] *Rabbinic Literature and Gospel Teachings*, p. 151.

that this is the worldly and prudential ethic of a book which stands, despite all its shrewd wisdom, on a lower spiritual plane than its companions in the Old Testament; but the Midrash could make no such concession. It therefore conveniently misunderstands the words to mean that the sinner is not to lose hope after one transgression, or imagine that the way of repentance is closed—an admirable sentiment, but scarcely what the writer said.[49] The Talmud passes over the difficulties of the text, and goes on to point out that a man who has made his breath smell foully by eating garlic does not cure his halitosis by the consumption of more garlic.[50] If the precise words used lack the burning and coercive zeal of Paul, they show clearly at least that Ecclesiastes is not to be made the excuse for any latudinarian ethic. Here the Talmud and the New Testament are solidly and impressively at one.

There are two main teachings on adultery which stem from Jesus. The Synoptic pronouncement: "Every one who looks at a woman lustfully has already committed adultery with her in his heart" may be paralleled many times in Talmud and Midrash, even though less impressively, for the Rabbis also realised that purity of mind is just as important as purity of body, and considerably more difficult to attain. It is roundly declared that mere meditation on sinful acts requires atonement.[51] Not only is a man to abstain from the slightest contact with a woman who is not his wife,[52] but his mental or imaginative sin is declared more harmful than would have been the actual transgression.[53] The lust of the eye, even when it is not accompanied by any outward act whatsoever, is still declared emphatically to be adultery.[54] The outward and inward standard of conduct prescribed is as high as that demanded by Jesus—only His marvellous insight went a little further, and placed these sins where they really belong, in the human heart.

The teaching above finds its necessary complement in the Johannine pericope on adultery—an almost certainly genuine Dominical occasion and utterance, the precise literary history of which is of no immediate concern. It may well have been

[49] Eccl. R. VII.17, I.
[50] Shab. 31 *b*. Cf. Kidd. 55 *b*; A. Zar. 2 *b*-3*a*.
[51] See above, p. 97, note 14.
[52] Ex. R. XVI.2.
[53] Yom. 29*a*.
[54] Lev. R. XXIII.12.

suppressed at one stage by Christians not sufficiently enlightened to receive it. The idea that there was forgiveness even for a fallen woman, and the incredible words: "Neither do I condemn you," stand in strange contrast to the vindictive brutality of the way the Rabbis talk, at least in the Halakhah, about the adulteress and the punishment appropriate for her.[55] Once again they are discussing penalties they had no power to inflict, and the ugly sentiments in their hearts have abundant Christian parallels. It need scarcely be pointed out that the pericope merely raises the possibility of forgiveness for what is past—it does not offer the slightest loophole for any lax views about a premeditated act of adultery, or conflict in the minutest particular with its complementary teaching above stated.

There are two comments which the Christian interpreter feels moved to make. Firstly, it must be conceded that the Rabbinic approach in the Haggadah is frequently less harsh and uncompromising than in the Halakhah. In an interesting passage of Gemara, for example, God is represented as determining the fate of sinful Israel by a test directly applied to His prophet Hosea. If Hosea will abandon his harlot wife Gomer and her children conceived in adultery, then God will abandon His people. But the prophet staunchly refuses, and God upholds His divine loyalty to His erring but still chosen people. This kind of sentiment breathes, even in metaphor, an altogether humbler and more wholesome spirit.[56] The second comment is that it is still difficult to clear certain Rabbis from the charge of harsh and merciless judgment based on an element of self-righteousness. Some of them are convinced that they have kept the whole law, and therefore possess the right to be very hard on a weaker sister or brother. (Yet all too little is said about the adulterer, in Rabbinic or in modern times.) It is never possible to read very far in the literature without finding some Rabbi rubbing his hands with joy over his own integrity and worth. The scathing parable of the Pharisee and the Publican praying in the Temple had lost none of its point for certain individual cases in the days of the Talmud. The following prayer is suggested as habitual for those leaving the House of

[55] Cf. Sot. 8^b, 9^a, II.1, etc.   [56] Pes. 87^{a,b}.

Study. "I give thanks before Thee, O Lord my God, that Thou hast appointed my steps with those who sit in the House of Study, and not with those who sit at street corners; for I rise early, and they do also, but I rise early for words of Torah, and they for words of idleness; I toil and they do also, but I receive a reward for my toil, they receive none; I run and they do also, but I run to the life of the world to come, they to the pit of destruction."[57] Abrahams has interesting comments both on the Talmudic passage and on the parable. Of the former, he says: "This prayer is simply a grateful recognition for good fortune; it in no sense implies (except quite indirectly) that the speaker prides himself on being a better man."[58] Two pages earlier, he had remarked: "Luke's Pharisee who thanked God that he was not as the Publican must have been an exceptional case, one of the weeds of ritualism, not one of its ordinary or natural fruits." This sounds rather like a piece of special pleading. No sane person would defend the thesis that all Rabbis were self-righteous hypocrites, but there is unquestionable New Testament and Talmudic proof that some undetermined number of them were. And it was from these in all probability that the harsher enactments of the Halakhah arose.

The Book of Proverbs declares that "death and life are in the power of the tongue,"[59] and the third chapter of the Epistle of James expands this into a remarkable piece of teaching, full of wisdom and sound psychology. The Rabbis were also aware of the importance of the matter, and they say some very emphatic and urgent things about the evils of slander, that poison which permeates like the serpent's bite, causing infinite harm to utterer, listener, and victim.[60] The tongue is capable of the best and highest, also of the worst and lowest—a fact illustrated by appropriate stories.[61] On another theme of James, the sinfulness of respect of persons, the Talmud does not take such a strong stand—it may even seem a little too subservient to rank and eminence on occasion;[62] but it does recognise that the ends of justice must not be perverted or shirked because a

[57] Ber. 28[b]. The tautology of the original is slightly pruned.
[58] *Studies in Pharisaism and the Gospels*, VOL. I, p. 59.
[59] Prov. XVIII.21.   [60] Lev. R. XXVI.2; Num. R. XIX.2.
[61] Lev. R. XXXIII.1.   [62] Cf. B.K. 86[a].

litigant is rich or powerful.[63] The words of James include and presuppose this specific matter in a principle of wider bearing, but every concrete application of it is to be welcomed.

It is familiar New Testament teaching that a man must not only abstain from sin in his own life and actions, but must also take especial care not to be a cause of stumbling to others through laxity or bad example.[64] The eternal and not only the temporal wellbeing of others is of paramount importance. A Rabbinic passage gathers together the fine flower of this teaching in a remarkable way. "How is it shown that he who causes a man to sin is worse than his slayer? This is because his slayer can kill him only in this world, whilst his portion in the world to come remains his own. But the man who causes him to sin slays him in this world, and in the world to come also."[65] This is an isolated saying in a late Midrash, but it reflects a mind grappling, just like Jesus and Paul, with man's deepest spiritual needs.

The Synoptic Gospels record that Jesus and the Pharisees clashed several times on issues connected with the Tradition of the Elders, inasmuch as that which was sin to the strict upholders of the Law was not recognised as such by the Teacher of Galilee. This is a large subject of considerable complexity, and it is not proposed to offer here more than a few comments on typical points. The curious reader may be referred to the larger Commentaries. The theme does, however, fall very clearly within the purview of this section.

There has been much discussion as to why Jesus approved, or at least failed to disapprove, of the fact that the disciples ate bread "with unwashen hands."[66] Washing before meals is urged today from the point of view of hygiene, even by the most irreligious. In the first century, food was taken by the hands from a common dish. The Pharisaic preoccupation was not, however, the physical disgust which a modern might feel, particularly if there was any obvious neglect of hygiene: it was the Levitical danger that particles of unclean or forbidden food might adhere to the uncleansed hands. (There are some

---

[63] Sanh. 6b.   [64] Cf. Rom. xiv.13; 1 Cor. viii; Mt. xviii.6; etc.
[65] Num. R. xxi.4.
[66] Mk. vii.5 and parallels. See, e.g., Montefiore, *Synoptic Gospels*, VOL. 1, pp. 130-44; Abrahams, *Studies in Pharisaism and the Gospels*, VOL. II, p. 199 f.

controversial questions of chronology and reference, which Montefiore discusses voluminously, but the preceding sentence is sufficiently accurate for immediate purposes.) There was much in the Jewish dietary laws which may have had an origin in taboo and superstition: this Jesus radically abrogated by the new principle that a man is defiled, not by what enters his mouth, but by what comes out of his mouth.[67] This is a principle, long become commonplace to Christians, which Jews no doubt will never fully accept so long as they adhere to Judaism. If Jesus sometimes sits a little lightly to the Tradition of the Elders, He maintains on the other hand a serious view of divorce as something totally contrary to God's original will and purpose, which goes far beyond Rabbinic or even certain Pentateuchal principles. The man who is more than a nominal Christian subscribes an immediate inward consent, for his religious upbringing has implanted in him a hatred of the broken marriage which the Jew does not normally feel in equal measure—though he too acknowledges the sadness of seeing a man parted from the wife of his youth. Montefiore sums up the issue by declaring that if a Jew is to be faithful to the Law, he must abstain from eating rabbits, which are Levitically unclean, and he must not under certain circumstances prohibit or belittle the permitted institution of divorce.[68] The Christian has little interest in the first count, and a majority would disagree on the second.

It may be of interest to mention three other points in the teaching of Jesus to which Montefiore as a Jew takes exception, for these are indicative of significant divergences between the two faiths. There is a widespread Christian belief, with adequate Dominical and apostolic authority, that in certain cases celibacy may be a higher choice than marriage for the man who would serve God. This opinion can be totally independent of any expectation that the end of the cosmic order is at hand, as the existence of the Roman priesthood abundantly confirms. This entire idea is roundly condemned by Montefiore as "distinctly anti-Jewish."[69] The second and complementary teaching that a man's religious vocation may override his

---

[67] Mk. vii.15, etc. Cf. Acts x.15, etc.   [68] *Synoptic Gospels*, VOL. II, p. 536.
[69] Mt. xix.12. Cf. Paul. Cf. Montefiore, *Synoptic Gospels*, VOL. II, p. 264.

family relationships and duties is similarly described as "out of harmony with Jewish feeling."[70] To those who do not feel it an inescapable religious duty to propagate a particular race, these are teachings of challenging nobility, counsels of perfection in a few special cases, not regulations for humanity. The world has been all the richer for certain men who have forsaken all to follow God alone. The third point is somewhat different. The teaching of Mt. vii.13, that many are lost and few saved, is dismissed by Montefiore as an "odious doctrine," and the Dominical predictions regarding the unhappy final fate of certain rich men in Mk. x.23 is called "harsh, unjustifiable and presumptuous."[71] Montefiore is of course openly universalistic in his theological sympathies—but the Rabbis are by no means always in line with him. The doctrine of Jesus, which is the doctrine of very many Jews, may according to conviction be odious or realistic—it cannot in any circumstances be palatable. But this theme belongs to a later chapter.

It would be an impertinence to conclude this section dogmatically on evidence so selected and so incomplete. It is clear, however, that the deepest teachings of the New Testament on sin are almost all echoed in the Rabbinic literature, at least in special cases. The originality of Jesus and of the Apostles consists frequently, though not exclusively, in the simplicity, profundity and comprehensiveness of their teachings.

[70] Mk. iii.31-35; Lk. xiv.26; etc.; Montefiore, *Synoptic Gospels*, VOL. II, p. 476.
[71] Montefiore, *Synoptic Gospels*, VOL. I, p. 245.

CHAPTER IX

THE MYSTERIOUS FIGURE
OF MELCHIZEDEK

THE last chapter concluded with some direct comparisons between Rabbinic and New Testament teachings, all connected with the doctrine of sin. There is another topic in which the two sets of teachings may be fruitfully compared, namely the interpretation of the mysterious and fascinating figure of Melchizedek. This chapter, though devoted to an independent and special theme, may be inserted here as supplementing the New Testament material which goes immediately before.

Melchizedek is significant in the New Testament because he is used in a very telling piece of typology. The first Adam as a type of the second, which is Christ, is a commonplace in Pauline theology. The non-Pauline Epistle to the Hebrews, above any other book in the New Testament, abounds in typology. There are numerous examples on the use of the figure in non-personal contexts. The Sabbath rest of the Creation story is a type of the rest of the people of God; the Old Covenant is a type of the New; the earthly Tabernacle and its furniture are types, albeit copies and shadows, of heavenly things; Sinai is a type of Zion; the faith of the Old Testament heroes is a type of the faith of Christians; the beasts burned outside the camp are a type of the Passion of Christ outside the Walls of Jerusalem; and so on. In each case, excepting perhaps the first, the anti-type is greater than the type. Above all Melchizedek, much more than the Levitical High Priest, is a type of Christ. The way in which his character is built up in the Epistle, largely by arguments from the silence of Scripture, is very reminiscent of Rabbinic methodology.

It is possible to spend much time on fruitless discussion as to whether Melchizedek is or is not an historical figure, and as to whether, assuming that he is historical, the particular argument of the Epistle to the Hebrews is logically valid and acceptable. The real purpose of the writer seems abundantly clear, and altogether independent of such considerations. For it is analogy he is interested in, not literal and mundane detail. The Levitical High Priesthood might be taken as a metaphor or symbol of the work and mission of Christ: but, argues the writer in effect, if you take the High Priesthood of Christ as being not Aaronic, but after the prior and higher order of Melchizedek, this fresh analogy will lead you to a deeper grasp of the same truth. It may be, as a modern scholar suggests, that the Epistle is addressed in polemic to some who believed strongly that the Aaronic priesthood and the Mosaic sacrifices were of eschatological as well as temporal significance, and who questioned the sacerdotal claims of Jesus on grounds of validity. The theory goes further, and regards these people as a group of converts drawn from the Dead Sea sect, but still unorthodox in their Christianity because of this former allegiance. This must not of course be taken as more than an individual opinion, although it is a most interesting one.[1] The teaching presented in the Epistle is as profound, suggestive, and significant as the more familiar analogy of Paul, and it leads to the very heart of the doctrine of the Person of Christ. It is of little consequence whether this Melchizedek, this early heathen priest-king of Jerusalem, be historical or legendary: he has captured the imagination of men, Jews as well as Christians, throughout the ages, and the spiritual truth of which his name has become the symbol remains unshaken. Yet the Old Testament mentions him only in a three-verse passage in its opening book, and in a single verse in a single short psalm.

There are two startlingly different Rabbinic interpretations of the character of Melchizedek, one favourable, the other the reverse. It is possible, for reasons which will be stated below, that the complimentary view is the earlier and original one, and the uncomplimentary one a change of front. The earlier view makes Melchizedek at least a pure and noble monotheist

---

[1] Y. Yadin, "The Scrolls and the Epistle to the Hebrews," in *Scripta Hierosolymitana*, IV (1958), pp. 36-55, esp. pp. 41-5.

H

of non-Jewish, or rather pre-Jewish race, a devout servant of God according to his lights. He is supposed to be one of the four workmen of Zechariah,[2] the righteous priest associated with Messiah ben-David, Messiah ben-Joseph, and Elijah, all of whom were reckoned somewhat more than mortal men.[3] He is supposed also to have been one of the co-authors, along with David, of the Book of Psalms.[4] He also acted, according to other authorities, as the guide and instructor of Abraham in a number of important matters. In a passage outside the sources surveyed in this volume Melchizedek, here tacitly identified with Shem the son of Noah,[5] teaches Abraham the meaning of charity and compassion. The patriarch expresses surprise that there was scope for such qualities in the restricted life of the Ark, so the needs and claims of the dumb animals on their human guardians are pointed out to him.[6] As men have always tended to exploit the animal kingdom with more greed than compassion, the notion is not unworthy of consideration. The most important passage[7] declares that Melchizedek was born circumcised—a fact deduced, to the satisfaction of the Rabbis if not of the grammarians, from a name etymology, and that he instructed Abraham both in the details of the Torah and in the duties and procedure of the priesthood. It need hardly be remarked that the Rabbis could conceive of no higher pinnacle of earthly honour on which to place him. If Melchizedek or Shem lived from the days of the Ark till the days of the Psalter, there is little need to be disturbed over the juxtaposition of Abraham and his rather remote ancestor—or over finding the same Shem or Melchizedek as a writer of psalms many centuries later. Are the Rabbis showing a mere sublime imperviousness to the difficulties of chronology? Or are they themselves implying in this earlier tradition that Melchizedek was one "having neither beginning of days nor end of life"?

Though he lived in the pre-documentary period, the writer to the Hebrews may well have been familiar with a set of

---

[2] Zech. 1.20 (11.3 M.T.).   [3] Sukk. 52ᵇ; Song of Sol. R. 11.13, 4.

[4] B.B. 14ᵇ. Cf. Eccl. R. vii.19, 4, where Melchizedek is supposed to be the correct reading.

[5] This common Rabbinic tradition will recur below.

[6] Midrash on Ps. xxxi, 7, cited in R.A., No. 1172.

[7] Gen. R. xliii.6.

Rabbinic traditions on Melchizedek following something of the above pattern. His own handling of the theme is bold, new, and original: he has outsoared his native Judaism without denying his starting-point. There is the interesting possibility that his famous statement about Melchizedek quoted in the paragraph above may have pinpointed a sentiment already vaguely felt in Judaism, but never hitherto so clearly and explicitly expressed.

Although the material and chronological evidence is a little meagre, it seems reasonably clear that a school of Rabbinic thought later arose which desired, for dialectical purposes, to strip Melchizedek of some of his glory, either discrediting him or else reducing him somewhat in stature. The later custom of identifying him with Shem the son of Noah, found in the Targumim as well as in the Rabbinic literature proper, may or may not have been intended to dissipate some of the awe and mystery surrounding him by attributing a clear mortal origin, though some of these passages are in no way derogatory. According to Christian evidence, certain Jews designated Melchizedek as the son of a prostitute.[8] If this statement is true, it reflects an unjustified vilification in the interests of polemic. Talmud and Midrash both stress that, according to the literal record of Genesis, Melchizedek blessed Abraham before blessing God—an oversight which was regarded as insulting to the Almighty, and which caused his priesthood to be transferred to the seed of Abraham.[9] The Midrash implies that he was immediately "unfrocked" in favour of Abraham, the Talmud rather that he kept his office during his lifetime, while his descendants lost what would have been their heritage. As this is free Haggadic material, it is useless to point out that the blessings may be very reasonably interpreted as climactic, or that Abraham was the direct descendant of Shem in any case. Melchizedek unquestionably became a highly controversial figure, both within the pale of Judaism and in Jewish-Christian controversy.

Two theories regarding the well-established Rabbinic

[8] Ginzberg, *Legends of the Jews*, VOL. v, p. 226, citing Epiphanius. Cf. also Marcel Simon, "Melchizedek dans la polemique entre juifs et chrétiens et dans la légende," in *Revue d'histoire et de philosophie religieuses*, 1937, p. 66.

[9] Ned. 32ᵇ; Lev. R. xxv.6. Cf. Herford, *Christianity in Talmud and Midrash*, pp. 338 ff.; Marcel Simon, *op cit.*, pp. 67-9.

identification of Melchizedek with Shem may be mentioned in passing, before the more general question of the later hostility towards the priest-king of Salem is discussed. According to one scholar, this identification is a mere "Midrashic conceit, which in the absence of any clear-cut chronology identifies any number of Biblical personages with one another, especially when there is no official 'obituary' in the Bible."[10] This is a forcible description of a familiar exegetical phenomenon; but that in no way excludes the possibility that there may be a little more to it in this case. Another scholar suggests that the pure monotheistic worship attributed to the non-Israelite Melchizedek and the subservience attributed to the mighty Abraham in the Genesis record were both highly distasteful to orthodox Judaism, and that Melchizedek was therefore identified with the direct if distant ancestor of Abraham in order that his deference might give no offence.[11]

The earlier Rabbinic reverence for Melchizedek, which is echoed in Philonic and other Jewish sources, seems more natural than the very different attitude which prevailed later. The phenomenon has been explained by many scholars in many ways, all of which fall into one or other of two broad categories; those which look for the clue inside Judaism itself, and those which search rather in the realms of Jewish polemic against the Christians.

Uncompromisingly in the first class are Windisch, Aptowitzer, and others, who maintain that the Rabbinic change of front with regard to Melchizedek has nothing whatever to do with Christianity. Kohler, who is of the same mind, regards the discrepancies as constituting an orthodox counterblast against certain Jews in Alexandria who were seeking to win converts without insisting on circumcision, and made much of the honour accorded to the uncircumcised Melchizedek in bolstering their claims.[12] It would be interesting to know more about these people, and to ascertain whether they had had any contact with Pauline Christianity. Petuchowski[13] puts forward another

[10] J. J. Petuchowski, "The controversial figure of Melchizedek," in *Hebrew Union College Annual*, XXVIII (1957).
[11] Marcel Simon, in *Revue d'histoire et de philosophie religieuses*, 1937, esp. pp. 60, 62, 63.
[12] *J.E.*, art. "Melchizedek."   [13] In *Hebrew Union College Annual*, XXVIII (1957).

Jewish explanation which is of considerable interest, whether it be accepted or not. The Hasmonean dynasty, he argues, made much of Psalm cx, which became their special charter of rights although doubtless it was first composed long before their time. Melchizedek was therefore exceedingly useful in their political propaganda. But the Rabbis were not partial to the Hasmoneans—there is a pointed reference to the "deadly silence on the subject of Maccabean glories in the Rabbinic literature." In the judgment of this scholar, the unquestioned change in the estimate of Melchizedek is due to factors not anti-Christian but anti-Hasmonean.

More widespread, and considerably more convincing, is the opinion that the Rabbinic passages which speak slightingly of Melchizedek are the direct fruit of propaganda against the teaching of the Epistle to the Hebrews.[14] The author of the most important passage[15] is Rabbi Ismael, who is, as Petuchowski points out, an uncompromising opponent of Christianity. Marcel Simon thinks the propaganda may be, not directly against the Epistle to the Hebrews, but against the references to Melchizedek in Justin Martyr.[16] This is a variant opinion which does not greatly affect the issue: after all, Justin's remarks are based on the Epistle.

This is not the place to enlarge at length on the Christian interpretation of Melchizedek: he is undoubtedly useful, not only as a type of Christ and a deeply suggestive one at that, but also as a propaganda exemplar in the Pauline movement of the infant Church against the requirement of circumcision for Gentile converts. All this, according to the more convincing school of thought, gave rise in its turn to counter-propaganda on the Jewish side against Melchizedek. According to Simon's way of putting it, the Jews were forced to abandon Melchizedek, to leave him in fact to the Christian side as a dubious ally for them.[17] The hostility which twisted the doctrine of the Virgin Birth into the fantastic story that Jesus was the son of Mary by

[14] See W. Bacher, *Die Agada der Tannaiten*, VOL. I, 2nd edn. Strassburg 1903; Herford, *Christianity in Talmud and Midrash*, pp. 265, 338 ff.; etc.

[15] Cf. note 9, p. 115.

[16] Justin Martyr, *Dialogue with Trypho*, Anti-Nicene Christian Library, VOL. II, Edinburgh 1867, XIX.32-3.

[17] Simon, in *Revue d'histoire et de philosophie religieuses*, 1937, p. 66.

a Roman legionary paramour[18] endeavoured by similar means and for similar reasons to discredit Melchizedek.

This chapter merely opens up an interesting topic, which the reader may or may not care to follow out for himself in the literature cited, and in the fuller references there given.

[18] Cf. J. Klausner, *Jesus of Nazareth*, New York 1927, pp. 18-54.

CHAPTER X

ATONEMENT

A FELT need for spiritual atonement presupposes a serious and contrite awareness of sin, which belongs to an advanced and reflective stage of religious thinking. Judaism certainly reached that stage long before the days of the Talmud, though the earlier and cruder vehicle of expiation, animal sacrifice, had remained in operation for some two generations after the death of Jesus Christ and might have continued much longer had the Temple not been destroyed in A.D. 70. The practical Rabbinic conception of atonement may, by circumstance rather than by desire, be totally divorced from the specific ritual of Temple and offering, but its roots are deeply embedded in the old sacrificial worship which the Talmud describes so minutely in all its anachronistic detail. These historical beginnings cannot therefore be ignored, but a very brief summary will serve here.

The broad general meaning of the term atonement will be clear to every reader. The ideas of expiating the sin, and of propitiating God whom the sinner has offended, are both included. There has been much scholastic discussion as to the precise meaning of the Hebrew root *kipper*, habitually translated "to atone." It makes little difference theologically whether it means to cover a sin, so blotting it out; or to wipe it away; or to make it white, so removing the blackness of guilt; or whether the verb be etymologically connected with the Hebrew noun meaning ransom. These have all been suggested,[1] and have all been used fruitfully in exegesis. They are all in

[1] Cf. W. Robertson Smith, *The Old Testament in the Jewish Church*, 2nd edn. London 1892, p. 381, footnote; *J.E.*, art. "Atonement," *init.*; S. R. Driver, *A Critical and Exegetical Commentary on Deuteronomy* (International Critical Commentary), Edinburgh 1895, pp. 243 f., 425 f.; B. Gray, *Sacrifice in the Old Testament*, Oxford 1925, pp. 67-77; etc.

harmony with the total conception of atonement, though none of them expresses it fully, and that conception is luminous to the religious mind without laboured definition.

Animal Sacrifice

The two points of immediate interest in a vast field are the probable reasons for the initiation of animal sacrifice—a theme which, fully considered, would extend far beyond the confines of Judaism; and the main ideas and purposes underlying the practice and procedure of the Herodian Temple, the last one to function in Jerusalem. This is necessary prolegomena to the proper theme of the chapter. The first topic may be sufficiently opened by a bare summary of the respective theories of two outstanding and representative scholars—though there are in fact numerous other names and views in this connexion. For the second topic, the sources themselves supply abundant material. A slight selection of distinctive ideas will be sufficient for the immediate needs of the reader.

The two scholarly doctrines concerning the earlier motivation of animal sacrifice which are selected for special attention here are the communion theory, pre-eminently associated with the name of W. Robertson Smith, and the gift theory, advocated, with a slightly different emphasis, by Buchanan Gray.[2] Each of these theories is fully outlined by its author in a single volume, and each volume is a theological classic.

Smith offended the orthodox opinion of his day by postulating the origins of sacrifice not in revealed religion, but in primitive animism, totemism, and ancestor worship. Unquestionably he refers these origins to a period long anterior to the organised Judaism of the Old Testament—but this did not mitigate the bitterness of the opposition of Scottish theological opinion to views for which it was completely unprepared. It is the precise theory, however, which is relevant here, not the emotional reactions of a bygone age. According to Smith, the earliest conception of holiness with which sacrifice was associated was not that of a spiritual or ethical force, but that of a physical

---

[2] W. Robertson Smith, *Religion of the Semites*, 2nd edn. London 1894; Gray, *Sacrifice in the Old Testament*.

contagion, closely connected with taboo and ritual uncleanness. Then sacrifice later developed into a pleasant public meal for the whole clan or kith. The deity, his worshippers, and the sacred or totem animal are regarded as being all of the same blood, and in this solemn yet frequently joyous act, their solidarity is reaffirmed while a particle of sacred life is conveyed by the blood to each participant. The central idea, it is urged, is one of communion, not of atonement: it is an elementary blunder to read into early sacrifice ideas which belong to a much later stage, and particularly to the Jewish faith.

Gray's book is closer to Biblical times in its theme and reference. He prefers to find the mainspring of sacrifice in the concept of a gift offered to the deity in his honour. The two theories need not necessarily be treated as contradictory: Smith could be right for the primitive era, Gray right for the period on the threshold of the Old Testament. Smith had indeed made full allowance for the gift theory, insisting only that it belongs to a later stage of sacrificial thinking such as that reflected by the Mosaic and post-Mosaic ordinances—a stage when the concept of property and ownership on an individual basis, something utterly foreign to the simplicity of primitive communities, had become fully developed. The first stage could very well pass by natural gradations into the second. Of greater interest is the consideration that a gift interpretation of sacrifice can lead by more obvious logical steps to those ideas so closely associated with important types of Old Testament offerings, namely expiation and atonement. Gray's emphasis therefore has a good deal to commend it from the point of view of the Biblical interpreter.

The second topic must now claim attention. Animal sacrifice had enjoyed a long history in Scriptural times, beginning before the Patriarchs, and continuing through the days of the Tabernacle, likewise of the First or Solomonic and all the later Temples. By the period of the Herodian Temple sin and guilt offerings, prompted by the desire for atonement, had a very special, though not an exclusive, importance. The Mishnah, in laying down the six purposes of sacrifice, allows for five which are not specifically expiatory.[3] These other purposes, however,

[3] Zeb. iv.6, 2ᵇ.

are not of immediate concern. The atonement envisaged was for ritual and unintentional rather than for ethical and witting transgressions, although it no doubt embraced all the lesser stumblings to which human beings in their weakness are very liable. It was rightly felt that a man could not commit serious sins with a high hand, and then procure full pardon by the purely material expiation of a Temple offering, which might represent a very small abnegation for the rich.[4] The Mishnah, embracing the general principles of the Old Testament, lays down the absolute necessity of penitence in all atonement: without this, sacrifice or any other form of expiation is meaningless.[5] The next Mishnah explains how futile it is to plan a sin and also the repentance which is to follow that sin. This is an attempt to mock God, a reduction of human contrition to mere caricature. The bringing of a sacrifice is scarcely regarded as appropriate at all for a wilful transgression.[6] With all its faults and imperfections, the system was never intended as a means of enjoying personal licence, and then escaping the consequences by means of a statutory payment, although the prophets and their spiritual successors may well have fulminated because men were perverting the entire system into these channels.

Though sacrifices can be both bloody and unbloody, the former are far and away the most important. The writer to the Hebrews states that almost all atonement under the Old Covenant was by means of blood (ix.22), while the Talmud declares uncompromisingly that there is no atonement except by blood[7]—though this view can scarcely have been pressed in all times, places, and exigencies. Some would insist further on the blood accompanying the departure of life.[8] Bloodless offerings of sundry kinds existed, but they were of minor expiatory importance.

The effectiveness of the Temple suffered from the limitations both of time and of geography. During its circumscribed existences, the morning and evening sacrifices might, as the Midrashist declares, enable everyone in Jerusalem to sleep

[4] Cf. A. B. Davidson, *Theology of the Old Testament*, pp. 310-15 ff.; J. P. E, Pedersen, *Israel*, VOL. IV, p. 359; Smith, *The Old Testament in the Jewish Church* p. 372.

[5] Yom. VIII.8.   [6] Yeb. 33 [b].

[7] Yom. 5 [a].   [8] Pes. 65 [a, b].

with untroubled conscience;[9] but this would scarcely help those who were born at the wrong time, or who dwelt in the far places of the Diaspora. Jewish sacrificial worship was generally considered valid only in its proper place in Jerusalem, and the other Temples on Mount Gerizim in Samaria and at Leontopolis in Egypt were always regarded as heretical by the orthodox. That was why the Babylonian exile was so bitter, and why it seemed the mark of God's blazing wrath against His people. Those who never saw Jerusalem in the flesh had to be content with paying the Temple tax, if there was a Temple. The whole sacrificial cult was unacceptable to some schools of thought long before A.D. 70. The writer of the fiftieth Psalm had declared the absurdity of offering a gift to the Giver of all, and the Prophets knew, long before the New Testament was written, that "it is impossible that the blood of bulls and goats should take away sins." Yet many, pious according to their lights, clung with affection to the old forms, and sincerely believed that their souls were cleansed thereby.

Two Rabbinic sidelights may be noted in passing. An attempt to save the old tradition was made by declaring earnestly that sacrifices offered on the site of the ruined Temple would still be valid, because the Solomonic consecration of the ground itself was effective for all time.[10] It is the place and not the building which this view stresses.

Certain Jerusalemites felt that, because of the cessation of animal sacrifice and the wine libation, they must no longer partake of meat or wine not properly consecrated, but mourn only for the loss of the glory of Israel. R. Joshua begins by pointing out to them that similar objections apply to the use of bread, fruit, and water—whereupon they plan to extend their asceticism further. Their instructor thereupon demonstrates that the process may be continued indefinitely, until everything that makes life possible becomes proscribed. At last they are persuaded to view the matter rationally, and to keep their mourning within reasonable limits.[11] After all Judaism did survive, and has continued to survive, the loss of the Temple and of the institution of animal sacrifice.

---

[9] Song of Sol. R. 1.9, 6.   [10] Eduy. VIII.6; Meg. 10^a; Zeb. 107^b.
[11] B.B. 60^b.

Substitutes for Animal Sacrifice after the Destruction of the Herodian Temple

At an earlier stage, the final destruction of the Jerusalem Temple might well have entailed the paralysis and death of the Jewish faith. By the year A.D. 70 Torah had already become as important as, if not more important than, the Temple ritual. Some individual Jews may have felt the one, some the other, more effective for the saving of their souls. The local synagogue was certainly the only centre of worship for myriads who had never set eyes on the Holy City, because the Diaspora extended over the then known world. Yet sacrifice and atonement were so deeply intertwined in many minds that fresh means of expiation were sometimes excogitated as recognised substitutes for animal sacrifice. It will be instructive to glance at some of the suggested alternatives for those who would once have salved their consciences by the offering of a lamb or a bullock.

The most surprising substitute atonement recommended by the Talmud is the enjoyment and prolongation of the pleasures of the table[12]—a procedure which might sound hedonistic rather than deeply expiatory. This is allegorised by later commentators to mean, not the selfish enjoyment of these delights, but the providing at a man's own table of sustenance for the poor and needy. This might be more pious and sacrificial, on the doubtful assumption that it is the real meaning of the Talmud text. Allegory is so frequently used to conform forcibly all extraneous or unwelcome views to those of the interpreter. The idea might equally well be a throwback to that pleasant if not unduly contrite primitive conception of the sacrifice as a joyous communal meal of fellowship with the Deity, an example of the ideas so vividly described by Smith operating at a much later date. The reader may make his own choice. Lavish gifts and hospitality to Rabbinic scholars constitutes another thoroughly acceptable substitute for animal sacrifice.[13]

The more serious plans for finding atonement without animal sacrifice, among those who had been preconditioned in that particular direction, fall into two classes, those which prescribe

[12] Ber. 55ᵃ; Men. 97ᵃ.   [13] Ber. 10ᵇ; Yom. 71ᵃ; Ket. 105ᵇ.

additional religious exercises, and those which advocate the mortification of the body.

Prominent in the first class, and very natural from the Rabbinic viewpoint, was the careful and meticulous study of the whole corpus of sacrificial law in Bible and Talmud[14]—an undertaking of truly formidable dimensions. The Jew regarded it as an exercise of religion in itself, and as a very necessary accomplishment should his cherished dream of the ultimate restoration of the Temple and of its ritual ever be realised in fact. The study of the Torah in general may be regarded as a variant of this.[15]

The most worth while of all the suggestions under this heading, and the one which possesses a universal appeal, is the practice of prayer,[16] which is declared to be better than sacrifice.[17] There is some controversy as to whether the institution of the main daily prayer, the Tefillah, is patriarchal, or whether it originated in the period between the two main Temples as a specific alternative for animal sacrifice.[18] The Rabbis took their statutory liturgical prayers very seriously—so much so that occasionally the ugly note of fanaticism creeps in. It was a mark of piety to say that prayer should not be interrupted to return the greeting even of a king—after all, God is greater than any earthly king; but to go on to the demand that a man should continue to pray even if a snake coils itself around his ankle[19]—meaning, presumably, that nothing short of death should disturb his orison—is a counsel open to grave moral objection. There is some evidence that although prayers were for the most part liturgical, free prayer was neither unknown nor unusual.[20] The beauty and majesty of the language of many of the Rabbinic prayers comes out, even in translation. The reader may judge of this for himself from the samples given in the appendix. One passage states specifically that to ensure ritual cleanliness, put on the phylacteries, and then recite the Shema and Tefillah is equivalent to building an altar and offering sacrifice thereon.[21] A detailed study of

---

[14] Cf. Men. 110ᵃ; Taan. 27ᵇ; Lev. R. vii.3; etc.
[15] Cf. Men. 110ᵃ.   [16] Ber. 26ᵃ.
[17] Ber. 32ᵇ.   [18] Ber. 26ᵇ.
[19] Ber. v.1, 32ᵇ-33ᵃ. Cf. Ex. R. ix.3.   [20] Ber. 12ᵇ, 16ᵇ-17ᵃ, iv.2, 29ᵇ.
[21] Ber. 15ᵃ.

Rabbinic prayer yields much fascinating material. Jews and Christians possess much in common in their prayer heritage. It so happens that most of the material is concentrated in the first Tractate of the Talmud, which, perhaps more than any other, would repay careful perusal by the reader.

There are sundry other ritual acts which one Rabbi or another happens to choose as his substitute for animal sacrifice, but these need not be examined in detail.[22]

Foremost under the second heading, mortification of the body, comes the common practice of fasting, which many Jews considered a very natural substitute for animal sacrifice. Rabbi Shesheth would fast and pray, concluding his devotional exercises with some words, perhaps of his own composition which, acceptable or unacceptable as they may be to the particular individual, undeniably contain the whole philosophy of a certain kind of contrite piety. The words are: "Lord of all being, it is manifest in Thy sight that at the time when the Temple was in existence, a man might sin and bring an offering, and though nothing was sacrificed from it save only its fat and its blood, nevertheless atonement was made for him. Now I have observed a fast, and my fat and my blood have become reduced. May it be Thy will that my fat and my blood which have been reduced be regarded as though they had been offered before Thee on the altar, and do Thou grant me Thy favour."[23] It is stated elsewhere that the blood of a wound may have atoning power, which links with the idea expressed above, but some would define and circumscribe the conditions of its effectiveness rather carefully.[24] The modern mind discerns greater insight in the statement that humility of spirit before God is equivalent in value to the bringing forward of all the stated offerings.[25] That is the teaching of prophetic Judaism, which Christianity may proudly recognise as ancestor.

This section has outlined typical conceptions of atonement amongst those who looked back nostalgically to the old, dead sacrificial cult, regarding that as the real Judaism could it only be restored. But there were others who looked forwards, not backwards, and new dimensions of thought, totally independent

[22] Cf. Sukk. 45[a, b].
[24] Hull. 7[b].
[23] Ber. 17[a]. Cf. Num. R. xviii.21.
[25] Sot. 5[b]; Sanh. 43[b].

of animal sacrifice, will appear in the rest of this chapter. For there were some undoubtedly who broke away completely from the desire for a restored Temple—and some who recognised, even while the building existed, that it represented but a facet of Jewish worship and never its total expression.

The Treasury of Merits, the Doctrine of Works, and Vicarious Atonement

The Treasury of Merits, briefly mentioned in Chapter II, is another important Rabbinic vehicle of atonement. The basic idea is very simple. If a man commits some particular trans-gression for which he has not made a full and separate expiation, his own virtuous actions in the past, or somebody else's virtue, or the merits of his ancestors, may make atonement for him. The doctrine is applicable to a community as well as to individuals. The paragraphs which immediately follow refer singly to separable aspects of the whole concept, which consists of a doctrine of works and a doctrine of vicarious atonement in combination. This affords important material for the com-parative study of Rabbinic Judaism and of Christianity.

The first axiom, which the Rabbis take for granted, is that certain human actions are absolutely and intrinsically meritorious, and that the performance of them vastly enhances the prestige of the agent. Saul the Pharisee might have thought along these lines, but Paul the Apostle would have rejected the idea with horror. The Mishnah stresses the temporal and eternal value of certain lines of conduct and activity, extolling above all others the study of the Torah, promising boldly the fruit or interest in this life and the capital in the life to come.[26] Some would argue, from this passage and others, that Matthew VI.19-21 is merely a re-statement of commonplace Jewish teaching, and Montefiore cites with this implication the rather outstanding example of King Monobazus mentioned below.[27] But the self-interest of this outwardly worthy gentleman is apparent in all his charity, even if it be enlightened and eschatological: he fails on analysis to measure up to the words

---

[26] Peah I.I; Kidd. 39 b.
[27] Montefiore, *Rabbinic Literature and Gospel Teachings*, p. 139.

of Jesus. Returning to the main theme of the paragraph, the Rabbis sometimes perceive merit, not in what appears to be the main or significant action but in some concomitant circumstance, the virtue of which is not immediately apparent to others. Thus the zeal evidenced by the act of running to attend Halakhic lectures, even when this might be held to desecrate the Sabbath, had greater importance for some people than the proper understanding of the lectures.[28] It is refreshing to find an admission that the fulfilling of a precept does not really confer any benefit on God, who is exalted far above all human assistance —it merely enables the pious individual to acquire merit by carrying it out faithfully.[29] Pauline theology would accept the first part of the statement while rejecting the second, teaching rather that man's merit is imputed or gifted, not acquired by his own effort.

From this first principle of intrinsic merit in certain actions the Rabbis go a stage further, postulating that God keeps an exact record of the merits and transgressions of each individual. On this view, every action which is not ethically neutral must increase either the credit or the debit balance in a man's heavenly bank account, and a man stands finally judged by whichever happens to be in excess of the other. As the two sides of the ledger may approach equality in a large number of human beings, one meritorious action or one sin, particularly on the eve of death, may make all the difference to a man's eternal destiny.[30] This is a familiar Christian heresy, based on the misunderstanding of passages such as Matthew VI.19-21, cited above, and the Parable of the Sheep and the Goats. The first passage really teaches that men should pay more heed to eternal than to merely temporal values, and the second that mundane actions should be regulated by the principle of love— neither of them matters subject to precise mathematical evaluation. The New Testament makes it clear, here and elsewhere, that the kind of merit God specially approves springs spontaneously from a man's intrinsic character, and is unconsidered by him. He does not "buy" eternal life by his terrestrial almsgiving, but the love which has prompted it

[28] Ber. 6ᵃ. Other examples in the same passage. [29] Num. R. xv.2.
[30] Eccl. R. x.1, 1.

fits him, all unbeknown to himself, for God's wondrous gift. A Christian counterpart to the Jewish doctrine of the Treasury of Merits is merely the spurious result of bad exegesis. Abraham is an outstanding example for emulation, according to the Rabbis—he began very early in life to invest heavily on the merit or credit side.[31] A man's good and evil deeds alike precede him into the world to come, the former helping, the latter hindering, his footsteps in the next life.[32] If a man feels so secure in his good deeds that he calls upon God for an unnecessary miracle, by gratuitously placing his life in danger for example, this miracle will be deducted from his credit balance of merits.[33] If his merits are insufficient and the miracle is withheld, it is to be presumed that he suffers the consequences of his folly. There were some healthy cynics who perceived the shallowness and absurdity of the doctrine. One Rabbi of the early fourth century declared roundly but all too briefly that a lifetime of good deeds will not enable a man to pay God even for the breath with which he has been endowed.[34] A little more of this man's theology might have proved wholesome. The selfsame paragraph stresses, again against all popular opinion, the non-heritable nature of merits—in other words, a scapegrace son cannot escape the moral consequences of his actions simply because of the piety of his father. This is a view in which most modern people would heartily concur.

A man who depends on his own merits for justification in the sight of God may be leaning on a very shaky stick: when he begins to count on the merits of others, alive or dead, his soul may be in yet greater danger. Unfortunately, it was widely taught that the man who was ethically insufficient in himself might draw on the credit balance both of his contemporaries and of his ancestors—a view which was much more popular than the contradictory one cited above. There are two separable ideas here, which must now be examined in turn, together with the refutations to be found in the same sources.

The first form of what might be called the extra-personal application of the Treasury of Merits, specific ethical dependence on those still living, occurs with surprising frequency,

---

[31] Gen. R. xxxix.3.
[33] Shab. 32ᵃ, 140ᵃ; Taan. 20ᵇ.
[32] A. Zar. 5ᵃ.
[34] Lev. R. iv.2.

I

both within the then contemporary Talmudic age and in retrospective reference to those of an earlier period. A man is not normally recognised as a saint within any slight temporal distance of his own lifetime, but certain of the Rabbis were credited with sufficient merit to compensate fully for the deficiencies of others—one was declared to protect the entire city in which he dwelt.[35] Class adulation from members of that same class is more or less equivalent to self-praise. On two occasions on which calamity was just averted from cities, salvation was erroneously ascribed to the virtues of great resident Rabbis. In each case the matter was declared too trifling for so outstanding a man, and the residents were said to have been saved through the merits of lesser mortals dwelling among them.[36] This is a more subtle form of flattery. When the High Priest officiated in the Holy of Holies on the Day of Atonement, he was accredited with merits enough and to spare, which were supposed to be available for the benefit of others.[37] The entire Exodus was supposed to have been accomplished because of the merits of the tribe of Levi.[38] These last two examples are of a "contemporary in the past" nature. Once again it is refreshing to find the lone voice dissenting from a shallow but understandably popular view: "If a man makes his plea depend on his own personal claim to merit, then it is made to depend on the merit of others; whereas if he relies on the merit of others, then he is constrained to rely on his own merit."[39] In other words, assistance is forthcoming for the man of honest endeavour, whereas the would-be parasite is thrown back on his own resources. A fixed desire to depend on other people is usually frustrated. The Christian may approve the emphasis, even if he rejects the underlying theology.

The merits of the Patriarchs were still more widely and confidently canvassed by certain schools of thought. Abraham is a popular choice,[40] likewise Moses and Aaron.[41] The combined merits of the fathers of the faithful are declared over and over again to be effective,[42] and even endless.[43] Two other passages, probably a little earlier in date, show respectively a

[35] Taan. 22[a].   [36] Taan. 21[b].   [37] Lev. R. xxi.6.
[38] Num. R. iii.6.   [39] Ber. 10[b].   [40] Gen. R. xliv.16.
[41] Ex. R. xv.3.   [42] Lev. R. xxix.7, etc.   [43] Lev. R. xxxvi.6.

little moderation, and a large measure of healthy scepticism. A man is said to forfeit the ancestral merit when he emigrates from Israel to another land.[44] A brave but possibly rather lonely voice declared that the merits of the Patriarchs were exhausted.[45] This teaching must have been salutory for many.

The channelling of the benefits deriving from the accumulated merits of others may be directed to a community as well as to individuals. A congregation is more richly endowed in this respect than any single member of it.[46] The good deeds of Israel are sometimes declared inadequate for her salvation,[47] sometimes she is declared to be redeemed through her elders. [48] The more popular view is that she stands by virtue of the Torah.[49] The idea of the Patriarchs praying and making intercession for Israel[50] is more beautiful and valuable than the preceding sentiments, and is not open to the same objections as a mechanical, self-exempting, and self-excusing doctrine of merits.

It is easy for the Christian interpreter to be unfair in assessing this particular ethical approach, because his whole Pauline training and background has preconditioned him to being a little unsympathetic. For him, it smacks too much of a *do ut des* attitude to the Deity. The best Jewish minds were not entirely satisfied with it either, as several of the passages cited above clearly show. And yet, viewed dispassionately, it compares quite favourably with Utilitarianism and other secular moral theories. It certainly pinpoints man's duty in the Godward and manward spheres quite sharply, and offers a working guide to conduct, even if it does not make for a religion of the highest and most spiritual type.

It is instructive in this field to compare the corresponding New Testament doctrines. Many have confused the issue by placing the teachings of Paul and of James in antithesis, as though one must be true, the other false. The epithet Luther applied to the work of James, "a right strawy epistle," has been more quoted than justified: Melancthon perceived with greater insight that there is no essential conflict between

---

[44] B.B. 91*a*. [45] Shab. 55*a*.
[46] A. Zar. 4*b*. [47] Ex. R. 1.35. [48] Ex. R. iii.8, xv.4, etc.
[49] Lev. R. xxxvi.2; Esth. R. vii.13. [50] Ex. R. xv.26.

Paul's doctrine of justification by faith and the special emphasis
on works in the theology of James. Paul never suggested that a
purely acquiescent and intellectual faith, acknowledging no
particular practical duty in this terrestrial sphere, is enough.
The place of works in his theology comes out clearly enough
in the thirteenth chapter of 1 Corinthians, the sixth and twelfth
of Romans, the sixth of Ephesians, and in many other places.
Even the doctrine of total depravity was meant not as an excuse
but as a challenge. Paul would have agreed heartily with the
Rabbi aforecited, who recognised that all the virtues of the
best of mortals cannot repay God for the breath with which
he has been endowed. Nevertheless, realising the fact of sin,
men still endeavour, and still fail to endeavour, to please God,
and stand judged thereby. The doctrine of works as an element
in rather than the essence of God's scheme of salvation for men
still has its place in theology; and James, along with Paul,
rightly has his niche in the canon of the New Testament. James
II.24 does not mean that faith is unimportant—merely that it
is fully effective only when accompanied by earnest human
striving. The next verse but one means that the mere body
of flesh has no significance apart from a rational mind and
immortal soul, and that in parallel a faith which fails to trans-
late itself into a practical way of life is no true faith. The
Rabbinic conception of a man obtaining justification and
atonement even by his own personal treasury of merits is
contrary to the New Testament, not because the Rabbis
regarded a man's works as important, but because they
regarded them as sufficient, therein failing to appreciate the
fact of sin quite seriously enough. It is right and proper that a
man should practise virtue and good deeds, but this is to please
God, not to repay Him or to create any obligation on His side.

The concept of vicarious atonement is perhaps of more
interest for the reader of the New Testament than the personal
treasury. The Patriarchs were glorious heroes of the faith, as
the writer to the Hebrews recognised, but Scripture teaches
also that they were fallible and occasionally sinful men. To
regard them as an example and an inspiration is one thing,
to treat them as ethical capital is another. The Rabbi who
declared their merits exhausted realised the spiritual dangers

of his compatriots. Equally false and even more unworthy is the notion that the heathen nations of Rabbinic or of earlier times will be cast into Gehinnom to make atonement for the sins of Israel[51]—others may pertinently ask, For what good reason? The Rabbis possessed, particularly in the Servant Songs of Isaiah, the basis for a more worthy concept of vicarious atonement, though they made less use of it than they might have done. Job is said to have been selected by God for temporary suffering so that Israel might be saved in the time of the Exodus.[52] Interesting also but equally dubious is the notion that the children of wicked parents should die young, thereby saving the older generation from eternal punishment. The Midrashist can even worm his way round the difficulties caused by the continued sins in this life of those who cannot mend their ways even after their progeny have died for them: the children make successful intercession in the next life, suggesting, at the instigation of Elijah, that God should permit the attribute of Grace to prevail over the attribute of Punishment.[53] Outside the blood bond, there is a clear statement that the righteousness of Abraham or of any of his descendants may operate vicariously on behalf of those of the same generation, the death of the righteous man being a necessary condition.[54] The innocent are of course regarded as making a more effective vicarious atonement than the guilty.[55] The passages taken as a whole are not very impressive, and many Christians are inclined to remain unconvinced.

Additional Virtue

In the Rabbinic way of life, virtue consists mainly in fulfilling prescribed actions and avoiding proscribed ones. Each type is so numerous that the burden seems to the Gentile well-nigh intolerable. Yet, difficult as it might appear to the outside observer, some scope was left for the zealous and eager to acquire additional merit or grace.

On any day of his life, a man might dispense additional charity, according to his pecuniary means; or undertake extra

---

[51] Ex. R. XI.2.   [52] Ex. R. XXI.7.   [53] Eccl. R. IV.I, I.
[54] Gen. R. XLIV.5. Cf. Ber. 62[b]; Lev. R. XX.12.   [55] Shebu. 14[a].

studies in the Torah, or additional prayers, according to the time he could spare without neglecting his work, if he did not happen to be a Rabbi. Each day carried for the faithful observer a fairly heavy programme of prescribed and liturgical prayer— yet some seem to have found time for further and less formal communion with God, using their own words. This, when it was well practised, was probably more worth while than the additional and optional Shema which a man could recite on his bed, thus earning the Rabbinic commendation.[56] The Sermon on the Mount indicates that a man's additional prayers could on occasion be mere ostentation and hypocrisy, but it is not suggested that this was true in all cases. A more punctilious respect or special honour to teacher or parent might also be included under these general principles. A specific case will be cited below.

The special circumstances wherein a man may, according to Rabbinic ideals, render himself a little more acceptable to God are legion. Most of them consist of some additional stringency or sacrifice in fulfilling an Halakhic requirement. A few examples are chosen at random.

Certain obligatory gifts, such as the leaving of the corners of fields ungleaned for the benefit of the poor, and certain particular Temple offerings, when these were in force, could be made with additional generosity, illustrating the principle that the Lord loveth a cheerful giver.[57] Special credit is accorded to the Jew who repays his debt in the seventh or Sabbatical year, even though the law specifically permits him to escape, and his creditor is willing to remit.[58] If a teacher is leaving a city, a pupil may, as a mark of honour, accompany him as far as he pleases beyond the minimum limit which courtesy demands.[59] The finder of lost property is permitted in certain circumstances to keep it—but he may go beyond his actual obligations in seeking out the owner in order to return it.[60]

These suggestions are typical of the sincere, if not highly imaginative, Rabbinic search for additional righteousness. A prevailing principle of love is much more effective than scattered counsels for circumstances which are sometimes rather hypothetical.

[56] Ber. 4ᵇ.　　　　　　[57] Peah. i.i.　　　　　　[58] Sheb. x.8, 9.
　　　　　　[59] Sot. 46ᵇ.　　　　　　[60] B.M. 24ᵇ.

The Day of Atonement

The Jews possessed a special Day of Atonement, mentioned already in these pages, on which they considered it fitting to seek a rather fuller and more comprehensive forgiveness from the burden of sins which beset them. In the period of the Temple of Herod, and much earlier, this was accompanied by a prescribed ritual set out in the sixteenth chapter of the book of Leviticus, and much elaborated in the Talmudic Tractate Yoma. After the final destruction of the Temple the nature of the ritual observances had to be radically altered, although the day never lost its importance in the Jewish sacred calendar. Certain passages of the New Testament assume a knowledge of the ritual on the part of the reader, and portions of it are important for historical perspective, notwithstanding the wise words of the writer to the Hebrews; "what is becoming obsolete and growing old is ready to vanish away." Much of the picture is reasonably clear, though details and dates may be controversial.

The reader knows that the early Tabernacle with its sacred Ark was followed by the successive Jerusalem Temples of Solomon, Zerubbabel, and Herod, though the second of these may have been a reconstruction of the partially ruined edifice of Solomon.[61] It would be tedious and unnecessary to try to trace the growth of ritual through these various sanctuaries, even if the facts were less uncertain. Many Jews like to claim that the ritual of the Day of Atonement as it was known in the Herodian Temple is of direct Mosaic ordinance; others assert that it began only after the completion of the Temple of Zerubbabel in 516 B.C.,[62] or else during the Exile.[63] More probably it is a final synthesis of very ancient elements.[64] The question might have some importance in a close study of the Epistle to the Hebrews but it is hardly appropriate in the present context.

The main interior portion of the Herodian Temple, as

[61] See W. O. E. Oesterley and T. H. Robinson, *History of Israel*, Oxford 1932, VOL. I, pp. 82 ff.
[62] Cf. M. M. Kalisch, *Leviticus*, VOL. II, London 1872, pp. 266-82.
[63] Oesterley and Robinson, *History of Israel*, p. 136.
[64] Cf. N. Micklem on Leviticus, in *The Interpreter's Bible*, VOL. II, New York and Nashville 1953, p. 77 f.

distinct from its outer courtyards, was divided into two sections, the Holy Place and the Holy of Holies. The latter was invested with very special taboos, which may or may not have been equally strict in the earlier sanctuaries. In the Herodian structure the Holy of Holies was separated from the Holy Place by two curtains placed a cubit apart, and known as the veil of the Temple. These replaced the double cedar doors of Solomon's building. The Holy of Holies was dark and empty, save for a stone, once associated with the Ark, on which to rest the censer. In this perfectly cubical room, half the size of the Holy Place, was supposed to dwell the nearer Presence of God; and there, on this single day of the year, the High Priest, and he alone, entered, with picturesque ritual and elaborate precaution, to act as special intermediary between God and His people.[65] He there made confession and atonement for his own sins and for the sins of the house of Israel, while all the people awaited his return with anxiety, and hailed it with thankfulness. It was a matter for reproof if the High Priest happened to prolong his prayer, for this caused affliction of mind to those who remained outside.[66] Any mistake in ritual or procedure might, according to the popular view, cause him to be blasted by the wrath of God. The Sadducees maintained that the incense must be set alight outside the Holy of Holies and carried in already smoking—no fire must be kindled in the place where dwelt the Real Presence of God. The Pharisees did not deny the reality of the Presence but laid greater stress on the Omnipresence, which made every spot sacred. Therefore, according to them, the incense must be set alight within the Holy of Holies. The Talmud records the sudden and horrible death of a Sadducean High Priest who acted in the manner of which the Pharisees disapproved.[67] The idea of a jealous God smiting His officiating minister for some error of outward ritual is not a pleasant one. It may have arisen from the accidental but natural death of some High Priest performing his annual duty.

The other main distinctive feature of the Day of Atonement

[65] *J.E.*, arts. under "Temple," art. "Holy of Holies."   [66] Yom. 53ᵇ.
[67] Yom. 19ᵇ. Cf. H. Loewe in *Judaism and Christianity*, ed. W. O. E. Oesterley, VOL. I, London 1937, p. 134.

was the ritual of the scapegoat. Two animals, equal in age and value, were brought to the High Priest, who then cast lots over them. In accordance with the guidance of the lots one animal was sacrificed to Yahweh, the other declared "for Azazel," a demonic power inferior to Satan.[68] The second goat was not actually sacrificed to Azazel—a notion which would have been considered blasphemous, idolatrous, and abhorrent —but was banished as the bearer of sins not its own to the darkness of his realm. Scripture and Talmud handle this concept with a little restraint, for it could easily lead to some ideas of a very un-Jewish nature. The High Priest would lay his hands on the head of the scapegoat, making full confession of sins, his own and those of the house of Israel, and the animal was then cast loose in the wilderness, or, according to other authorities, hurled to death over a precipice. This is a further and very important conception of vicarious atonement. There are traces of a further idea which is not without its interest. A scrap of crimson wool was placed on the Temple door, or on the animal itself, or perhaps on both—the Talmudic evidence is confused and contradictory. If this wool turned miraculously white, thus illustrating the words of Isaiah 1.18, God's forgiveness was demonstrated in a practical way for those who accepted the sign.[69]

The ritual of the old Jewish Temple lingers in the New Testament in symbol and analogy, though not, after the earliest stages, in actual worship. The familiar rent veil of the Temple in the Passion narrative has been interpreted both literally and metaphorically, but its essential meaning is clear. This links with the more elaborate and typological expression of the same teaching in the Epistle to the Hebrews. The writer goes back in his thoughts to the early Tabernacle: its furnishings and its ministry become the bricks of his symbolism. It may be that what he says about the Holy of Holies is more strictly applicable to the later Temple, and something of an anachronism in respect to the Tabernacle[70]—this depends on the accuracy of those scholars who assign the taboo to a much

[68] Lev. XVI. See *J.E.*, art. "Azazel"; also art. "Atonement," VOL. II, p. 280, col. 2, *et seq.*
[69] Cf. Shab. IX.3; Yom. IV.2, VI.8, 39ᵃ; R.Sh. 31ᵇ.   [70] Heb. IX.7.

later date. The writer had the whole ritual history of Judaism to draw on for his archetypes, and in the wider sense he undoubtedly does not blunder, for dead chronological details are not of the stuff of which vital allegories are made. The special teaching or *gnosis* of the epistle is that Christ's one sacrifice has removed the taboo and all barriers which separate man from God—which is precisely the import of the Gospel passage about the veil of the Temple.

Another matter of exegetical interest calls for a few words, namely the Midrashic statement that the earthly Holy of Holies is exactly opposite its heavenly counterpart.[71] This symbolism may be a little crude and localised, but it links in an interesting way with another dominant theme in the Epistle to the Hebrews, namely that the earthly Tabernacle and all its concomitants are but copies and shadows of heavenly things[72]—a thought which would apply equally to the Temple. The same imagery is used in the comparison of Law and Gospel.[73] This profound and suggestive idea is in keeping with the writer's whole emphasis on archetype and ectype, and on the things unseen, which may have vastly more importance than the things seen. The Midrashic passage fails to reach this lofty level, but it expresses a kindred thought.

The scapegoat is not used quite so directly as a vehicle of New Testament teaching, but it is an implicit background concept. The red wool is mentioned in a more general context in Hebrews IX.19, though without the Talmudic embroideries. Significantly, the ceremony of the scapegoat reached its climax outside the camp, or outside the gate (Hebrews XIII.11-13). This links with another ceremony, the burning of the Red Heifer, and the subsequent mingling of its ashes with water, to be used for purposes of ritual purification. This also happened outside the camp.[74] There is a direct reference to the Red Heifer in Hebrews IX.13, and both ceremonies require mention in the full exegesis of Hebrews XIII.11-13. The writer is of course comparing all these ineffectual and outward struggles for ritual purity with the one sufficient and effective sacrifice of Christ, which makes real purity attainable for all.

---

[71] Song of Sol. R. III.10, 4; IV.4, 9.   [72] Cf. esp. Heb. VIII.5.
[73] Heb. X.1.   [74] *J.E.*, arts. "Red Heifer," "Parah."

This completes the survey of what might be called the semi-official channels of atonement in the Rabbinic theology. In the period which followed the final destruction of the Herodian Temple, the ritual described above became a mere memory. The modern practice of slaying a cock on the eve of Atonement, praying that it may be the vicarious burden-bearer of sin, looks like a throwback to animal sacrifice, but it lacks all the Halakhic prerequisites, and may be explained in other ways. It is also deprecated or condemned in many schools of Jewish thought.[75] The Day of Atonement continued to be observed scrupulously, but penitence, fasting, prayer, and charity form perhaps a more valuable replacement of the earlier elements. The essential meaning of the time and occasion remained unaltered.

Some Further Rabbinic Teachings on Atonement

This section gathers up a few isolated but relevant teachings not previously mentioned, each with some intrinsic interest.

In a curious passage of the Gemara, Abraham and Jacob are said to acquiesce in God's plan to wipe out the children of Israel because of their sins, while Isaac becomes mediator and offers some mathematical pleading. Man's average life is seventy years. In the first twenty years—other Jewish authorities would say thirteen—he is immature, and exempt from the penalty for his sins, so fifty years only are under judgment. Twenty-five of these years—in mathematical value, that is, not chronologically—are taken up with the nights and sleep. Twelve and a half of the remaining years are taken up with prayer, eating, and natural functions, and are therefore likewise free from sin. So there are only twelve and a half years for which a man needs to make atonement, and the situation is not nearly so bad as it sounds when these factors are unconsidered.[76]

An uncircumcised male is declared to be incapable of making atonement for his transgressions until such time as he rectifies this particular sin of omission.[77] From the usage of the word, it is clear that the reference is primarily, if not exclusively, to those of Jewish race, and there is no certain ground for deducing anything concerning the Gentiles from this context.

---

[75] *J.E.*, VOL. II, p. 282, col. 2; also VOL. VII, art. "Kapparah."
[76] Shab. 89*b*.　　　　　[77] Pes. 62*a*.

Some Rabbis were deeply conscious of the graciousness and availability of God. If a man sins, and offers contrite prayer, God is satisfied by his mere words, though other human beings smarting under a sense of wrong would not be so easily pacified.[78] This is a gracious teaching, admirable within its limits.

The next passage would afford a significant echo of the best prophetic Judaism, were it less restricted in its reference. The Gemara is discussing the sin of the house of Eli, which "shall not be expiated by sacrifice or offering for ever."[79] Although the priestly ceremonial expiations will not avail, it is declared that Torah and charitable deeds will avail.[80] It is a pity that the Talmud does not add the note of repentance, which is stressed in other contexts, and then universalise the implication throughout the realm of human conduct—this would raise the teaching to a very exalted level.

The last passage calling for mention here is a surprising *volte-face*. The destruction of the Temple, so loudly and so bitterly lamented elsewhere, is declared to have given Israel atonement for all her sins.[81] A more usual reaction is deep concern as to the very possibility of atonement without the Temple cults. From the modern point of view the movement away from animal sacrifice and everything connected with it is a healthy one.

The preceding sections open up most of the topics belonging to the doctrine of atonement proper. Some reference was made also in passing to the kindred theme of prayer, a main and self-expressing vehicle of the heart seeking atonement. For the Christian reader nothing can illuminate Rabbinic practice better than the main elements of the liturgy they actually used, and which Jews still use today. A translation, which the Jewish reader may ignore, is added in an appendix to this book.

[78] Yom. 86[b]. Cf. Hos. xiv.2.   [79] I Sam. iii.14.
[80] R.Sh. 18[a].   [81] Lev. R. xi.7.

CHAPTER XI

IMMORTALITY

THE cry of the stricken Job: "If a man die, shall he live again?" has been echoed in countless hearts throughout the generations, and few human questionings have exercised greater fascination or led to more probing speculation. The Rabbis, like most groups of religious people, were profoundly interested in the subject, and few themes recur so frequently in their writings.

The historical background of the thinking on immortality of the Rabbinic and New Testament writers alike lies in the Old Testament, the Apocrypha, and the Pseudepigrapha. Once again, the evidence has been variously interpreted by different scholars, and any adequate summary of the controversial issues would be out of place in a volume dealing with the Rabbinic material. A very bald synopsis will serve present purposes.

Most peoples of ancient times believed that human beings survived mortal death in a shadowy and unsatisfying Sheol, sharing an equal fate there, totally unaffected by the virtuous or evil conduct which had characterised their earthly lives. Such a belief in immortality, if it be worthy of the name, was shared by Israel from the earliest times; but this Sheol, equivalent to the Greek Hades, was not recognised as being within the domain of Yahweh. This kind of view appears as a freak survival even in the Rabbinic literature. It is almost startling to read in the Talmud a passage expressing a clear philosophy of "Eat, drink, and be merry, for tomorrow we die," and to note its strenuous denial that there is any happiness in the grave.[1] This reads like a throwback to the tone and spirit of certain passages in Ecclesiastes.

[1] Erub. 54^a.

It is widely asserted that the Old Testament almost in its entirety is concerned exclusively with the everlasting continuance of the nation Israel, and agnostic or wholly indifferent regarding the fact or nature of personal survival beyond the tacit minimal belief mentioned above. Almost at the very end of the Old Testament period, on this theory, the problem of undeserved suffering, classically exemplified by Job, led certain late writers to question the naïve presuppositions of the earlier theology. The righteous, as any impartial critic might observe, were not necessarily rewarded, nor the wicked unvaryingly punished, in this temporal sphere, as all Judaism felt that they ought to be; therefore this settled doctrine must have exceptions or deeper implications, and therefore the concept of a richer and more significant personal immortality was born, that the wrongs of this world might be righted in the next. It is postulated by some that a survival of this kind is foreshadowed only in a few very late books of the Old Testament, while others see the intimations of such an immortality, incipient or concretely felt, glimmering or shining all through the sacred record.

Souls and Spirits

There are two main conceptions of human immortality, logically separate, but frequently blended in human thinking, be it Jewish or Christian. There is the essentially Hebraic notion of the resurrection of the body, and the essentially Greek one of immortal spirit. While the resurrection concept is more Rabbinic, in fact more Jewish, there is abundant evidence of the far-reaching influence of the Greek ideas in Talmud and Midrash, though these are transmuted into a more Jewish pattern. Philo Judaeus and other writers of the wider Graeco-Roman world undoubtedly contributed to this situation. The more conservative Judaism of Palestine and Babylonia may have felt some suspicion and hostility towards anything that savoured of Greek philosophy, but influences, even unwelcome ones, may sometimes be too strong for effective total resistance.

A doctrine of souls or spirits is no innovation in Judaism, for it is clearly discernible in the later books of the Old Testament.

Daniel XII.1-4 obviously teaches resurrection either to bliss or to punishment, according to the deeds done in this mortal life. It is equally obvious that portions of Psalms XLIX and LXXIII, together with Job XXXIV.14, Ecclesiastes XII.7 and other passages, teach the redemption of the soul from Sheol by God, or its return to Him, and approximate to the Greek notion. In the Apocrypha and Pseudepigrapha, both doctrines are developed and extended.[2] By this time they are part and parcel at least of Pharisaic Judaism, though the Sadducees remained fiercely hostile to any notion of human immortality so long as they had a Temple and a voice in the religion of the nation.[3]

The last paragraph should be qualified by the fact that there is a distinction in meaning between soul and spirit, though the resemblance is fairly close. The differentiation sharpens slightly in the later writings of the Old Testament canon. The soul of man means to begin with the breath which gives him life—possibly even the blood[4]—but certainly the animating principle which he shares with the lower creation. Then it comes to mean his whole personality. Then two aspects of personality come to be distinguished—the functions of breathing, eating, propagating, and so forth, which man shares with the animal, and in contradistinction those higher intellectual capacities which he alone possesses in the created order, particularly manifested in his awareness of and seeking after God. This latter element in man comes to be known as his spirit. Then the question arises as to whether the spirit is merely the noblest part of the soul, or something separate from it. On the first view, man's nature becomes a dichotomy of body and soul, on the second, a trichotomy of body, soul, and spirit. Whichever metaphysical scheme be preferred, it is essential to keep the distinctions clear, and not equate the terms.[5]

It is not necessary to examine the impact of the soul-spirit

---

[2] Cf. R. H. Charles, *Religious Development between the Old and the New Testaments*, London 1914, pp. 123 ff.; W. Hirsch, *Rabbinic Psychology*, London 1947, Chap. IV.

[3] Cf. Ber. IX.5. For an interesting sociological discussion of this cleavage of opinion, see E. Finkelstein, *The Pharisees*, Philadelphia 1946, Chap. VIII. This writer argues ably for a bitter class struggle between the Sadducees, rich, arrogant, powerful in this world, interested only in its affairs, and the poor but pious Pharisees, awaiting the fulfilment of all their hopes in the next world.

[4] Cf. Hirsch, *Rabbinic Psychology*, p. 57.

[5] Cf. Hirsch, *op. cit.*, p. 94.

teaching on the Rabbinic literature in detail, as the resurrection doctrine is more typical and important. Nevertheless the far-reaching effects of the Greek approach are of sufficient interest for brief demonstration. It is, however, a modified Grecianism which percolates into Judaism, because for that religion the body is neither inherently evil, nor the tomb of a restless spirit only eager to escape. The body may involve men in temptations, but if the Rabbis considered it intrinsically foul, they would scarcely hope to have it raised from the dead.

Certain Rabbis at least believed in the pre-existence of the soul, for the souls and spirits of the unborn are said to dwell in the seventh heaven, in symbolic proximity to righteousness and justice.[6] The reader has already met the declaration, oft repeated, that Messiah will not come till all the souls of the unborn have attained their sojourn upon earth.[7] The doctrine of survival is reflected in the declaration that the souls of the righteous dead are hidden under the Throne of Glory, while those of the wicked suffer.[8] The divine affinity of the soul is asserted in many respects in a lengthy passage, declaring among other things its purity, its superiority to sleep, and the fact that it outlasts the body.[9] If these passages do not claim eternal existence for the soul in specific terms, they travel at least some considerable distance in that direction.

The view of man as a dichotomy of soul and body is common, both in the Rabbinic literature and in the New Testament, and needs no special exemplification. The less recurrent trichotomy appears in the passage cited just above concerning the unborn souls and spirits in the seventh heaven. Another context, speaking of the divine-human partnership in the formation of the embryo, ascribes to God the creation of soul and spirit as His prerogative.[10] The reader will perceive that there is enough material here to form the foundation of a full-fledged theology of this type. The resurrection teaching is, however, considerably more voluminous and typical.

---

[6] Hag. 12 ^{b}.

[7] See above Chapter IV, p. 47, n. 1. See also A. Zar. 5 ^{a}; Nidd. 13 ^{b}.

[8] Shab. 152 ^{b}. In the same folio, the soul is said to be free to pass between heaven and earth for twelve months after death.

[9] Lev. R. IV.8. More briefly Ber. 10 ^{a}.

[10] Nidd. 31 ^{a}. Cf. 1 Thess. v.23; Heb. IV.12.

The Reference of the Life after Death

One question this section would seek to explore is what kind of immortality, if any, the Rabbis envisaged for the Gentiles— who, after all, considerably outnumbered the Jews. Unfortunately, the answer remains indeterminate because of the conflicting nature of the evidence. Just as the social attitude of Jews to Gentiles, always coloured by personal experience, varied from fanatical and intolerant hatred to complete absence of ill will, so did the estimate of their post-mortal future—though few in Talmudic times would predict for them the joys of Paradise. The opposition of Jews to the conversion of any of their family to Christianity, or to the marriage of any of their offspring to Gentiles, is well known even today, and these sentiments find close parallels in other religious groups. Many persons of other cultures are inclined to take bitter exception to rigorous exclusiveness. Yet it cannot be denied that it reflects basic loyalties, and often a deeply spiritual view of life. There is a kind of religious toleration which springs from a fine humanity, and a kind which springs from mere indifference.

Some extreme Rabbis may have felt that all men would be resurrected from the dead, a few elect Jews to eternal bliss, and all the rest—many of Israel, and all the Gentiles—to everlasting punishment, much in the spirit of Holy Willie's Prayer. In fact, the exceptions allowed might reasonably be considered deliberate modifications of the harshness of a doctrine so intolerable and so contrary to much of the prevailing spirit of Judaism.

Total oblivion after death is obviously a lesser penalty than eternal torture, and the Rabbis sometimes name persons to whom the privilege may be conceded. The destroyers of the Temple are considered to repent—the case is obviously hypothetical. Their guilt in profaning the sanctuary is so enormous that they cannot be resurrected to bliss; nevertheless for their repentance they are permitted oblivion without punishment. The same concession is granted to the children of the Gentiles who die in their youthful innocence, to the soldiers of Nebuchadnezzar,[11] and, in some contexts, to the generation of the Flood,

[11] Ruth R. III.2; Eccl. R. IX.4, 1.

K

who are regarded as having suffered sufficiently already to pay the penalty for their sins.[12] (Yet other passages declare that the waters of the Deluge will be specially boiled for their more exquisite torture in Gehinnom.)[13]

It was probably reaction against the ugliness of an extreme doctrine of retribution that prompted the notion of punishment in Gehinnom being limited to twelve months,[14] or which declared alternatively that a prolonged period of torture is reserved only for those of quite exceptional wickedness.[15] This opinion was not universal. A tidy and speculative mind divides men into three classes on the day of judgment: the distinctively righteous, who will inherit the joys of Paradise; the thoroughly evil, who will be condemned to everlasting torture in Gehinnom; and the intermediate in guilt, who will suffer for twelve months, and then be relieved by annihilation.[16] The mundane psychology is interesting, whatever the reader may think of the eschatology.

The duration of the pains of Gehenna, and the fate of the Gentiles, whether oblivion or torture, are clearly subjects open to differences of personal opinion. A typical reaction may be reflected in the declaration that Israel may escape punishment for certain sins, whereas Gentiles guilty in precisely the same direction cannot and will not escape.[17] This is of course an appeal to privilege.

In order to secure a blessed immortality, a man must normally be a Jew, for Israel is the heir[18]—or at least, by somewhat grudging concession, a circumcised proselyte. The normal lack of cordiality towards proselytes reaches its extreme form when they are shockingly likened to a sore on the skin of Israel,[19] though other passages of a more generous nature may be found. All Jews should have this happy expectation; yet they may, despite their birthright, exclude themselves by certain sins, such as denial of the fact that resurrection is taught in the Pentateuch.[20] Isaac is said to sit constantly at the entrance to

[12] Gen. R. xxxii.1; Lev. R. iv.1.   [13] Gen. R. xxviii.8; Lev. R. vii.6.
[14] Shab. 33 b; Eduy. ii.10; Lam. R. 1.40.   [15] Cf. B.M. 58 b; Gen. R. xxvi.2.
[16] R.Sh. 16 b-17 a.
[17] Ruth R. Proem 1; Song of Sol. R. ii.1, 1, viii.8, 1.
[18] Ex. R. xv.27.   [19] Yeb. 109 b.
[20] Sanh. xi.1, etc. See p. 153 f.

Gehinnom to deliver all his descendants from entering therein.[21] But this is qualified elsewhere. The circumcised foreskin is normally the guarantee of entry. But for those guilty of exceptional carnal sin, or extreme doctrinal obliquity, there are ways of dealing with the matter. A guardian Abraham, while diverting almost all his descendants from the gates of Gehinnom, may nevertheless cut a few foreskins from uncircumcised babes, and graft them onto the members of Israelites deserving condemnation[22]—or, if Abraham be too busy, the angel may stretch the foreskin so thoroughly as to remove the appearance of circumcision altogether.[23] These unpleasant ideas may have had some historical prompting. Certain Jews, attracted by foreign cultures, were known to remove the physical vestiges of circumcision, thus repudiating, both spiritually and politically, their ancestral ties. The horror engendered in loyal compatriots by this apostasy possibly finds some echo in the passages just cited. The Rabbis would naturally concede no salvation for the fortuitous or surgical circumcision practised amongst Gentiles for hygienic reasons, as this would possess no sacramental significance in their eyes. It is sad to find the redeemed actually pictured as gloating over the misfortunes of the rejected.[24] In all cultures the pursuit of salvation is potentially fine, but may in individual cases degenerate into selfishness.

If a man is not a Jew, the Rabbis, in many of their teachings, do not hold out for him any hope of a blessed hereafter, even if he be endowed with every conceivable virtue, and even if he be Cyrus, the great benefactor of the Jewish race.[25] He cannot save himself by the supreme Jewish virtue of charity—his heathen status makes this valueless, and he is considered to do it solely for his own reward or glory.[26] In accordance with these convictions, Rabbis declare that certain foods are proscribed to the Jews because of their lofty spiritual destiny—God has not troubled to forbid them to Gentiles, who do not fall within His saving purpose.[27] In the Messianic age and in the life to come the gate is barred to proselytes, as indicated in Chapter III.

---

[21] Song of Sol. R. viii.9, 3.   [22] Gen. R. xlviii.8.

[23] Ex. R. xix.4.   [24] Lev. R. xxxii.1.   [25] R.Sh. 3 b-4 a.

[26] B.B. 10 b, misunderstanding Prov. xiv.34.   [27] Lev. R. xiii.2.

This is a common attitude in the period surveyed, although exceptions are allowed.

The individual Gentiles to whom salvation is conceded have generally performed some outstanding service to one of the Rabbis. Thus the Roman Emperor " Antoninus " is brought secretly within the fold, and another secures eternal bliss at the point of death by circumcision, self-administered in haste, and by leaving all his worldly goods to Rabbis.[28] When Rabbi Gamaliel was sentenced to death, a high-ranking Roman officer expressed willingness to accord him earthly safety in return for the promise of heavenly life for himself. On receiving the solemn word required, the officer hurled himself from the roof, knowing that the Romans would not desire two deaths at once and that his suicide would cause them to rescind their death sentence against the Jew. The man's portion in the world to come was thereupon assured by a Bath-Qol.[29] One cannot but wonder whether Rabbi Gamaliel really arrogated to himself the power of granting eternal life to others, or whether he merely saved his own skin at the expense of a credulous pagan. In a similar situation another Rabbi, not perceiving the implied discredit to his own order, merely laments that some should acquire eternal life so "cheaply," whilst others must labour in Torah for many years.[30] The real point of these certainly unhistorical incidents is that the salvation of a heathen soul is, in a large consensus of Rabbinic opinion, a phenomenon so exceptional as to call for full explanation. And yet the same Rabbis declare elsewhere that many Gentiles will be saved, not for especial virtue or humanity but solely because they happened in their lifetime to abstain from pork.[31]

The Qualifications for Future Bliss

Assuming that a man's Jewish faith makes him eligible in Rabbinic eyes for the joys of Paradise, he must still behave in the manner his preceptors approve if he is to assure his final qualification. The actions which are especially to be desired

---

[28] A. Zar. 10[b].   [29] Taan. 29[a].
[30] A. Zar. 18[a].   [31] Eccl. R. 1.9, 1.

on his part fall into two categories: those concerned with the outward observances of religion, and those of a more ethical or personal nature.

Prominent in the first group of virtues is the study of the Torah.[32] Equally to be commended is the teaching of Torah, whether to a man's own sons,[33] or to compatriots.[34] It is also highly worthy to make a long journey specifically to hear lectures on Torah.[35] The careful observance of Halakhic restrictions,[36] the devotional recitation of Halakhic laws,[37] and the keeping of divine commandments[38] all link closely with the precepts above. This kind of advice is frequently reiterated in eschatological emphasis in greater or lesser detail.[39] Eternal bliss may be secured by reciting Psalm CXLV thrice daily,[40] or by lifelong abstinence from pork,[41] or by the possibly quite fortuitous circumstance of being present at the death of a Rabbi.[42] Residence in Israel is also a great help.[43]

The more ethical of the numerous Rabbinic gateways to a blessed hereafter are frequently those which might be expected from the Old Testament, and are therefore more reasonable to the wider world. These include meekness and humility,[44] charity,[45] suffering and chastisement,[46] piety,[47] confession,[48] good deeds,[49] rightful conduct towards parents,[50] and other virtues of like tenor.

Two teachings only call for brief special comment in this section.

The Midrash lays down the essential innocence of those illegitimately born—the sin is not theirs, but another's. Bastards, therefore, though not necessarily of the elect any more than others, are as eligible for ultimate acceptance as anybody else, and may even be accorded some preference to make up for the unfair disabilities they have suffered in

[32] Peah I.1; Ab. II.7; A. Zar. 3ᵇ; etc. [33] Pes. 113ᵃ.
[34] Sanh. 92ᵃ. [35] Song of Sol. R. II.5, 3.
[36] Nidd. 16ᵇ. [37] Nidd. 73ᵃ.
[38] Ex. R. XXX.24; Num. R. XIV.6. [39] Cf. Hull. 44ᵇ; Men. 44ᵃ; etc.
[40] Ber. 4ᵇ. [41] Eccl. R. I.9, 1.
[42] Ket. 103ᵇ. [43] Pes. 113ᵃ.
[44] Sanh. 88ᵇ. [45] Pes. 8ᵃ, etc.
[46] Gen. R. IX.8; Lev. R. XXX.2. [47] Num. R. XIX.1.
[48] Sanh. VI.2; Num. R. IX.17. [49] A. Zar. 4ᵇ, 5ᵃ; Gen. R. IX.9.
[50] Peah I.1; Shab. 127ᵃ; Deut. R. I.15; etc.

life.[51] There is a fair-mindedness and even nobility in this teaching which makes an immediate appeal.

The Talmud offers a most interesting parallel to Matthew VI.19-21, which is worth quoting.[52] The translation is shorn of the voluminous Scriptural proof-texts of the original. "The Rabbis taught: It is reported of King Monobazus that he squandered his own hoarded treasure and that of his fathers. His brothers and those of his father's household joined in protest against him, and said to him: 'Your immediate ancestors saved, and added to the treasures of their fathers, which you are simply squandering.' He answered them: 'My fathers saved for this world below, I am saving for the world above. . . . My fathers saved in a place where the hand of man has power over their possessions, while I am saving in a place where the hand of man has no such power. . . . My fathers saved something which does not bring forth any fruits, while I have saved something which does. . . . My fathers saved worldly wealth, but I have saved treasures of souls. . . . My fathers saved for others, but I have saved for myself. . . . My fathers saved for this world, I have saved for the world to come.' "

No student of the New Testament can read this passage without perceiving its interest, but the parallel to the Matthean verses is not quite so close as Montefiore would have us believe. King Monobazus may be criticised on two counts. He was the steward, not the owner, of the treasures of his kingdom; and his subjects, his relatives, and his possible successors would all have a measure of grievance if he really left the kingdom impoverished to an unwarrantable extent. It would also seem that the king's chief preoccupation was the salvation of his own soul, and therefore basically selfish. The kind of practical human love praised by Jesus is done for its own sake, out of the spontaneous goodness of the heart, and for God's glory only, never for that of the ego. But the story throws an interesting sidelight on the Rabbinic view of good works as an earnest of salvation.

[51] Eccl. R. IV.I, I. Cf. Lev. R. XXXII.8.
[52] B.B. 11ᵃ. Cf. Montefiore, *Rabbinic Literature and Gospel Teachings*, p. 139. Cf. also *J.E.*, art. "Adiabene."

Conduct leading to Future Punishment

Salvation may have sounded rather easy in some parts of the last section, but the Rabbis point out many possible stumbling blocks. Some of those ethically or Rabbinically obvious may be dismissed with a bare mention. These include idolatry,[53] derogatory remarks about deceased scholars,[54] loss of temper,[55] flattery,[56] all the sins of pride and arrogance,[57] slander,[58] adultery of the body,[59] adultery of the eye,[60] frivolous and unnecessary conversation with one's wife,[61] accepting advice from one's wife,[62] wrongful legal judgment,[63] lewd speech,[64] departing from the Torah,[65] or denying even a single point in its text,[66] reading books which are uncanonical and hence forbidden,[67] or putting a neighbour to shame.[68] Some of these topics are familiar from earlier chapters.

The reader has already seen that the Rabbis may consider exempted from Gehinnom those who have suffered grievously in mortal life, even if they qualify in other respects. Such good fortune may befall the very poor, those afflicted with bowel disease, and those who have suffered at the hands of the Romans. There is some discussion as to whether the husband of a bad wife should or should not be included. The sufficiency of his earthly martyrdom is a little doubtful, unless he is genuinely too poor to afford a divorce: in the latter case, his misfortunes may make atonement for his sins.[69] On the other hand certain classes, such as the rich men of Babylon, are confidently assigned to all the tortures to come.[70] Surely, one context would argue, the students of Torah should be exempt even from the thought of future punishment.[71] On the contrary, it is asserted elsewhere, their sins, if they be sinful, will bring

---

[53] Taan. 5[a].
[54] Ber. 19[a].
[55] Ned. 22[a].
[56] Sot. 41[b].
[57] B.B. 10[b], 78[b]; A. Zar. 18[b]; Ab. v.20.
[58] Arak. 15[b].
[59] Sot. 4[b] f.; Num. R. ix.12; Lev. R. ix.5; etc.
[60] Ber. 61[a]; Erub. 18[b]; Kidd. 81[a]; Esth. R. vii.9; etc.
[61] Ab. i.5.
[62] B.M. 59[a].
[63] Song of Sol. R. iii.7, 3, etc. The converse is stated in Ex. R. xxx.17.
[64] Shab. 33[a].
[65] B.B. 79[a].
[66] Sanh. 99[a].
[67] Sanh. xi.1; Num. R. xiv.4.
[68] B.M. 59[a]. Cf. Gen. R. i.5.
[69] Erub. 41[b].
[70] Betz. 32[b].
[71] Hag. 27[a].

them a double Gehinnom, as they of all people have the least excuse.[72] For any who are in danger of condemnation, there is the possibility of escape through the practice of certain virtuous actions such as the visitation of the sick,[73] or through the cultivation of certain mental attitudes such as the fear of God[74] and repentance.[75] In other words the individual may change his course in an upward or downward direction at any particular moment.

Very frequently reiterated is the sentiment that the righteous are fully punished in this world for their minor transgressions while the wicked are fully rewarded, also in this temporal sphere, for their minor virtues, so that the fullest measure of bliss and woe may be accorded to each hereafter.[76] This may be regarded as a fresh solution, on new data, to the problem of undeserved suffering. Some would regard this teaching as harsh. Closely analogous is the notion that each individual possesses within himself a portion of good, corresponding to the Garden of Eden, and a portion of evil, corresponding to Gehenna. The predominantly righteous man will in time to come be allowed by God to take possession of his evil neighbour's portion of good and so qualify for bliss, while the predominantly evil man will be forced by God to bear his neighbour's portion of sin and so qualify for punishment.[77] Many will be tempted to pronounce unfair both this teaching and the closely parallel sentiments of Matthew xxv.29, and the entire parable from which that verse is drawn. Western minds are seldom fully at home with Eastern symbolism. Much of the difficulty disappears when it is realised that Jesus and the Rabbis are describing, not deliberate and dubious actions on the part of the Deity, but rather deep underlying psychological facts of human nature and experience. What they really mean to teach is that when men set out, whether in the way of righteousness or of sin, there is a certain unescapable momentum of circumstance which generally tends to keep them travelling in that same direction, until the destiny of their lives is fulfilled.

Men may be condemned to Gehenna simply because they

---

[72] Yom. 72[b]. Cf. the long debate in Hag. 15[b].

[73] Ned. 40[a].

[74] Yeb. 102[b].

[75] Eccl. R. vii.14, 1.

[76] Taan. 11[a]; Kidd. 40[b]; Gen. R. xxxiii.1; etc.

[77] Hag. 15[a].

have neglected available opportunities of doing good, and without being guilty of specific transgression.[78] This is a practical and very wholesome reminder that there are positive as well as negative aspects in the search after righteousness.

Another partial New Testament analogy may be found in the parable of the king who bids many guests to his feast, ordering each to bring something for his own comfort in sitting. Some appear properly equipped, others bring unseemly pieces of wood or stone and then grumble at the king, who becomes furiously angry. These people are exactly like the man without a wedding garment in the second part of the familiar parable in Matthew XXII.1-14. The fault, for those who are uncomfortable, lies in their own lack of suitable provision: so, for those who suffer in Gehinnom, the fault lies in their own actions in the course of their earthly lives.[79]

It would seem then in Rabbinic opinion that even the Jew may boast little more than a chance of reaching Paradise: there remain for him, despite his birthright, many possible snares and stumbles by the way.

The Concept of Resurrection

However much or little individual Rabbis may have dabbled in Greek philosophy, it is clear that the majority of them looked beyond this life in the expectation, not of an immortal soul, but of a resurrected body. This is the common belief, which calls for further study.

One of the primary articles in the Rabbinic creed, mentioned above, is that the resurrection of the dead is explicitly taught in Torah, and that whosoever denies this will be excluded from the world to come.[80] The exegetical devices by which this conclusion is "proved" are many and various. For example commandment is given in Numbers XVIII.28 that heave-offering must be paid to Aaron the priest, who never in his mortal state so much as reached the Holy Land: this therefore demonstrates the resurrection of Aaron, and, by implication, of others.[81] From the juxtaposition of grave and womb in Proverbs XXX.16,

[78] Esth. R. VIII.6.
[79] Eccl. R. III.9, 1.
[80] Sanh. XI.1; A. Zar. 18[a]; etc.
[81] Sanh. 90[b].

it is argued that, just as the womb takes in semen and gives forth a child, so also the grave takes in its corpse, and gives forth a resurrected body. This likewise "proves" that just as the child is born with loud cries, so also the body will be raised with loud cries.[82] As the Hebrew text refers specifically to the barrenness (literally "restraint") of the womb, the logic is strange. From these and from many similar arguments[83] it is repeatedly demonstrated that the Old Testament contains intimations of immortality on almost every page—a fact which many Christians accept on entirely different presuppositions. The doctrine of resurrection simply must be true, for the adequate reward of those good Jews who fulfil many precepts depends on its reality.[84]

The Rabbis are not in harmony with those who believe wholeheartedly in the fact of resurrection, but base their faith on something other than the Jewish Scriptures. There may have been controversies with those Christians who denied that there was any hope of human immortality before Christ rose from the dead. It is urged against all opponents that proof of resurrection is to be found in Torah (here, Pentateuch) Prophets, and Hagiographa.[85]

Should any still feel doubts on the issue of resurrection itself, the Rabbis would bid him consider the phenomenon of awaking from sleep, a daily minor resurrection. In this smaller miracle, he will see the larger one clearly reflected.[86] This is a good metaphor, though scarcely a formal proof. Among seven suggested explanations of the quickening of the dead bones in Ezekiel xxxvii is the thesis that those raised were persons who had in life denied the fact of the resurrection and now found themselves confuted in this dramatic way.[87] There is imagination and boldness in this striking interpretation. The unusual note of final doubt sounds indeed strangely, but nevertheless a certain Rabbi, seeing the tongue of his martyred colleague in the mouth of a dog, is moved to a sombre expression of

---

[82] Ber. 15^a. Cf. Eccl. R. iii.2, 1.
[83] Pes. 68^a; Hull. 142^a; Gen. R. xx.11.
[84] Kidd. 39^b.
[85] Sanh. 90^b. See Soncino translation, p. 604, n. 12.
[86] Gen. R. lxxviii.1; Lev. R. iii.23, 8.
[87] Sanh. 92^b. Cf. also Gen. R. xiv.5; Lev. R. xiv.9.

scepticism and pessimism.[88] But this attitude is the very reverse of typical.

The power of resurrecting the body is the prerogative of God. The Midrash expresses this by declaring that He holds the key, a fact deduced from the reference to God opening graves in Ezekiel xxxvii.13.[89] The physical means proposed is interesting. According to the Rabbis, there is one bone in the body superior to the attacks of water, stone, fire, and iron, therefore utterly indestructible. They call this the nut of the spinal column, meaning presumably the coccyx. When all the rest of the body has been destroyed, this bone, sufficient for God's purposes, will remain undamaged.[90] According to some authorities, God raises bodies from the dead only in the land of Israel: but His ingenuity is equal to the challenge, for the bodies of faithful believers buried elsewhere will be rolled through underground cavities to the Holy Land. Loewe argues in an interesting note that this whole notion is a conflation of two ideas—re-burial in Palestine of the bodies of Jews who have died elsewhere, which is quite Hebraic and normal, and metempsychosis, which is a doctrine alien to Judaism. A discussion follows as to whether it was really necessary to carry the body of Jacob from Egypt to Canaan. According to one reading, Jacob feared he might not be found sufficiently righteous to be rolled underground: according to a variant reading in the Gemara, he resented the anticipated discomfort of such a journey. Such is the virtue of Israel's soil that there is salvation even for a Canaanite bondwoman buried therein.[91] According to this view, and in supplementary reference to an earlier section of this chapter, there would be no resurrection for Gentiles outside Israel, and even there God will not trouble to raise the illiterate.[92] This would suggest that resurrection is the privilege, or, in the event of condemnation, the misfortune, of a limited number of people. But the evidence is too conflicting for any dogmatic statement as to the prevailing belief.

Following up the hint of Hosea vi.2, it is declared that resurrection will take place after three days. The Dominical prediction and the Passion narrative will at once spring to the

---

[88] Ruth R. vi.4.   [89] Deut. R. vii.6.   [90] Lev. R. xviii.1; Eccl. R. xii.5, 1.
[91] Ket. 111[a]. See also *R.A.*, pp. 650 ff.   [92] Ket. 111[b].

reader's mind. According to a Midrashic commentator, this period is counted "from the beginning of the final judgment."[93] This would suggest that a human being sinks into oblivion at the moment of death, and remains unconscious of the phenomenon of life until he is raised at the final judgment. This notion is probably a little more widespread than the postulate of death being the immediate gateway into a new sentient life, but both views are discernible in Rabbinic and Christian sources.

The dead will arise afflicted in the first instance with all the blemishes and disabilities which marked them at the time of death, blindness, lameness, or whatever they might be. There will be speedy healing for God's elect—the arrangement is merely for the convenience of recognition.[94] The wicked, however, will be bereft of the power of speech.[95] The righteous will rise clothed with the very garments they wore in mortal life—for wheat, by an argument from minor to major, is buried naked and sprouts up covered; how much more, therefore, will the dead who are buried in their own clothes rise from the grave suitably invested.[96] The modern western mind would regard this as something of a *non sequitur*, but it is good Rabbinic logic.

The Rabbis have their answer for any who would argue that the task of raising the body is too difficult for God. He has already fashioned man from water—that is to say, from the drop of sperm or semen. Will He not the more easily re-fashion him from the dust or clay to which he returns, and which possesses a greater solidity? Glass vessels blown by the craft of man may be broken; yet the constituent glass is melted down, and blown once more into a fresh vessel. Is it any more difficult for God to re-create the human body which has perished? And there are many more examples of a like nature.[97]

The reader will perceive from the material above that many Rabbis believed firmly in the resurrection of the body. But there was also, as the last section of this chapter will indicate,

---

[93] Esth. R. ix.2. See Soncino translation, p. 112, n. 4.
[94] Gen. R. xcv.1; Eccl. R. i.4, 2.   [95] Eccl. R. ix.10, 2.
[96] Ket. 111ᵇ; Sanh. 90ᵇ. Cf. 1 Cor. xv.36 ff. Cf. also Eccl. R. v.10, 1.
[97] Sanh. 91ᵃ. Cf. Gen. R. xiv.7.

a school of thought which accepted the resurrection terminology, yet virtually denied to the raised body any corporeality which could link it in any way with human experience.

The Nature of Gehinnom

The valley of Ge-Hinnom lies fairly close to the Old City of Jerusalem, and is visible from the summit of the Mount of Olives, or from the dusty road beyond the Pool of Siloam. Today the boundary between the new state of Israel and the Hashemite Kingdom of Jordan splits it in half, and Israeli-Arab tensions make it difficult to get close to it. The writer attempted to walk boldly up the valley from the lower or Arab end, when a local youth called out in broken English: "You go up there, you die!" It is quite certain that there was nothing of the symbolic or eschatological in his intention, but the words, just in that place, had a strange associative ring. For it was there that in ancient days children were sacrificed to Moloch, and because of that horrible association the place became accursed in Jewish thought, mentally linked to the domain of future retribution. Rabbinic observers reported the incidence of smoke arising between two palm trees in this valley—a phenomenon probably due to causes entirely natural, but quite enough to start a story.[98] Gehenna is the grecised form of the Hebrew Ge-Hinnam, and Gehenna and Gehinnom are used indiscriminately; and the nomenclature of this section generally follows the usage of the particular passage cited. This place was reputed to have three gates, one in the wilderness, one in the sea, and one in Jerusalem. It was argued that the Jerusalem gate was in fact the spot where smoke ascended in the neighbouring Gehinnom, which would otherwise be a fourth.[99] It was commonly believed that Gehenna was situated underground, though alternative suggestions occur.[100] Its dimensions were supposed to be truly vast. The world and Gehenna are compared respectively to a lid and pot, though the precise large number of times the latter exceeds the former in size is variously computed.[101] There are obvious topological difficulties in the concept, unless

---

[98] Sukk. 32^b.
[99] Erub. 19^a. Cf. Sukk. 32^b.
[100] Cf. Tam. 32^b.
[101] Pes. 94^a; Song of Sol. R. vi.9, 3. Cf. Taan. 10^a.

the image adopted be that of a tenement building in reverse, with numerous floors descending from earth level. But it is unlikely that such matters were investigated in mathematical terms.

It is declared in more than one context that God created Gehinnom.[102] Despite possible difficulties this admission is a wise one, for the notion of a place of punishment not in the hands of God would be worse a thousandfold. The earlier views of Sheol mentioned above were long discarded by the days of the Talmud.

There are conflicting views as to the precise moment when Gehenna came into being. The narrative of the second day of Creation (Genesis 1.6-8) fails, unlike the others, to assert that the work of God was good—therefore, according to some Rabbis, Gehenna, an evil place, must have been created that day.[103] An alternative theory is that the fire of Gehenna was created on the sixth day, the eve of Sabbath.[104] Yet others would argue that it preceded the world altogether in the order of creation.[105] In other words the matter remains indeterminate.

Opinions as to the duration of Gehenna are most confused and contradictory. It is not made clear whether the twelve months of punishment frequently postulated is to start from the death of the individual, or from a final judgment aeons hence.[106] Passages may be found to support either view, but the evidence is not sufficiently consistent to form a doctrine. And the twelve months' period is not consistently asserted. On the notion that the place of torment is immediately available for the wicked at death, a Rabbi is taken to a crack in the earth which emits smoke strong and hot enough to singe wet clipped wool. By listening attentively he can, he professes, hear the followers of Korah in torture in Gehenna repeating over and over again that Moses was right and they were wrong. His companion informs him that these unfortunate people are turned every thirty days, like flesh in a pot.[107] Strikingly different in its eschatological implication is the teaching that in the time to come the sun, withdrawn from its sheath, will shine on the just and on the unjust, but with very different results—the righteous

---

[102] Sot. 22ᵃ; B. B. 16ᵃ.   [103] Gen. R. iv.6; Ex. R. xv.22. Cf. Gen. R. xxi.9.
[104] Pes. 54ᵃ.   [105] Ned. 39ᵇ; Pes. 54ᵃ.
[106] See p. 146.   [107] B.B. 74ᵃ; Sanh. 110ᵃ, ᵇ; Num. R. xviii.20.

will be pleasantly warmed, the wicked annihilated.[108] Common also is the view that twelve months is a sufficient period of punishment for most people, but not for those exceptional either in wickedness or in doctrinal perversity. The Emperor Titus, regarded as outstanding in the first class, is cheerfully consigned to a particularly loathsome and horrible death, followed by a lasting term of punishment hereafter.[109] There is a longer list containing persons of both classes which probably, though not certainly, implies the inclusion of Christians as belonging in contemporary Jewish eyes to the latter category. Whatever be the political occasion of this, the Christians are not singled out, but included with a number of other categories.[110] It may be that the Rabbinic mind in its more humane moments recoiled from the idea of eternal punishment even for others, yet welcomed it again when sufficiently aroused by the passions of circumstance or controversy.

Amongst the alleged facts concerning Gehenna which receive a more passing mention the following may be briefly recorded. Gehenna has seven divisions.[111] It is a place of darkness,[112] from which the darkness which plagued Egypt was taken.[113] And yet its fires are sixty times hotter than any known on earth,[114] while its mouth is narrow so that the torturing heat and smoke may not escape.[115] The wicked are said to be punished naked,[116] and Gehenna to be ever hungry for fresh victims.[117] There the wicked learn at last to praise God, and their tears of regret are so copious that even the fires of torment are cooled somewhat.[118] The Pharaoh of the Exodus is declared in certain Rabbinic sources not surveyed in this book to have escaped death at the Red Sea, and to have taken up a permanent stance at the portals of Gehenna to bear witness to the power of God and to warn other delinquents.[119]

A few remaining ideas are of sufficient interest or curiosity to merit a brief paragraph apiece.

[108] A. Zar. 3ᵇ; Ned. 8ᵇ; Gen. R. vi.6; etc.
[109] Eccl. R. v.8, 4.
[110] R.Sh. 17ᵃ. See Soncino edn., p. 64, n. 1.
[111] Sot. 10ᵇ.
[112] Yeb. 109ᵇ; Gen. R. xxxiii.1.
[113] Ex. R. xiv.2.
[114] Ber. 57ᵇ.
[115] Men. 99ᵇ, et seq.
[116] Esth. R. iii.14.
[117] Shab. 104ᵃ.
[118] Ex. R. vii.4.
[119] Ginzberg, Legends of the Jews, VOL. III, p. 50, VOL. VI, p. 54, n. 10.

The people of Tiberias possessed thermal springs of such temperature that cold water passed through them in a pipe could be usefully heated without fire. The Mishnah forbids them to use this natural facility on the Sabbath. The Gemara at first objects, disputing the necessity of prohibiting an object merely heated by the sun, when this is normally permitted on the Sabbath as on other days. The hot springs are thereupon declared to owe their existence to the fires of Gehenna—the water thereupon becomes an object heated by fire, and must be prohibited on the Sabbath.[120] The question at issue is merely one of casuistry: there is not the slightest objection to using the presumed fires of Gehenna for mortal convenience and economy, so long as no infringement of the Sabbath law is involved.

Gehinnom and Paradise are declared to be adjacent, so that the one is clearly visible from the other.[121] The implied teaching is that part of a condemned man's punishment consists in the Tantalus-like contemplation of the joy he has missed and can now never attain. Such is the fate of the condemned rich man who beholds the saved Lazarus in the Gospel parable (Luke XVI.19 ff.). It is possible that there is some echo here of a common Jewish tradition. The revolting converse, that the righteous in Paradise should behold with equanimity or even joy the tortures of the damned, is not unknown in Christian sources, and may be hinted at in the Midrashic passage cited in note 24 above.

There is an interesting statement to the effect that sunrise derives its colouring from the roses of Eden, sunset from the fires of Gehenna.[122] This notion is of poetic rather than theological significance, and scarcely calls for further comment.

Out of the welter of contradictory opinions, it is roughly true to say that Rabbinic Judaism inclines mostly to the view that the wicked and unsaved, or some of them, will be temporarily punished after death—whether immediately after, or aeons after, at the final judgment, is not made quite clear, and will thereafter be consigned to oblivion. A very few suffer an eternity of punishment. Elect Jews have immortality, and later Judaism came to include with them righteous Gentiles.[123]

[120] Shab. III.4, 39ᵃ.   [121] Eccl. R. VII.14, 3.
[122] B.B. 84ᵃ.   [123] See *R.A.*, p. 603 f.

The Nature of Paradise

It was stated in an earlier chapter that Rabbinic Judaism usually distinguishes and separates the Messianic Age from the world to come, though trifling implied exceptions may be found.[124] In other words, the Messianic Age is merely a period of especial worldly prosperity for Israel under a divinely appointed leader, while the world to come belongs to the realm of eschatology. This is a fundamental distinction.

There are two significant and sharply contrasted opinions on the nature of the life to be lived in the realms of Paradise. These reflect respectively the temperaments of the ascetic and the hedonist, the subjugator of the body and the frank lover of the good things of the flesh.

According to the first or stricter view, the things which men particularly enjoy in the flesh have no place or significance in the world to come. In that higher life there will be no eating, drinking, or propagating, and all the baser human emotions will be entirely eliminated.[125] Also to be found is the opposite opinion, namely, that Paradise is a place of heavenly banqueting, with table delights far surpassing those of earth.[126] Wine, which by its nature may cause human delinquency, will be stripped of any menace, presumably that it may be enjoyed without any tedious need for moderation.[127] Other Rabbinic tastes seem to run to pleasures forbidden to good Jews on earth, such as wild beast contests and meat not ritually slaughtered.[128] These last passages may well reflect the ancestry of the Islamic conceptions of a carnal Paradise. This tension between the fleshly and the spiritual, the worldly and the other-worldly, is familiar in all religious experience, corporate and individual. There is no logical argument for either position: to the truly ascetic mind the idea of a carnal Paradise is abhorrent, to the carnal mind the idea of an ascetic Paradise is dull. But finite brains are not really competent to speculate on a plane of existence far above anything they can accurately conceive.

---

[124] See above Chapter IV, p. 50, and nn. 21, 22.
[125] Ber. 17ᵃ. Cf. Gen. R. XLVIII.14. Cf. Mt. XXII.30.
[126] Esth. R. II.4, 5. Cf. Ruth R. v.6.   [127] Lev. R. XII.5.
[128] Lev. R. XIII.3.

L

In accordance with the more sensuous of these views, Paradise will possess a fruitfulness inconceivable on earth. There, a single grape which a man harvests will produce a quantity of wine which sounds to mortal ears very much more than is good for him, and its stalk will provide abundant firewood.[129] Job is said to have enjoyed a foretaste of the world to come. This is deduced from Job 1.14, a passage which means, according to Rabbinic exegesis, that ploughing and reaping took place at one and the same time—a happy state of affairs known only in a better world than this. The same kind of phenomenon is foretold, the Rabbis assert, in Amos ix.13,[130] and is reflected in the similar experience of Jacob recorded in Genesis xxx.43.[131] But these are only picturesque imaginings, and such fruitfulness would in any case be pointless for those who held the more ascetic view.

There is a more significant group of Rabbinic teachings to the general effect that a man's destiny in the world to come is completely and finally determined by his conduct in this mortal life: in other words this temporal sojourn is specifically a probation for the next life. This is expressed in several ways, and usually in a manner theologically acceptable. The reader may feel inclined to quarrel with the occasional point of view. It is declared in one passage, for example, that a man who is a common labourer in this world cannot join the ranks of the scholars in the world to come, even if he has performed services for a Rabbi: it is firmly decreed that he must remain with his fellow craftsmen throughout eternity, and he looks in vain for any promotion.[132] Christianity would altogether divorce a man's spiritual worth from his intellectual attainments. The teaching loses something of its harshness when it is remembered how specifically sacred an occupation the study of Torah was in Rabbinic eyes. Nevertheless every religion needs to leave room for a sincere piety which is lacking in intellectual gifts. Much less open to question is the general statement that a man may reform his character while he is alive in this world, whereas he can do nothing whatsoever in that direction hereafter. In other words repentance after

---

[129] Ket. 111 *b*.   [130] Lev. R. xvii.4; Ruth R. ii.10. Cf. B.B. 15 *b*, *et seq.*
[131] Gen. R. lxxiii.11.   [132] Eccl. R. iii.9, 1.

death comes too late to be of any service.[133] This is also an orthodox Christian teaching, however frequently it may be forgotten.

The same thought is sometimes expressed in a more poetic and striking manner. Rank in the next world will be bestowed strictly according to ethical merit, and will not depend on the social status that a man has acquired in this world.[134] Despite the fact that the Shekinah will be manifest to all,[135] it is nevertheless laid down that those who attain to the life beyond will have a bright or dim view of the glory of God strictly according to the degree of excellence of their personal character.[136] This would specifically postulate social inequalities in the community of the redeemed, a notion which the parable of the labourers in the vineyard (Matthew xx.1-16) would seem to contradict emphatically. This is a profound and pertinent issue, with deeper implications than those of right- or left-wing politics.

This concludes the survey of those Rabbinic teachings on Paradise which have some ethical significance. It may be true that angels have no backs, and face in all directions at once.[137] It may even be true that in the better land winds blow in opposite directions at one and the same time.[138] The modern reader may feel some surprise at the postulates, but, lacking data, he is little inclined to argue. Many of the notions above are to be found somewhere or other in Christian thinking.

[133] Ruth R. iii.1, 3.   [134] Pes. 50ᵃ.
[135] Lev. R. i.14.   [136] Sukk. 45ᵇ.
[137] Hag. 15ᵃ.   [138] Lev. R. ix.16; Song of Sol. R. iv.16, 1.

CHAPTER XII

THE RABBINIC ESTIMATE OF MAN

THE subject of this chapter has pervaded in some measure the entire book. A good deal has been said already on the Rabbinic view of Jewish man, and it need not be repeated here. Opinions regarding Gentile man are sometimes vague, sometimes spiteful, sometimes unfocused: in other words a teacher, conscious of his Jewish environment and audience, may say things about Israelites which he himself would also regard as true of men in general, though he has not declared this in so many words. This chapter selects a few representative teachings which are anthropological in the widest sense. It is not so much the survey of a new theme as a supplementary gathering together of some important material so far omitted.

There are three main types of estimate of man: those which stress his greatness or goodness; those which emphasise his impotence or evil; and those which more discerningly perceive both his potential and his weakness, or which stress the alternative choices confronting him in the journey of life. Particular Rabbis perceived man in all these ways, both inside and outside the framework of revealed religion. This chapter considers the more general and less specifically religious appraisal, particularly from the three viewpoints mentioned. The whole Rabbinic view is inevitably coloured by the excessive importance attached to the small section of humanity which was specifically Jewish: but this kind of emphasis is not uncommon in other religious cultures, despite the fact that it may be very unpalatable to those not in immediate sympathy.

The Greatness of Man

The Talmud does not fail to stress the dignity of man,[1] which,

[1] B.K. 79 *b*.

for the particular kind of human being who observes the Jewish law, may even override a negative precept[2]—a considerable concession indeed. It was for the sake of man's greater prestige that God removed the tail with which, like all the animals, he had originally been endowed.[3] As man possesses a soul of heavenly origin,[4] given by God in purity in the first instance but laying heavy responsibilities upon its owner,[5] this claim is no more than might be expected. The greatness and wonder of man's being are physically manifested by the fact that he possesses a body full of holes and orifices and yet, miracle of miracles, the breath that is in him does not escape.[6] As an uncorked bottle remains full of air, and as man's respiratory system is nearly identical with that of the humblest quadruped, including exhalation as well as inhalation, the special miracle is a little hard to discern. Man's greatness is not to be minimised by derogatory comparisons of living persons to great men of the past, for even the greatest are replaceable;[7] those now at the helm are to be accorded equal rank with their predecessors,[8] and good men can attain to superhuman powers, as the example of the prophets shows.[9]

God's thorough competence in the task of creating man, which has made such a good job of him, is frequently stressed with arguments sometimes more, sometimes less cogent. The minting of coins from one mould by human workers results in absolute uniformity and identity. Yet although God created all men from the same original mould, namely Adam, each is individual and different from all his fellows.[10] This is a good thought, starting from the wrong premises. Mould is scarcely the most appropriate metaphor for the first parent of the human race. Furthermore it would be more fitting to stress the wonder of the origin of *homo sapiens*, and the continued wonder of the discrete personality of so many myriads of the human species. But the underlying idea is good.

On this same theme it is declared that God's workmanship in creating the human body is perfect and beautiful. If a man

[2] Men. 37 b.　　　　　[3] Gen. R. xiv.10.
[4] Eccl. R. vi.6, 1.　　　[5] Nidd. 30 b; Eccl. R. xii.7, 1.
[6] Gen. R. i.3.　　　　　[7] Eccl. R. i.5, 1.
[8] Eccl. R. i.4, 4.　　　　[9] Deut. R. x.2, 3.
[10] Sanh. 38 a.

builds a house and places a waterspout above the door, the result is unsightly. Yet God placed the human nose above the mouth, and the results are aesthetically pleasing.[11] Such is the argument, unfortunate as certain possible interpretations might be. There are two explanations as to why so many of man's organs go in pairs—eyes, ears, hands, feet, etc. One idea is that God and His heavenly colleagues, after due consideration and voting, arranged man's anatomy on the most aesthetically pleasing pattern that was possible, their judgment being final.[12] The other explanation rests on the claim that God foresaw the wisdom of Solomon in dealing with the rival mothers who were claimants to the one child, and arranged man's anatomy expressly so that the king could display his astuteness.[13]

If a man happens to be God-fearing, an additional guardian angel is appointed to his entourage each time he faithfully performs a precept.[14] This statement leaves little for the commentator to say. Very much more fruitful and beautiful is the thought that the worshipper of God grows in likeness to his Maker.[15] This is a proved fact of all genuine religious experience, whether it be Jewish or Christian.

It is to the credit of the Rabbis that the passages belonging to this section are not numerous. For unqualified praise is very rarely appropriate to man's mortal estate, whether it be considered from the individual or the collective point of view.

The Smallness of Man

Very much more numerous than the panegyrics on man are those teachings which recognise his limitation in potential, ethical or practical, or which acknowledge his essential littleness. A few representative ideas will be sufficient here.

A small number of passages state or imply that man's corporeal frame and its physical functions are aesthetically disgusting, though this idea is not common. It is foreign to the normal spirit of Judaism, and also open to grave biological objection. In accordance with this infrequent outlook man's

---

[11] Gen. R. xii.1.
[12] Eccl. R. ii.12, 1.
[13] Eccl. R. x.16, 1, on 1 Kings iii.16-28.
[14] Ex. R. xxxii.6.
[15] Deut. R. i.12.

physical origin is said to be a drop of putrid semen supplied by his immediate parents, while his appointed destination at the end of life's journey is with worm, dust, and maggot.[16] Man is created with excretory organs to curb his potential arrogance, the implication being that these render him rather foul.[17] As gnats preceded man in the order of creation, he has in any case little claim to pride.[18] These arguments state unalterable facts but use them foolishly: the mysteries of man's primary origin and ultimate destiny cannot be resolved by cheap jibes based on adventitious circumstances, and such dignity as man may legitimately claim is not to be lessened in that particular way. Equally foreign to the normal Rabbinic outlook are the Midrashic Seven Stages of Man, which liken the human animal successively to pig, kid, horse, ass, dog, and ape, implying steady degeneration following life's glorious and regal inauguration in babyhood. These stages are considerably more depressing than their Shakespearean counterparts, though the situation is declared to be just a little better for students of Torah.[19]

A more interesting passage discusses the shares of God and of the father and mother in the formation of the child. The parts of the physical frame deriving respectively from the paternal or maternal semen are explicitly detailed. The kernel of the passage is the declaration that everything which renders the body something of greater significance than a mere lifeless mass derives from God. This is what God takes away at death: the physical part alone remains and suffers corruption.[20] This passage contains at least the sound beginnings of a philosophy of body and soul.

Certain teachings suggest that man is, or has become, a rather tragic figure. In this spirit, God Himself is declared to have mourned the loss of man's immortality when he was expelled from Eden—which is a close approximation to the doctrine of the Fall.[21] It is sometimes pondered, on the basis of Genesis vi.6, whether God did not make an unfortunate error in creating man at all.[22] Death is now incontrovertibly the destiny of all

---

[16] Ab. III.1; Lev. R. XVIII.1; Eccl. R. XII.1, 1; etc.   [17] B.B. 75ᵃ.
[18] Sanh. 38ᵃ.   [19] Eccl. R. I.2, 1.
[20] Nidd. 31ᵃ; Eccl. R. V.10, 2.   [21] Gen. R. XXI.2.   [22] Gen. R. XXVII.4.

men—a limitation which applied even to Moses in his time;[23] and no man may appoint a substitute for himself, or delay the hour of his passing.[24]

Numerous passages point out the mental and physical limitations of the mortal state. Man must toil, unlike the angels,[25] for without work he cannot have bread.[26] This statement has been approximately accurate all through the ages of man's history. Exceptions based on inheritance, determined vagrancy, or some other factor are fortuitous and atypical. Man, unlike the angels, can yield only an imperfect obedience to God.[27] The very finite and circumscribed capacity of his brain is illustrated by the fact that he cannot follow intelligently the conversation of two persons talking at the same time, while God can hear and comprehend simultaneously the prayers of all who address Him.[28] This is a meaningful thought of considerable beauty and power. Unspeakable is the folly of mortal men who have tried to claim divinity.[29] After all, the combined efforts of all mankind cannot endow a single insect with life,[30] and all the magicians in the world are incapable of turning morning into evening before the appointed hour.[31] In all the statements of this paragraph the modern reader will concur wholeheartedly with the Rabbis.

The extreme of pessimism is reached when life is parabolically compared to the experience of a fox who longs to enter a fenced vineyard stocked with particularly luscious grapes. Unfortunately there is only one hole, rather on the small side, but capable of admitting him after a period of voluntary but grievous fasting. Reynard fasts, enters, and feasts—but he has to go all through the tedious process of fasting again before he can get out through the same hole, and he sadly asks himself what he has really gained by all his trouble. Such, in the estimation of this particular Rabbi, is the sum total of the profit to be derived from the living of a human life.[32] It is a truism that man brings no earthly possession into the world, and that he can take none out—but whether this justifies so final a

---

[23] Deut. R. xi.8.
[24] Deut. R. ix.3.
[25] Gen. R. ii.2.
[26] Gen. R. xiv.10; Eccl. R. ii.17, i.
[27] Lev. R. i.i.
[28] Ex. R. xxi.4.
[29] Ex. R. viii.2.
[30] Gen. R. xxxix.14, lxxxiv.4.
[31] Num. R. xviii.4.
[32] Eccl. R. v.14, i.

cynicism as that of the fox is an individual decision to which many return a negative answer. Some would stress the value of the courageous living of the life, and they or others would underline the undying human hope of life immortal.

The Dual Potential of Man

Most of the teachings so far cited in this chapter press some element of truth in a particular direction, and would give but a very distorted impression if they claimed to be the whole story. Man, as he is known in life and experience, is always a mixture of strength and weakness, of good and evil, of conflicting potentials, of higher and lower tendencies. Unreserved approval or censure of him is seldom fully appropriate, and the truest estimates, whether in Rabbinic thinking or elsewhere, are those which recognise his dual capacity.

The Rabbinic belief in some measure of human free will has appeared already in these pages. It is frequently suggested that man possesses a large element of choice in what he makes of his life. His physical characteristics, even the poverty or wealth which will attend his earthly life, may be foreordained, but his moral nature is left by divine intention to his own shaping. This carries the unexpressed corollary that the totality of his life affords a basis for judgment.[33] Certain less percipient exponents of this view maintain that so many years are allocated to a man at birth, and that this number may be extended for good conduct, or reduced for any improper behaviour—in other words, divinely adjusted and regulated by the specific use that a man makes of his free will.[34] These theorists might well be advised to use their eyes in daily living, and also to gain a clearer understanding of the message of the Book of Job.

There are many other passages of like tenor. Man cannot control what he sees, hears, or smells, for dominion over his own eyes, ears, and nose has not been granted to him. But his mouth, hands, and feet he does control: his mouth is capable of repeating either precepts of Torah or blasphemies; his hands may dispense alms or commit murder; his feet may carry him to synagogue or circus, the latter representing grievous sin in

---

[33] Nidd. 16 b.   [34] Eccl. R. III.2, 3.

the eyes of the Rabbis.[35] (The circus means the regular gladiatorial shows of the Roman amphitheatres, where human as well as animal life was sacrificed very freely for the entertainment of the crowd.) The potentialities of the heart are numerous —some of them are detailed, and men may make very different choices.[36] The righteous are in control of the heart or passions, the wicked are in subjection to them, and this again is a matter of character-forming choice.[37] The same idea recurs in quaint medical terminology, for man's body is said to be in balance, half water and half blood. But the exact and healthful proportions are maintained only as a reward for virtue. If a man sins, either the water will exceed the blood, causing dropsy, or the blood will exceed the water, causing leprosy.[38]

It is a commonplace of Rabbinic thought that man possesses likeness both to the ministering angels of God's nearer presence, and to the dumb animals of the lower creation;[39] both to the angelic hosts and to the accursed demons.[40] The precise likenesses postulated by the Rabbis are listed more fully in the fifth chapter. It comes to the same thing to say that there are both celestial and terrestrial elements in the amalgam of man's personality and character.[41] This is a religious way of putting an everyday truth accepted even in secular circles, namely, that man has close physical links with the animal world, and yet remains sharply differentiated from it. That is part of the mystery of his being.

Leadership, and willingness to be led, are essential factors of human community, some individuals possessing capacity for the one, some for the other—a fact which is pungently expressed in one of the more excellent of the Rabbinic parables. The tail of the serpent, jealous of the supremacy of the head, demanded and was granted a period of control, only to discover that it lacked utterly the capacity to avoid water, fire, thorns, and other perils, and could not therefore be supreme. The masses are as incapable of leadership as the tail of the serpent, and any pandering to them in this respect by their appointed rulers

[35] Gen. R. LXVII.3.   [36] Eccl. R. 1.16, 1.
[37] Gen. R. XXXIV.10.   [38] Lev. R. xv.2.
[39] Gen. R. VIII.11, XIV.3.   [40] Hag. 16ᵃ.
[41] Gen. R. XII.8; Lev. R. IX.9.

is fraught with grave danger for the community.[42] This is a differentiation of certain men from certain other men rather than a contribution to the abstract total phenomenon of human personality. But it is an idea of intrinsic interest, whatever the colour of the individual politician who may consider its import.

The schools of Shammai and Hillel once had a serious debate as to whether it would or would not have been better for man to have remained uncreated. After two and a half years of discussion, they voted that it would; adding a rider to the effect that, accepting the misfortune of his creation, man must nevertheless act with constant deliberation.[43] The modern reader may agree or disagree with the verdict according to the essential pessimism or optimism of his nature. There must have been some leanings towards the brighter view in that the matter was at least considered open for debate, and discussed over so long a period.

Human judgments are usually subjective. A man often sees the best qualities in those who agree with him, and the worst in those of an opposite opinion. Judgments on one's fellows in general are apt to be equally fallacious, but those which perceive both the good and the evil, or which compare potential and performance, may possibly be nearer the truth. With such brief comment, the foregoing teachings may be left to speak for themselves.

[42] Deut. R. 1.10.   [43] Erub. 13 b.

CHAPTER XIII

APOLOGIA AND EPILOGUE

In the preceding twelve chapters the writer has endeavoured to be as objective as possible: he has tried also not to intrude his own personality and opinions more than he could help. No human author ever achieved complete success in such aims. If a man were to be capable of evaluating another faith quite dispassionately, with absolute fairness, he would almost need to be without religious convictions of his own. The present writer is an evangelical Christian, holding firmly to all the doctrines of the Apostles' Creed. This has inevitably coloured his appraisal of Rabbinic religion, just as the books of Montefiore and others on Christian themes have been coloured by their Judaism. If in this book the writer has in any way misrepresented or underestimated the other side, he herewith makes humble apology.

The reader has seen that in certain fields of enquiry Judaism and Christianity share the same unresolved difficulties, in others their interpretations diverge widely. The most important headings will be recapitulated here, but without the detail of the relevant preceding chapters. Then a few concluding words will be said on the quality of the Rabbinic religion as a whole.

In the doctrine of Holy Scripture reflected in their exegesis of the Hebrew Bible, the Rabbis exhibit precisely the same schools of thought as do the Christian exegetes who range over both Testaments. On both sides there are fundamentalists holding to the most rigid canons of verbal inerrancy, liberals or modernists of quite advanced views, and every possible shade of opinion in between. It is interesting and instructive to discover that the problem presents the same parallel features in both faiths.

There is a second major common field of this kind. The reader is familiar with the contention that if God is omniscient, men cannot be free, and if men are free, God cannot be omniscient. This troublesome paradox or dilemma belongs to all humanity, not to one particular creed or sect. The Rabbinic approach to the problem was discussed at some length in the second chapter, and it was freely admitted that Jewish and Christian theologians have frequently found themselves bogged in the self-same mire in equal measure, simply because they have tried over-zealously either to exalt the power of God or to exalt the freedom of men. There is no detailed and final answer to this query in the mortal state, though the shape of a reasonable solution probably lies along the lines that God, while remaining omniscient, fore-ordains only certain things, leaving the human will free in limited and particular respects. It is important for a convincing theology to leave man partially free without in the least binding God, and to leave God wholly free without completely binding man. On this crucial issue, the Jew and the Christian meet each other once again in a measure of shared failure and shared bewilderment.

Without undue repetition of the material of earlier chapters, it may be stated broadly that the Christian accepts much of the Jewish teaching on the doctrines of God, creation, sin, atonement, and immortality, rejecting certain concepts and adding others of cardinal importance. The two faiths speak the same language, but with considerable differences of dialect. Yet there are residual and inescapable incompatibilities. Three main ones may be isolated and underlined, though the first preconditions and outweighs all the others.

For the Jew, Jesus Christ may be a teacher or a prophet—for the Christian, He is God. A Jew cannot accept Christ and remain a Jew: neither can a modernist argue away His divinity and remain a Christian. This is the first and fundamental incompatibility between the two faiths.

The Christian view of sin and atonement is sterner, more realistic, and more inward than the Jewish one. Its outward rules are fewer, less related to specific circumstance, centred in greater measure in the intangible realm of the human heart— which makes its canons loftier and more difficult for the observer. Much of what the Christian regards as sin might be re-defined as insufficiency of love, Godward or manward. When the laws of love are broken, the sensitive transgressor knows this very well without the yardstick of precept or case law. It follows from this that a Jew may sometimes feel a satisfaction with his life and conduct which is impossible for the Christian, because the law of love is always so much more demanding than his personal attainment. If ever a Jew looks for some divine reward for his virtues, a Christian can look only for divine pardon for his sins. This is the second major discrepancy.

The Jew rejects the authority of the New Testament. In his faith, as in that of the Roman Catholic, tradition is believed to be the reliable interpreter of Scripture. The reader has already met the claim that tradition also goes back to God's revelation to Moses on Mount Sinai. The Protestant conviction builds life, faith, and doctrine on the revealed Word of God, which includes both Testaments but no other source, oral or written. Herein lies the third major discrepancy.

From the root concept of the divinity of Christ—to go no further in Trinitarian thinking—it is clear that no amalgam or accommodation is possible between genuine Judaism and genuine Christianity. The two are antithetic, and must remain so throughout their separate temporal existence. Many nominal Christians deny Christ in their actions and thinking today. Yet strangely enough they do not revert to Judaism, which might be logically reasonable and theologically preferable to the alternatives chosen: racial antipathy or political prejudice prompts them rather to become Unitarians or agnostics, secret or avowed. The Cross confronts Christians, even as Sinai confronts Jews, with a challenge and a choice—they cannot have it both ways.

It is the writer's duty now to say a few concluding words on his estimate—which must naturally be a personal one—of Rabbinic Judaism from a religious point of view. This is not easy. Modern Judaism is a living force with a contemporary impact: the material surveyed in this volume belongs, not by any means to a dead faith, but to a bygone manifestation of one that has radically changed. Talmud and Midrash are perhaps as

familiar to most modern Jews—and certainly to all modern
Christians excepting only a handful of theological research
students—as the lost books of Livy.

For the Christian student, familiar with the Old Testament
and just beginning Rabbinic studies, the first reaction is
inevitably one of disappointment. It needs much patient search
to find the gems and excellences in a field which is quite foreign
to him, and in an idiom which conveys little meaning to the
tyro. Whatever meed of praise may be searched out for the
academies of Sura, Pumbeditha, and Nehardea, it can scarcely
be denied that by the time of the Talmud the best days of the
Old Covenant were undoubtedly and for ever past. Gone was
the bright morn of Judaism, with the trump of battle, the
commanding and pristine vigour of the first Law, the right
hand and stretched-out arm of an omnipotent Yahweh, at
whose command the waters of the Red Sea or the walls of
Jericho sprang to obedience; gone was the high noon, with the
stern yet splendid clarion of the prophet and the sweet notes of
the Psalmist; gone was the tragic yet golden afternoon, when a
Maccabee might give even an Antiochus to think, and a godless
Roman minion might find that his ten martyrs had bred a
thousand more; gone were these things, and the sunset glow
had come. Was there then merely a tame and truncated present,
with the memory of a mighty past? That sunset glow was
endowed with some strange and unaccountable perpetuity, for
persecution, deportation, mass murder, and all the rolling
centuries have failed to bring on the expected night. The sheer
permanence and vitality of Judaism is something at which all
the world has wondered.

The reader has perceived already how the three parts of the
Hebrew Bible all make their contribution to the Rabbinic
literature, though there is much additional and independent
material. The Torah or Pentateuch is the ancestor of nearly all
the Halakhoth, which are pre-eminent in importance to the
Rabbi, of lesser worth to most other people. It is not in this
field that Judaism has bequeathed its most precious legacy to
posterity. The Prophets—giving the word the coverage of the
Hebrew rather than of the English Bible—are remarkable for
their more broadly ethical teachings, their reiterated calls to

repentance, their fierce denunciations of the backsliding and ungodly, and their hammer-like emphasis on the lessons of history. Unquestionably these elements are all reflected in the Rabbinic literature, although there may be nothing to compare with the personal grandeur of an Amos or a Jeremiah. The same remark may be made concerning the more diversified elements of the Hagiographa—the penitence, courage and God-consciousness of the Psalms, the hard wisdom of Ecclesiastes or Proverbs, the apocalyptic of Daniel, and many others. Speaking very broadly, and allowing for numerous exceptions, it may be said that the Rabbinic teachings inspired by the Torah are not always, though they may sometimes be, of especial value to this modern age, whereas very many of those with a thought ancestry in the Prophets or Hagiographa have a universal and timeless appeal. Were it legitimate to expunge the puerile, the casuistical, the unworthy, the tedious, and the iterative, then the residual Rabbinic theology would reflect a monotheistic faith as lofty, noble, and spiritual as anything to be found outside the inspired canon of Holy Scripture.

The ardent modern oecumenical reformer may feel that the study of Rabbinics is too arid and academic to merit his serious attention. If he has little leisure, and looks for quick returns in the form of organic religious union, he is doubtless correct. During a prolonged study of the frequently dreary folios of the Talmud, the writer has alternated between impatience at their ineptitudes, and the thrill of joy in seeing those men of fifteen or more centuries ago come to life, and prove so very like their modern counterparts, puzzling mixtures of good and evil. A deeper comprehension of all that is involved in a shared humanity may be less than the ultimate oecumenical goal, but it is a very essential first step.

The brotherhood of Jew and Christian in the human family was never more pungently and memorably expressed than by Shylock, when he said: "Hath not a Jew eyes? hath not a Jew hands, organs, dimensions, senses, affections, passions?—fed with the same food, hurt with the same weapons, subject to the same diseases, healed by the same means, warmed and cooled by the same winter and summer, as a Christian is? If you prick us, do we not bleed? if you tickle us, do we not laugh? if you poison us, do we not die? and if you wrong us, shall we not revenge?" In Shakespeare's play, these basic facts of universal human existence were invoked in a spirit of hate and contempt, as happens so frequently in real life. Could they but be re-written in love, expanded to cover all races, creeds, and colours, and understood by all, then a better and finer world might be born. Intractable religious differences may still be a barrier to organic union, but they need be no barrier to friendship, or even to joint labour for the good of humanity.

APPENDIX

THE STATUTORY DAILY PRAYERS

The first major element of the daily Rabbinic liturgy was the Shema, the core of which consisted of the three Scripture passages Deuteronomy VI.4-9, XI.13-21; Numbers XV.37-41. This was said morning and evening with the accompanying Benedictions, two preceding and one following in the morning, two preceding and two following in the evening. The morning recital was considerably longer. Independently of this, the Tephillah or Eighteen Benedictions was said thrice daily. Much of this ancient material is incorporated in the modern Hebrew Prayer Book, and is still recited verbatim in every Synagogue.

The prayers follow in full, in their proper order, with their divisions indicated. The Hebrew text translated is that of D. W. Staerk, *Altjüdische liturgische Gebete*, pp. 4-14, but the same material will be found in the Hebrew Prayer Book.[1]

THE TWO BENEDICTIONS BEFORE MORNING SHEMA

1. *a.* Blessed art thou, O Lord our God, King of the world, fashioner of light and creator of darkness, maker of peace and creator of everything, who in mercy causest light to shine on the earth and on them that dwell thereon, and in goodness renewest every day continually the work of creation. *b.* How manifold are thy works, O Lord! All of them hast thou made in wisdom, the earth is replete with thy possessions (Psalm CIV.24). O King, who wast alone exalted from ancient time, lauded and magnified and glorified from days of old, God of eternity, in thine abounding mercies have mercy upon us,[2] Lord of our fortitude, Rock of our refuge, Shield of our salvation, Refuge for us! The blessed God, great in wisdom, provided and created the brightness of the sun, a good thing he fashioned, a glory to his Name. He appointed the luminaries to encompass his strength. The leaders of his hosts are holy beings who extol the Almighty and continually rehearse the

---

[1] D. W. Staerk, *Altjüdische liturgische Gebete*, Bonn 1910, pp. 4-6; *Authorised Prayer Book*, ed. S. Singer, pp. 37-40.

[2] There are four rhymes to this word in the next line, strengthened by identity of first plural suffix. The effect is most pleasing. Then twenty-two successive words begin acrostically with the successive letters of the Hebrew alphabet.

glory of God and his holiness. Blessed be thou, O God, for the perfection of the work of thy hands, and for the shining luminaries which thou hast made. They shall glorify thee for ever and aye. *c.* Blessed be thou, our Rock, our King and our Redeemer,[3] Creator of holy angelic beings, may thy Name be magnified for ever, O our King, who createst innumerable ministering spirits, all of whom stand at the world's topmost limit, and with awe announce together aloud the things concerning the living God and eternal King. They are all beloved, they are all undefiled, they are all mighty; and all of them with fear and reverence do the will of their Creator. And all of them open their mouths in holiness and purity, with hymn and psalm, blessing and lauding, glorifying and praising with awe, ascribing sanctity and kingship to the Name of God the King, great and mighty and feared, holy is he! And all of them accept for themselves, one from the other, the yoke of the kingdom of heaven, and give authority one to the other to hallow their Creator. In tranquillity of spirit, in clear speech and with holy melody they all make answer with one accord, and say with reverence, Holy, holy, holy is the Lord of Hosts! the whole earth is full of his glory! (Is. VI.3). And the Ophannim and the holy Hayyoth[4] with a great quivering uplift themselves towards the Seraphim, and utter praises close by them and say, Blessed be the glory of the Lord from his place. To the blessed God they proffer melodies, to the King, the living and enduring God, they utter hymns and make their praises heard, for he alone doeth deeds of valour, and maketh new things, the Lord of battles, the sower of righteousness, he that bringeth forth salvation, the instigator of healings, he that is revered in songs of praise, the Lord of wondrous acts. In his goodness he reneweth the work of creation every day continually, as it is said, To him that maketh great lights, for his mercy endureth for ever (Ps. CXXXVI.7). O make a new light to shine upon Zion, and may we all attain soon to be worthy of its brightness. Blessed art thou, O Lord, fashioner of the luminaries!

2.   With mighty love hast thou loved us, O Lord our God, with unstinted compassion hast thou pitied us. Our Father, our

---

[3] These three epithets all rhyme in Hebrew—same suffix as above.

[4] Literally "wheels" and "living beings." Kinds of angels are meant. See Ezek. I.

King, for the sake of our fathers who trusted in thee and to whom thou didst teach the statutes of life, even so show thy gracious favour unto us and teach us. Our Father, pitying and compassionate Father, have pity upon us, and instil into our hearts the capacity to discern and to act prudently, to hear, to learn, to instruct, to observe, to do, and to fulfil in love the words of the teaching of thy Torah. Grant light to our eyes in thy Torah, and make our hearts cleave to thy commandments. Unite our hearts in the love and fear of thy Name, and may we never at any time be put to shame. Because we have trusted in thy Name, holy and great and revered, let us rejoice and be glad in thy salvation. Make us to come in peace from the four corners of the earth, and make us go with heads high to our Land, for thou art a God that accomplisheth salvation. Even us hast thou chosen from every nation and tongue, and hast for ever brought us near to thy great Name in faithfulness, to give thanks to thee, and declare thy unity in love. Blessed art thou, O Lord, who choosest thy people Israel in love.

At this point the worshipper recites the three passages of Scripture mentioned above. It is for this very purpose that the entire prayer is designed.

THE ONE BENEDICTION FOLLOWING MORNING SHEMA [5]

True and constant, established and lasting, just and trustworthy, beloved and cherished, desired and delightful, revered and majestic, rightly ordained and acceptable, good and beautiful is this thy word unto us for ever and aye.[6] Verily the God of the world is our King, the Rock of Jacob, the Shield of our salvation. He endureth for ever and ever, and his Name endureth. His throne is established, and his kingdom and his faithfulness are for ever and aye. Moreover his words are living and enduring, faithful and desired for ever and to all eternity, unto our fathers and unto us, unto our children and unto our generations, and unto all the generations of the seed of Israel his servants. For the first and for the last of these, thy word is good and enduring for ever and aye. Truth and steadfastness is the essence of thy statute, and it shall not pass away. Verily thou art indeed the Lord our God and the

[5] Staerk, pp. 6-7; Singer, pp. 42-4.

[6] This sentence obviously refers to the preceding passages of the Shema. The Hebrew devotes fifteen conjunctions to the sixteen epithets.

God of our fathers, our King, our fathers' King, our Redeemer, our fathers' Redeemer, our Creator, the Rock of our salvation, our Deliverer and Rescuer from everlasting is thy name. There is no God except thee. *b*. Thou hast been the succour of our fathers from olden time, a protection and a saviour to their children after them in every generation. In the high places of the earth is thy habitation, and thy judgments and thy righteousness extend to the extremities of the earth. Blessed is the man who hearkeneth to thy commandments, and layeth up thy Law and thy words in his heart. Verily thou art the Lord of thy people, and a mighty King to defend their cause. Verily thou art the First and the Last, and apart from thee there is no King, Redeemer and Saviour for us. *c*. From Egypt didst thou deliver us, O Lord our God, and from the house of slaves didst thou cause us to be ransomed. All their firstborn didst thou slay, but thine own firstborn didst thou redeem. The Red Sea too didst thou cleave, and didst drown the presumptuous. The beloved didst thou lead across, and the waters covered their adversaries—not one of them was left. For this cause the beloved glorified and exalted God, and the dear ones uttered hymns, songs and panegyrics, blessings and thanksgivings to God the King, the living and enduring one, who is high and lifted up, great and revered, who humiliateth the proud and exalteth the lowly, who leadeth forth captives and redeemeth the meek, who helpeth the poor and answereth his people when they cry unto him. Praises to the Most High God, blessed and to be blessed is he. Moses and the children of Israel sang a song unto thee with great gladness, and said, all of them, Who is like unto thee, O Lord, amongst the gods, Who is like thee, glorious in holiness, revered in praises, doing wondrous works? (Ex. xv.11). In a new song did the redeemed ones offer glory unto thy Name at the sea shore, all of them gave thanks together, and ascribed sovereignty and said, The Lord shall reign for ever and ever (Ex. xv.18). *d*. O Rock of Israel, arise to the succour of Israel, and redeem Judah and Israel according to thy word. He is our Redeemer, the Lord of Hosts is his name, the Holy One of Israel (Is. xL.4). Blessed art thou, O Lord, who hast redeemed Israel.

This completes the morning orison. The four evening Benedictions follow. The appointed Scripture passages are said between the second and the third of these.[7]

---

[7] Staerk, pp. 8, 9; Singer, pp. 96, 98-100.

THE FOUR BENEDICTIONS AT EVENING SHEMA

1. Blessed art thou, O Lord our God, King of eternity, who by thy word makest the evenings to advance, who with wisdom openest the gates of heaven, who with understanding makest the seasons to recur and alterest the times, who arrangest the stars in their watches in the firmament according to thy will, who createst the day and the night, who rollest away the light from before the darkness and the darkness from before the light, who makest the day to pass away and bringest on the night, who dividest between the day and the night—the Lord of Hosts is thy name. Thou, living and enduring God, art King over us continually and for ever and ever. Blessed art thou, O Lord, who makest the evenings to advance.[8]

2. With everlasting love hast thou loved the house of Israel thy people, Torah and commandments, statutes and judgments hast thou taught us. Therefore, O Lord our God, we will meditate on thy statutes, when we lie down and when we rise up, and we will rejoice in the words of thy Torah and of thy commandments for ever and aye. For they, even they, are our life and the length of our days, and on them will we meditate day and night. And thy love mayest thou never remove from us. Blessed art thou, O Lord, who lovest thy people Israel.

Truth and firm faith is all this, and it is established with us that he is the Lord our God, there is none other beside him, and we, Israel, are his people. He it is who delivered us from the hand of kings, who redeemed us from the clutch of all ruthless men, the God who, on our behalf, exacted punishment from our adversaries and imposed a due requital on all the enemies of our soul, who doeth great deeds unsearchable and miracles innumerable, who maintaineth our soul in life and relinquisheth not our feet unto slipping, who hath made us to walk on the high places of our enemies and hath exalted our horn over all them that hate us; who wrought for us

---

[8] The reader may have observed already a tendency to alternate between second and third personal pronouns in respect to God. In this section the alternation is rather more pronounced. For English euphony, the second person is used throughout in translation.

miracles and vengeance on Pharaoh, signs and wonders in
the land of the children of Ham, who smote in his passing-over
all the firstborn of Egypt and brought forth his people Israel
from the midst of them to everlasting liberty, who made his
children pass between the parts of the Red Sea and drowned
their pursuers and those that hated them in the depths. His
children preceived his might. They gave praise and thanks
unto his Name, and willingly accepted his sovereignty over
them. Moses and the children of Israel sang a song unto thee
with great joy, and said, all of them, Who is like unto thee,
O Lord, amongst the gods? Who is like thee, glorious in
holiness, revered in praises, doing wondrous works? (Ex. xv.11).
Thy sovereign power did thy children behold even as thou
didst cleave the sea before Moses, and they cried, This is my
God! (Ex. xv.2) and said, The Lord shall reign for ever and
ever! (Ex. xv.18). It is said furthermore, For the Lord hath
delivered Jacob and redeemed him from the hand of him that
was stronger than he (Jer. xxxi.10, Hebrew). Blessed be thou,
O Lord, who hast redeemed Israel.

4. Make us, O Lord our God, to lie down in peace, and cause
us to rise up, O our King, unto life. Spread over us the
tabernacle of thy peace, and establish us aright by good
counsel from before thee. Save us for thy Name's sake, and
protect us round about. Remove from among us any enemy,
plague, sword, famine, or grief. Remove also the adversary
from before us and from behind us, and in the shadow of thy
wings conceal us. For it is thou, O God, who dost watch over
us and deliver us, for thou, O God, art a King, gracious and
compassionate. Guard our going out and our coming in unto
life and unto peace, from now and even for evermore. Blessed
art thou, O Lord, who guardest thy people Israel for evermore.

THE TEPHILLAH OR EIGHTEEN BENEDICTIONS—THRICE DAILY [9]

O Lord, open thou my lips, and my mouth shall show forth
thy praise (Ps. li.17).

1. Blessed art thou, O Lord our God, the God of our fathers,

[9] Staerk, pp. 11-14 gives a bad text, with several misprints. There is a better
text in O. Holtzmann, *Berakot*, Giessen 1912 (*Die Mischna, Text, Übersetzung und
Erklärung*, ed. G. Beer and O. Holtzmann).

the God of Abraham, the God of Isaac, and the God of Jacob, the great, mighty and revered God, the Most High God, owner of heaven and earth, our Shield and the Shield of our fathers, our confidence from generation to generation. Blessed art thou, O Lord, the Shield of Abraham.

2. Thou art mighty, bringing low the proud, strong, and the judge of the ruthless, living for evermore and raising the dead; making the wind to return and the dew to fall; nourishing the living and making alive the dead; bringing forth salvation for us in the blinking of an eyelid. Blessed art thou, O Lord, who makest alive the dead.

3. Holy art thou, and revered is thy name. There is none other God beside thee. Blessed art thou, O Lord, the holy God.

4. Favour us, O our Father, with knowledge of thee, and with understanding and sagacity from thy Torah. Blessed art thou, O Lord, who favourest with knowledge.

5. Bring us back, O Lord, unto thee, and may we return. Renew our days as aforetime. Blessed art thou, who takest delight in repentance.

6. Pardon us, our Father, for we have sinned against thee. Wipe out and remove our transgressions from before thine eyes, for great are thy mercies. Blessed art thou, O Lord, who aboundest in forgiving.

7. Look on our afflictions and defend our cause, and redeem us for thy Name's sake. Blessed art thou, O Lord, the Redeemer of Israel.

8. Heal us, O Lord our God, from the affliction of our hearts, and remove sorrow and sighing from us, and bring healing for our stripes. Blessed art thou, the healer of the sick of thy people Israel.

9. Bless this year to us for good, O Lord our God, in every kind of its increase, and bring speedily near the year of the fulfilment of our redemption. Grant the dew and the rain on the face of the earth, and make full the world from the storehouse of

thy goodness. Grant blessing on the works of our hands. Blessed art thou, O Lord, who blessest the years.

10. Blow on a great trumpet for our liberty, and raise a standard for the gathering together of our exiles. Blessed art thou, O Lord, who gatherest together the banished ones of thy people Israel.

11. Restore our judges as at the first, and our counsellors as in the beginning, and mayest thou alone reign over us. Blessed art thou, O Lord, who lovest judgment.

12. For apostates let there be no hope, and the kingship of presumption mayest thou speedily destroy in our days. May Christians and heretics perish in a moment, may they be blotted out from the book of the living, and not be written down with the righteous. Blessed art thou, O Lord, that humblest the proud.

13. On righteous proselytes may thy compassions be moved, and grant us a good reward with them that do thy will. Blessed art thou, O Lord, a confidence for the righteous.

14. Have compassion, O Lord our God, in thine abounding compassion on Israel thy people, and on Jerusalem, and on Zion the tabernacle of thy glory, on thy Holy Place and on thy Temple, and on thy kingdom of the House of David. Blessed art thou, O Lord, the builder of Jerusalem.[10]

15. Hearken, O Lord our God, to the voice of our prayer, and have compassion on us, for thou art a gracious and compassionate God. Blessed art thou, O Lord, who hearest prayer.

16. Be pleased, O Lord our God, to dwell in Zion, and thy servants will serve thee in Jerusalem. Blessed art thou, O Lord, whom we will serve in fear.

17. We give thee thanks. Thou art the Lord our God and the God of our fathers. For all good things, for grace and compassion

[10] The wording offers clear presumption of a date prior to A.D. 70. The form used today is expressed a little differently.

which thou has dealt out unto us and done unto us, and unto our fathers before us—and if we say, Our foot has slipped, the Lord will sustain us—blessed be thou, O Lord, to thee be the praise.

18. Give thy peace to Israel thy people, and unto thy city and thy possession. Bless us, each and every one. Blessed be thou, O Lord, who makest peace.

These prayers have been translated in full for the benefit of the Christian reader, because they form for him the best possible commentary on Rabbinic practice. The originals possess a majesty, a sonority, a beauty which a translation can echo only very imperfectly. The arrangement and emphasis are characteristically Jewish, yet there is much that a Christian could appropriately say in his own orisons, and little, apart from the twelfth Benediction of the Tephillah, to which he could take reasonable exception. That particular passage is an unfortunate echo of time and circumstance not necessarily endorsed today. One is reminded of the explicit statement in the Westminster Confession of Faith that the Pope is the Antichrist, the man of perdition. The most protesting Protestant of today, however loyally he accepted the substance of the Confession, might hesitate to go so far as that.

BIBLIOGRAPHY

Note

Certain lacunae in this Bibliography, particularly in the realm of modern literature about Rabbinics, are due to the fact that the book was written almost entirely in Cairo, where there was no access to any good public library of Judaica. Several good friends helped out my private resources with particular books, but other volumes I would have desired to consult were unobtainable, or became unobtainable through the departure of their owners. The mention, for example, of only one of the volumes of W. Bacher does not mean that the others are unimportant, merely that the one specified was the only one in my possession. The final revision of the manuscript was more than half typed when I returned to Scotland. Certain additional books were then used, but not so fully as they might have been at an earlier stage. One or two volumes are mentioned because they were of great value in earlier Rabbinic studies, before this book was contemplated. The prefixing of an asterisk to any title is intended to acknowledge a larger and more direct debt to that particular work. This applies most of all to the sources, from which the bricks used to build the chapters are taken.

The threefold division of the Bibliography will explain itself.

A. SOURCES, SUBSIDIARY SOURCES, TRANSLATIONS

Apocrypha, The. Revised Standard Version.
Biblia Hebraica, ed. R. Kittel. 4th edn.   Stuttgart 1949.
Biblia Rabbinica, 4 vols.   Warsaw 1860-9 (for text of Targumim).
Justin Martyr. *Dialogue with Trypho*. Anti-Nicene Christian Library, vol. ii. Edinburgh 1867.
*Midrash Rabbah, in Hebrew. 2 vols.   Stettin 1863.
*Midrash Rabbah, in English, edd. H. Freedman and M. Simon. 10 vols.   Soncino edn., London 1939.
*Mishnah, in English, tr. H. Danby.   Oxford 1933.
A Rabbinic Anthology, edd. C. G. Montefiore and H. Loewe. London 1938.
Septuagint. *The Old Testament in Greek*, ed. H. B. Swete. 3 vols. 4th edn. Cambridge 1909-12.
Staerk, D. W. *Altjüdische liturgische Gebete*. Bonn 1910.

*Talmud, The. English translation, ed. I. Epstein. Soncino edn. 34 vols. plus Index vol. London 1935-52.

*Talmud, Der babylonische. Hebrew and Aramaic text, with German translation, ed. L. Goldschmidt. 9 vols. The Hague 1933-5.

B. LEXICAL AND GRAMMATICAL HELPS

DALMAN, G. Grammatik des jüdisch-palästinischen Aramäisch. 2nd edn. Leipzig 1905.

*GESENIUS, F. H. W., KAUTZSCH, E. and COWLEY, A. E. Hebrew Grammar. 26th edn. Oxford 1910.

GROSSMANN, R., SACHS, H. and SEGAL, M. H. Compendious Hebrew-English Dictionary. Tel-Aviv 1946.

*JASTROW, M. Dictionary of the Talmud. London and New York 1903.

LEVY, J. Chaldäisches Wörterbuch über die Targumim. 2 vols. Leipzig 1868.

——Neuhebräisches und chaldäisches Wörterbuch über die Talmudim und Midraschim. 4 vols. Leipzig 1876-89.

MARGOLIS, M. L. Aramaic Language of the Babylonian Talmud (in English). Munich 1910.

*SEGAL, M. H. A Grammar of Mishnaic Hebrew. Oxford 1927.

*STEVENSON, W. B. Grammar of Palestinian Jewish Aramaic. Oxford 1924.

(Note. The serious student would find himself well equipped with Jastrow, Segal, and Stevenson.)

C. WORKS OF REFERENCE AND MODERN LITERATURE

ABELSON, J. The Immanence of God in Rabbinic Literature. London 1912.

ABRAHAMS, I. Studies in Pharisaism and the Gospels. 2 vols. Cambridge 1917, 1924.

ALBRIGHT, W. F. Archaeology and the Religion of Israel. Baltimore 1942.

——From the Stone Age to Christianity. Baltimore 1940.

BACHER, W. Die Agada der Tannaiten. VOL. I. 2nd edn. Strassburg 1903.

BOUSSET, D. W. Die Religion des Judenthums. 2nd edn. Berlin 1908.

COHEN, A. Le Talmud (French translation). Paris 1950.

DAVIDSON, A. B. Theology of the Old Testament. Edinburgh 1904.

Encyclopaedia of Religion and Ethics. 13 vols. Edinburgh 1904.

Epstein, I. *Judaism.* Harmondsworth 1959.
Epstein, L. M. *Marriage Laws in Bible and Talmud.* Cambridge, Mass. 1942.
Finkelstein, E. *The Pharisees.* 2 vols. Philadelphia 1946.
Ginzberg, L. *Legends of the Jews.* 6 vols. Philadelphia 1913-28.
Gray, B. *Sacrifice in the Old Testament.* Oxford 1925.
Hastings' *Dictionary of the Bible*, edd. J. Hastings, J. A. Selbie, and others. 5 vols. Edinburgh 1900-04.
Herford, R. Travers. *Christianity in Talmud and Midrash.* London 1903.
——*Talmud and Apocrypha.* London 1933.
Hirsch, W. *Rabbinic Psychology.* London 1947.
*Jewish Encyclopaedia, edd. I. Singer and others. 12 vols. New York 1901-6.
Jocz, J. *The Jewish People and Jesus Christ.* London 1947.
Klausner, J. *Jesus of Nazareth.* Trans. from Hebrew by H. Danby. New York 1927.
——*From Jesus to Paul.* Trans. from Hebrew by W. F. Stinespring. London 1942.
——*The Messianic Idea in Israel.* Trans. from Hebrew. London 1956.
Langton, E. *Essentials of Demonology.* London 1949.
Loewe, R. "Alexander Neckam's knowledge of Hebrew," in *Mediaeval and Renaissance Studies*, edd. R. Hunt and R. Klibansky, Warburg Institute, vol. iv, London 1958.
Montefiore, C. G. *Rabbinic Literature and Gospel Teachings.* London 1930.
——*The Synoptic Gospels.* 2 vols. London 1927.
Moore, G. F. *Judaism.* 3 vols. Cambridge, Mass. 1932. Index 1940.
Oesterley, W. O. E. and Robinson, T. H. *Hebrew Religion.* 2nd edn. London 1947.
——*History of Israel.* 2 vols. Oxford 1932.
Pedersen, J. P. E. *Israel.* 4 vols. London 1926.
Petuchowski, J. J. "The controversial figure of Melchizedek," in *Hebrew Union College Annual*, xxviii (1957).
Schechter, S. *Some Aspects of Rabbinic Theology.* London 1909.
——*Studies in Judaism.* 3 vols. Philadelphia 1945.
Schoeps, H. J. *Aus frühchristlicher Zeit.* Tübingen 1950.
Schürer, E. *History of the Jewish People in the Time of Jesus Christ.* Trans. from German by J. Macpherson, S. Taylor, and P. Christie. Edinburgh 1900-01.

SIMON, M. "Melchisédeck dans la polémique entre juifs et chrétiens et dans la légende," in *Revue d'histoire et de philosophie religieuses*, 1937.

SMITH, W. ROBERTSON. *The Old Testament in the Jewish Church.* 2nd edn. London 1892.

——*The Religion of the Semites.* 2nd edn. London 1894.

STRACK, H. L. and BILLERBECK, P. *Kommentar zum Neuen Testament aus Talmud und Midrasch.* 5 vols. Munich 1922-8. Index 1956.

STRACK, H. L. *Introduction to Talmud and Midrash.* Philadelphia 1945. Trans. of *Einleitung in Talmud and Midras*, Munich 1921.

WÜNSCHE, A. *Erläuterung der Evangelien aus Talmud und Midrasch.* Göttingen 1878.

YADIN, Y. "The Scrolls and the Epistle to the Hebrews," in *Scripta Hierosolymitana*, IV (1958).

GENERAL INDEX

Technical terms like Talmud, etc. are listed only when the text defines them, or gives some descriptive information. The inclusion or omission of biblical names depends largely on their Rabbinic significance. The name of Paul is not found, because the reader will extract the relevant material more conveniently from the Index of Biblical Passages.

N

INDEX OF RABBINIC PASSAGES

As the number of references in this volume is enormous, the list subjoined has been confined to the first citation in each footnote—all the others may be discovered by looking up the first one. Exact parallels follow without comment: "Cf." denotes analogous rather than identical material. References to the same folio or paragraph in different places do not necessarily denote the same passage—there may be two or more sets of parallels.

A. MISHNAH

B. GEMARA

C. MIDRASH

INDEX OF SCRIPTURE PASSAGES

A. THE HEBREW BIBLE

PRINTED IN GREAT BRITAIN BY
OLIVER AND BOYD LTD.
EDINBURGH